ERASMUS IN THE FOOTSTEPS OF PAUL

ERASMUS IN THE FOOTSTEPS OF PAUL

A Pauline Theologian

GRETA GRACE KROEKER

UNIVERSITY OF TORONTO PRESS
Toronto Buffalo London

ISBN 978-1-4426-9266-3

Erasmus Studies

Library and Archives Canada Cataloguing in Publication

Kroeker, Greta Grace
Erasmus in the footsteps of·Paul : a Pauline theologian /
Greta Grace Kroeker.

(Erasmus studies)
Includes bibliographical references and index.
ISBN 978-0-8020-9266-3

1. Erasmus, Desiderius, d. 1536 – Criticism and interpretation.
2. Bible. N.T. Roman – Criticism, interpretation, etc. – History –
16th century.   I. Title.   II. Series: Erasmus studies

BS2665.K76 2011   227'.107   C2011-902657-0

This book has been published with the assistance of a grant
from Virginia Polytechnic Institute and State University.

University of Toronto Press acknowledges the financial support for its
publishing activities of the Government of Canada through the Book
Publishing Industry Development Program (BPIDP).

University of Toronto Press acknowledges the financial assistance
to its Publishing program of the Canada Council for the Arts
and the Ontario Arts Council.

Canada Council   Conseil des Arts
for the Arts   du Canada

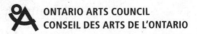

ONTARIO ARTS COUNCIL
CONSEIL DES ARTS DE L'ONTARIO

Contents

Abbreviations

CC   Corpus Catholicorum
CR   Corpus Reformatorum
CWE   Collected Works of Erasmus
LB   Erasmus, *Opera omnia*
NRSV   New Revised Standard Version (of the Bible)
St.A   *Philipp Melanchthon: Werke in Auswahl*
WA   *D. Martin Luthers Werke, Kritische Gesamtausgabe*

Preface

This project is an initial attempt to explore the nature of Erasmus's quest to understand the teaching of St Paul within the context of the Reformation debate. The project began as a paper in Thomas A. Brady's seminar at the University of California, Berkeley. I explored what appeared to me to be the inconsistent way Erasmus used New Testament scriptural evidence in his polemical exchange with Martin Luther about the freedom and the bondage of the human will. I found that Erasmus sometimes altered the wording of particular New Testament verses in order to bolster his arguments and defend the freedom of the will as Christian truth. Among the new questions this discovery posed to me, most persistent and vexing was why Erasmus, an outstanding philologist, a superb rhetorician, and an excellent New Testament scholar, would need to manipulate verses in order to support his arguments with Luther. The question drove my increasingly critical attitude towards a prominent theme in the modern literature on Erasmus: that he was something of a dilettante in theological matters. Erasmus's repeated efforts to understand and write about Paul seemed to contradict this view.

Professor Brady supported my efforts to further investigate this apparent contradiction and, with the support of a Mellon Summer Research Grant, sent me to consult James Tracy at the University of Minnesota, Minneapolis. Professor Tracy generously provided me with a copy of his 1968 conference paper, 'Luther's Influence on Erasmus' Concept of Faith,' which investigated the problem of, to borrow John B. Payne's terminology, 'Lutheranizing changes' in sequential editions of Erasmus's *Paraphrase on Romans*. Professor Tracy's paper not only inspired me to further pursue my questions about Erasmus's relationship to Luther's theology, but also provided me with solid evidence and wonderful leads for my quest.

This study presents only partial answers to the questions that drove that quest. It is limited to an investigation of Erasmus's use of St. Paul's Epistle to the Romans in the *Annotations*, the *Paraphrases*, and the three texts of Erasmus's polemic with Luther, *De libero arbitrio* and *Hyperaspistes I* and *II*. The project required me to collate the various editions of Erasmus's paraphrases on Paul's Epistle to the Romans because, as Professor John Bateman wisely advised, one should never trust anyone else's collation. I then used the collation to create a database of places where Erasmus's changes to the *Paraphrases* corresponded to changes in the *Annotations on Romans* and uses of Romans in *De libero arbitrio* as well as corresponding uses in Luther's *De servo arbitrio* – the major blows in their polemical exchange of 1524–5. I later added evidence from the *Hyperaspistes I* and *II* as well as data on how these verses were used by Philipp Melanchthon, Georg Witzel, and Johannes Cochlaeus and on how they appeared in the *Glossa ordinaria*, the medieval commentary on the Vulgate with references to patristic sources.

This study addresses the changing nature of Erasmus's encounter with Paul within the context of the early Protestant Reformation. It provides something of a snapshot of Erasmus's theological journey at the height of the Reformation crisis and is therefore limited in scope. For this reason, other very important subjects can only be mentioned or cursorily treated in this work. Erasmus's intellectual and theological relationship to other reformers, both Catholic and Protestant, is addressed only briefly. So is his relationship to his scholastic background, for I touch only peripherally on the Augustinian tradition as backdrop to the Reformation debate on justification by faith. Ultimately, a comprehensive reassessment of Erasmus's role in sixteenth-century thought requires a deeper analysis of his relationship to the traditions of ancient and medieval Christian teachings. Beyond that lies the more intimidating task of looking anew at humanism's place in the Age of Reformation. My study does suggest, however, a need to challenge the conventional dichotomy between 'new humanists' and 'old humanists' with respect to the Reformation.

This book is therefore a beginning, a first step towards reassessing the relationships between Renaissance humanism and Reformation theology as two closely related streams of a common

theological enterprise. The evidence for Erasmus's changing interpretation of Paul points unmistakably towards this very large
question. I hope that this project serves as a starting point for a
broader challenge to the marginalization of Erasmus's theological
works in modern assessments of his life and contributions.

Acknowledgments

Many people have generously helped me to complete this book. First, I wish to thank Professor Thomas A. Brady Jr for his remarkable and unfailing support, understanding, and encouragement. Without him, I would never have attempted this project and certainly would never have succeeded in completing it. I would also like to express my heartfelt gratitude to Kathy Brady for her friendship and encouragement. I would like to thank Professor James Tracy for his intellectual generosity and essential insights into Erasmus's Pauline scholarship. Professor Christopher Ocker not only read the manuscript and offered essential expertise but also patiently answered the infinite number of questions with which I relentlessly peppered him. The Department of History of the University of California, Berkeley, provided financial support, academic resources, and the most amazing of academic environments for the initial iteration of this project.

The research upon which this project rests would never have been possible without the two years I spent in Basel, Switzerland. Professor Kaspar von Greyerz's many kindnesses and amazing advocacy made it possible for me to live, work, and study in Basel. The Historisches Seminar of the Universität Basel provided not only the infrastructure for the project but also the camaraderie and companionship that made it such a joy to live in Basel and so difficult to leave. I also wish to express my gratitude to the staff of the Special Collections Reading Room at the University of Basel Library for their expertise and assistance. I would like to thank Professor Hans Medick and Professor Peer Schmidt, who through the University of Erfurt, Germany, and the Carl Schurz Fellowship provided the financial and institutional support for me to write and research in Erfurt.

I owe a debt of gratitude to Professor Charles Nauert for teaching me to handle humanists with care and that my reach should exceed my grasp; to Professor Frances Sternberg, whose own dedication to her craft has so influenced and inspired me; and to the late Professor John Stack, who saw a little light in me. Many others – professors, friends, and peers alike – have inspired, aided, and sustained me: Jan Austerlitz, Nicole Balin, Kristan Whelihan, Professor William Taylor, Jeanne Grant, Rachel Chico, Julie Tanaka, Professor Dr Hartmut Lehmann and Dr Silke Lehmann, Professor John Bateman, Beat Immenhauser, Barbara Studer, Claudia Barth, Yvonne Fankhauser, Tom Ewing, Janell Watson, Steven Bednarski, Julia Roberts, Tracy Penny Light, Jeff Nilsson, and Caley McCarthy. I am profoundly thankful to Amy Nelson, whose remarkable support and example sustained me at Virginia Tech. The two years I spent there ended with great sadness, and I will never forget those who were taken so painfully and tragically in April 2007. I am grateful to my current department at the University of Waterloo for welcoming me to Canada and offering their support for this project, and to Jane Forgay, librarian extraordinaire.

I am deeply indebted and wholly grateful to my husband, Karl Larson, for the endless hours of discussion, research, travel, hand-holding, and careful editing he contributed to this project and the many sacrifices he made to make the research and writing of the book possible. You are without equal. I wish to thank my sisters, Tirza, Tamara, and Kerry, whose support and love are as essential to my scholarship as they are to my life, and my brother, Mark, a true Erasmian, for his steadfast support and encouragement. I wish to dedicate this book to my loving parents, Lois and Duane Kroeker, who have given me so much in life, including Erasmus, and taught me to love words and ideas and to respect the power they carry. No humanist could have hoped for a better sodality of intellectual sustenance and support.

ERASMUS IN THE FOOTSTEPS OF PAUL

Introduction

This is a study of Erasmus as a theologian who worked in the footsteps of St Paul. Its starting point is Erasmus's defence of free will in his controversy of 1524–5 with Martin Luther. The growth of his Pauline theology is then followed through his biblical paraphrases and annotations between 1524 and his death in 1536. The changes, which are tracked through Erasmus's successive treatments of Paul's Epistle to the Romans, reveal a progressively more Pauline theology that has many similarities to, though is not identical with, Luther's teachings.[1]

This project examines Erasmus's employment of passages from Romans in his polemic with Luther and compares them with changes made to the *Annotations* in 1527 and 1535 and the *Paraphrases* in 1532. The *Annotations* encompassed Erasmus's philological and grammatical examination of scripture as he edited the New Testament based on both the evidence he found in Greek and Latin manuscripts of the Bible and the use of the texts in the writings of the Church Fathers. Though primarily philological in content, the *Annotations* were full of theological implications. Erasmus edited the *Annotations* several times, and each subsequent edition added more evidence from a variety of patristic and manuscript sources to bolster his philological changes to scripture. Erasmus hoped that the *Paraphrases* would be used as a study tool for students and believers interested in learning more about the true meaning of scripture. In them, he summarized verses and provided exegesis for readers in order to make them more accessible. The *Paraphrases*, too, appeared in several editions, often with changes influenced by his philological studies evidenced in the *Annotations*.

Erasmus's treatment of Romans in the latter half of his life indicates his growing fascination with Paulinism and Pauline theology.[2] The changes he introduced to his work on Romans in the 1520s and 1530s, furthermore, reflect his growing concern with the issues of grace, justification, and free will. Erasmus searched in Paul's Epistles for answers to the theological debates caused by the eruptions of the Reformation. Erasmus's theological trajectory during the Reformation years demonstrates that he searched in Paul – and in Paul's Epistle to the Romans, in particular – for a biblical theology that would answer the central questions raised by the reform-minded thinkers of his age, including the role of the Catholic hierarchy in the spirituality of believers, the role of the will in human salvation, and the process of justification by faith – in the context of the existing Church. As a result, his Pauline theology was tempered by the patristic tradition and the history of the Church.

Focusing on Erasmus's Paulinism helps in placing his theological development within the context of the Reformation. Erasmus's efforts to develop his own Paulinism and his construction of a theology of grace reveal him to have been a spiritually dedicated, if not entirely self-assured, theologian and scholar. Furthermore, his theological development has implications for the study of the Reformation more generally. Indeed, Erasmus's special position in the public polemics of the Reformation, caught as he was somewhere between his Catholic critics and his Lutheran foes, as well as his theological journey documented in the *Paraphrases* and *Annotations*, demonstrate that the Reformation did not take place in two camps fought along a clear line of 'reformed' and not yet fully defined 'orthodox' theological principles. The Reformation itself, like the men who fought its theological battles, engaged around a continuum of ideas within the context of both a long tradition of theological thought and the radical 'newness' of reinterpretation.[3] Just as Luther, Melanchthon, and other reformers revisited their theological positions and sometimes altered them during the height of the Protestant Reformation, so, too, did Erasmus.

A JOURNEY WITH PAUL

Some time before 13 May 1525 Erasmus of Rotterdam received bad news. Word had come to him that Alberto Pio, the former Prince of Carpi, was spreading rumours that undermined Erasmus's credibility and questioned his orthodoxy.[4] As Myron P. Gilmore explains, the prince argued 'that Erasmus was neither a philosopher nor a theologian and that there was no sound doctrine in him.' Furthermore, Alberto accused Erasmus of being the source of the 'Lutheran Revolt.' Erasmus vigorously denied the charges and asserted that Alberto had misunderstood his writings, particularly the *Paraphrases* on the New Testament.[5] In his famous response, Alberto argued, 'either Erasmus Lutherizes or Luther Erasmusizes,'[6] and he pointed to the *Paraphrases* as having 'provided material for the Lutherans.' For Alberto, Erasmus's continuing 'attacks on theologians, monks, good works, and the cult of the Virgin' unquestionably demonstrated his sympathy with the Lutheran cause.[7] The conflict between the two men plagued them throughout their last years.

Although Erasmus continued to defend his loyalty to the Church and attacked the prince and his claims even after Alberto had died, his reputation had been damaged by Alberto's challenge to his orthodoxy. While many modern historians have attempted to rehabilitate Erasmus as a Catholic[8] or have denied the possible connection between Erasmus and Luther precisely because Erasmus failed to break with Rome,[9] the controversy with Alberto Pio is a stark reminder that, even in his own time, Erasmus's name was closely associated with the outbreak of Luther's 'revolt.'

Erasmus's use, and sometimes unpredictable manipulation, of Paul's Letter to the Romans allows a glimpse of a gifted scholar who utilized his spectacular skills to seek answers to the spiritual questions and doubts common to his age. His renown, status, connections, and talents did not make the spiritual crisis that culminated in the Reformation period any more clearly cut for him than for other, lesser-known people. If anything, his prominent position made his personal interactions with Reformation issues public, often inflammatory, and sometimes dangerous.

Erasmus's concern about the spiritual health of the Church and the Christian community led him to Paul. The crisis of the early modern Church, which Erasmus had again and again addressed in works such as *The Handbook of the Christian Soldier* (1503),[10] *On the Education of Children* (1508?), *In Praise of Folly* (1511), and most strongly in *Ratio verae theologiae* (1519), demonstrated his concern with the salvation of believers and their dependence on a corrupt Church. He recognized that the freedom of the will underpinned this dependence on the Church, because the conduit between human action and God lay in the hands of the penitential cycle and its administration by Church officials. His original suggestion for a solution to this problem emphasized the spiritual renewal of the individual through the *philosophia Christi*, which stressed inner spiritual transformation, reliance on scripture, and the critique of ceremonies. Erasmus's confidence that the tenets of the *philosophia Christi* could regenerate the Church from the ground up, however, gave way by the mid-1520s to a conviction that it was not the gift of human reason but the divine gift of grace that could lead believers to salvation and the Church to renewal. In this way, he refused to abandon the renewal of the Church, but he placed its corporate health and salvation on the shoulders of the spiritual regeneration of the individual through grace instead of in the changeable grasp of the human will. Erasmus's understanding of grace, unlike Luther's, required a response in the individual, one that could be directed towards individual and corporate spiritual restoration. Furthermore, Erasmus's vision of the role of grace in the transformation of the Church remained unwaveringly grounded in his understanding of the historical community of faith, one embodied in the Church and grounded in the theology of the Church Fathers.

Erasmus was on his own journey with Paul, which at times coincided with the wider Reformation debate. At other times, Erasmus may have found himself on the same road with Luther, searching for the path left by Paul. Yet Erasmus's humanist background, scholastic training, fellowship with the Church Fathers, dedication to Greek manuscript sources, and his own form of flexible piety ensured that his solution would differ from that of Luther.

Despite the similarity of many of the changes Erasmus made between 1527 and 1532 to Luther's theology of grace, his theological approach and perspective differed drastically from Luther's. To Luther, the link between revelation and the gospel was experiential, and grace was simultaneously historical and current.[11] By contrast, Erasmus believed that tradition informed theology and gave it roots, context, and meaning. Scripture was thus grounded in and hinged on the contexts and traditions through which it had travelled. For Erasmus, theology – even Pauline theology – was like water filtered over the rocks of a riverbed on its way to the sea: forever changed by that over which it had flowed.[12] For Luther, theology was in the raindrops: imminent, experiential, and personal,[13] either all-encompassing or entirely absent. Given Erasmus's training,

knowledge, and deeply personal Reformation, this type of understanding was impossible. He could not ignore tradition, nor could
he break the ties with his fellows, the Church Fathers, the tradition
and legacy they had built, and the authority of the Church.[14]

As it is detailed so thoughtfully on paper, Erasmus's theological
development demonstrates that Luther's Paul was not the only
Paul for a careful seeker in the early modern period. Therefore,
there was not one Reformation – that of Luther, Zwingli, and
Calvin – taking place in the early sixteenth century. Indeed, there
were thousands, perhaps more, of individual reformations of personal and public theologies occurring across Europe. Erasmus's
was one of them.[15]

Erasmus's Reformation experience points to the ways in which
we must challenge the idea that the Reformation took place on an
almost unstoppable trajectory leading to the break with Rome, the
confessionalization of Europe, the Thirty Years' War, and many
other developments that historians often cast as the inevitable
outcomes of a world broken apart by Luther's genius.[16] Although
Erasmus and many of the reformers shared common humanistic
interests, skills (e.g., classical rhetoric and textual criticism), and
concerns (e.g., the role of critical philology in exegesis), and
though they applied them to the same questions of free will, grace,
and justification, these preoccupations did not necessarily produce Protestant doctrine.[17]

Through his repeated engagements with Paul, Erasmus's characterization of the gospel as the 'philosophy of Christ'[18] seems to fall
away to reveal a new, emerging, occasionally unbalanced and inconsistent but always considered Pauline theology. Contrary to the
outmoded characterization of Erasmus as a theological amateur or
even a theological invertebrate, his theological works demonstrate
that he was neither a defender of orthodox piety nor a pagan philologist in search of grammatical gaps in scripture nor an intellectual too cowardly to stand up for change. Rather, when Erasmus's
theological works are viewed and studied in their entirety, his vision of the New Testament appears complex, nuanced, even mal-
leable, and his search for understanding a lifelong endeavour.

In the following chapters, I illustrate the diverse and sometimes
conflicting strains of Erasmus's treatments of Paul in the *Annotations*,
De libero arbitrio, the *Hyperaspistes I* and *II*, and the *Paraphrases*.
Chapter 1, 'Justification, Grace, and the Will,' frames the context for
the debate on the will, grace, and justification from the early Church

Fathers to the Reformation. Luther himself saw this issue as the very heart of the Reformation debate, and Erasmus's increasing preoccupation with Paul's presentation of the debate demonstrates the centrality of this theological touchstone in the first half of the sixteenth century.

Chapter 2, 'Erasmus on Romans: Texts and Authorities,' offers a general introduction to the works in which Erasmus engaged with Romans and to the Church Fathers on whom he relied in his interpretations. In this sense, Erasmus's changing and increasingly 'unorthodox' interpretation of Paul grants insight into the development of a unique and yet historically sensible radical Pauline theology of grace and the will.

Chapter 3, 'Reconsideration,' focuses on the verses in Romans that Erasmus altered in both the 1532 *Paraphrases* and either the 1527 or the 1535 *Annotations*. The verses and Erasmus's exegesis of them in the form of the *Annotations* and *Paraphrases* are presented with commentary on the ways in which Erasmus made alterations and relied on patristic sources, especially Chrysostom, as he reconsidered his own interpretation of the Pauline message. Chapter 4, 'Reassessment,' looks at verses that Erasmus altered only in the *Paraphrases* or only in the *Annotations*. Chapter 5, 'Controversy,' investigates Erasmus's use of scripture in the light of his controversy with Luther. While the encounter with Luther was one aspect of his theological development but not the cause, it instigated a theological crisis for Erasmus on many levels. As a result of this social, political, and religious crisis, Erasmus was forced to contend with his own translations in the light of Luther's insistence on the bondage of the will. This chapter demonstrates how Erasmus explained Paul's Letter to the Romans in *De libero arbitrio* very differently than he did in the later *Paraphrases* and *Annotations*.

This project emphasizes Erasmus's role as a theologian. Like other recent work that has endeavoured to highlight the importance of the theological activities of early modern humanists and the application of their *ad fontes* approach to scriptural and theological undertakings, it seeks to trace Erasmus's theological struggle within the heightened sensitivity with which he and others approached biblical studies and theology during the Reformation.[19] Erasmus dealt with the challenges faced by the Church and his concern with the consequences of Luther's Reformation through repeated engagements with Paul as he developed his own theology of grace.

ONE

Justification, Grace, and the Will

Erasmus's relationship with Paul began long before he sat down to annotate or paraphrase his work. Indeed, as a child, he was schooled by the religious (whether the Brethren of the Common Life is a matter of some debate)[1] at Deventer, whose rector, Alexander Hegius, was 'a pioneer of humanist education.' After his parents' death, Erasmus's guardians pressured him to enter the monastery, and he chose the Augustinian Canons at Steyn. There, he pursued his love of Latin authors and humanistic philological studies. Disappointed in what he viewed as his fellow monks' lack of appreciation for classical learning and apparently ill suited for the monastic life, Erasmus was ordained as a priest in 1492. After he obtained permission to leave his cloister, he served Hendrik van Bergen, the Bishop of Cambrai, as his Latin secretary.[2] This position seems to have given Erasmus ample time for his intellectual pursuits, primarily classical studies and written defences of humanistic interest in pagan sources. He eventually left his position with Hendrik van Bergen and entered the University of Paris. There, between 1495 and 1499, Erasmus became increasingly interested in applying his humanistic skills to theological and biblical questions.[3]

His scholastic education at the University of Paris expanded his experience with biblical texts, and he received his bachelor's degree in theology in 1498. It is often thought that a 1499 visit to England during which he attended a lecture on Paul by John Colet sparked Erasmus's interest in scriptural interpretation.[4] However, John Gleason has shown that it is unlikely that this alone stimulated Erasmus's theological development. Still, Colet was, like

Erasmus, a humanist interested in exegesis and theology, and his example may have influenced Erasmus's path.[5]

Erasmus had to grow into his Paulinism. Preserved Smith has reminded us: 'There was nothing precocious about the genius of Erasmus. When he was thirty he had produced hardly anything. Had he died at the age of forty he would scarce be remembered now.'[6] Smith's observation is especially true of Erasmus's theological work, and his intellectual and spiritual journey is most evident in his work on Paul.

Though it is difficult to ascertain the exact moment Erasmus turned towards Pauline studies, it is clear that Lorenzo Valla (1407–57), the Italian humanist and biblical philologist, played an important role in confirming Erasmus's interest in biblical studies. Erasmus believed that Valla had 'rescued literature from the barbarians.'[7] This initial interest led Erasmus to publish Valla's notes on the New Testament. Erika Rummel argues, however, that while Erasmus may have relied on Valla's model in his own work on the New Testament, 'for inspiration and guidance he looked beyond Valla to the Church Fathers.' She continues: 'In Ep 149, which contains a programmatic statement on biblical studies, Erasmus declared that his own inclination was "to follow the path to which I am beckoned by St Jerome and the glorious choir of all those ancient writers" (Ep 149:62–3). In the preface to the *Annotations* he once again asserted that he had revised the New Testament according to the Greek sources, "advised to do so by Jerome and Augustine" (Ep 373:19).' And while Valla's work informed his own, Erasmus had written a commentary on the Pauline epistles in Greek four years prior to his publication of Valla's notes on the New Testament. It appears that as early as 1501 Erasmus had already committed himself to learning Greek to further his biblical studies.[8]

Once armed with the skills obtained through the careful study of classical texts, Erasmus applied his learning to biblical texts with immense energy and precision. Beginning with the *philosophia Christi*, as outlined in the *Enchiridion* and culminating in a remarkable revision of the *Paraphrases* for the 1532 edition, Erasmus's reputation and notoriety grew as he engaged in New Testament scholarship with the tools of philology and the mindset of a searching believer. Erasmus's goal in the *Annotations* was not mere grammatical perfection, nor did he wish simply to create palatable aphorisms in his *Paraphrases*. To the contrary, he wanted to discover the truth, or, more accurately, what he believed Paul really intended to tell the followers of Jesus Christ. Furthermore, Erasmus's Pauline studies played an important role in his debate with Luther over free will. While Luther continually asserted the efficacy of a *sola scriptura* approach to theology,[9] Erasmus worked to situate the free will debate within the multifaceted context of Pauline scripture, patristic sources, and medieval and early modern Church tradition. For Erasmus, the justification debate had a long history that had to be considered in his polemic with Luther. That tradition included not only the early Church Fathers, but also medieval thinkers.

MEDIEVAL TRADITION

Experts generally agree that the issue of justification did not occupy a place distinct from the broader soteriological debates in the theological context of the Middle Ages. Karlfried Froehlich notes:

> The patristic and medieval tradition did not show interest in a separate treatise *De iustificatione*. Lutheran historians of the nineteenth century regarded this fact as supporting the impression of a 'dark' Middle Ages and pointed with pride to the rediscovery of the doctrine by the Reformers. Catholic historians, on the other hand, used the marginal role of justification during the Middle Ages as an indication that it did not belong in the center of the church's doctrinal concerns until the sixteenth-century challenge by the Protestants made an official definition necessary. The absence of formal interest should not deceive us, however. Theologians today generally agree that justification language signals central Christian concerns which were discussed in countless ways from the very beginning. Justification touches on the fundamental structure of the relationship between God and human beings; it speaks of their role in this relationship and determines the very definition of salvation.[10]

Justification thus occupied an important part of the lexicon employed to describe the relationship between the Christian sinner and God. As Hubert Jedin notes in his study of the Council of Trent, Augustine's attack against the Pelagians highlighted the complexity of the issue for Christian thinkers, and from that time, 'the theme of justification had never ceased to occupy western theologians.'[11] Augustine had irrevocably linked Pauline language to the debate on justification and human freedom and consequently to the essence of the relationship between God and the believer. Augustine's influence continued throughout the Middle Ages as medieval exegetes incorporated 'Pauline-Augustinian language' into their work on justification.[12]

Medieval thinkers applied themselves to what Froehlich calls 'a main problem in the reading of Paul: the determination of the contribution of God and human beings to the process of salvation' in the light of Augustine's anti-Pelagian assertions. Indeed, 'Augustine's insistence on the impotence of the fallen will, and therefore on the absolute priority of God's helping grace (*auxilium gratiae*), did not fully answer the question.' Froehlich elaborates: 'It established the indispensability of grace, but there was room for new thought about the extent to which human nature was left intact or "wounded" (Luke 19:30, 34), capable of participating and starting the process or at least preparing itself for God's gracious intervention just as matter must be disposed to form.'[13]

Throughout the medieval period, theologians formulated theologies of justification that fit within a religious and pastoral context that urged human discipline and perfectibility and linked those ideas to both tradition and scripture. At times, this led to presentations of the process of justification that connected it to the sacrament of penance.[14] Theologians established this link more firmly when, in the twelfth century, 'the idea of merit as changing something not owed into a legal or moral debt which is owed' developed, and 'a distinction began to be made between 'congruous' or proportionate and 'condign' or fully deserved merit.'[15] Thus, Froehlich notes, 'Late medieval theology accepted the basic understanding of justification as the initial process of the Christian life, its first beginning in baptism and its renewed beginning in penance.' Yet how this justification was worked out in connection with salvation and to what extent it involved human effort remained an issue for late medieval theologians.[16]

Erik Saak, too, recognizes the complicated nature of the Augustinian picture in late medieval and early modern theology, and he underscores the importance of 'a renewed anti-Pelagian Augustinian theology' in the fourteenth century, particularly in the works of Thomas Bradwardine and Gregory of Rimini. Yet

Saak notes that, while 'the hallmark of Augustine's "Augustinian theology" is generally agreed to have been his doctrine of grace and love,' the fourteenth-century program of Augustinian theology was manifested in 'a multi-dimensional Augustinian theology on all levels.'[17] The exact trajectory that program took and its influence on Luther is, as noted earlier, the subject of rigorous historical debate. Froehlich writes that, given the broad range of theological interpretations about justification, grace, and free will, theologians exhibited 'renewed interest in the roots from which justification language in the western tradition had emerged: Paul's epistles.' He adds: 'It seems no mere coincidence that Martin Luther claimed his discovery of the true meaning of justification as the fruit of his exegetical endeavors.'[18] The late medieval Augustinian theological program influenced Luther, and it influenced Erasmus, too.

EARLY MODERN THOUGHT

Charles Trinkaus notes that this late medieval debate on justification received fresh attention from Renaissance humanists even before Luther made it the centre of his reform program. Indeed, Trinkaus sees the debate as an integral part of the wider 'cultural problem of the Renaissance and Reformation' rooted in efforts to 'reinforce the Church's claim to universality.' The medieval debates on the issue of human freedom in justification carried over into humanistic debates concerned with 'a separation of the material.' Trinkaus elaborates: 'For some, freedom of will was possible in the world of material relations but not where spiritual well-being or salvation was concerned. For others, man possessed spiritual freedom but no power over external events.'[19]

Influenced alternately by Stoicism and Neoplatonism, humanists from Petrarch to Ficino and Pico to Erasmus struggled to synthesize medieval religious concerns about free will and justification with Renaissance preoccupations with classical emphases on human potential.[20] When Erasmus attacked Luther on the subject of free will, he did so not only within the context of late medieval theological debates on the subject but also within the framework of early modern humanist interest in it. As Trinkaus notes, 'Erasmus was a humanist, and his religious reform program was a humanistic one, which in many ways was lost sight of in the debate over free will. But for Erasmus a humanistic reform program was more than a method of combat and was in fact part of a deeply conceived theological and philosophical position. Essential to it was both the doctrine of free will and that of grace, but the position itself was a broader one and provided the matrix within which these specific theological points became critical.' That broader context, according to Trinkaus, included the historical path of the debate on free will from Augustine through the medieval context as presented by the nominalists up to and including the humanistic concerns of the Renaissance,[21] through which Erasmus arrived at 'a pastoral and rhetorical theology, not ignorant of the systematic, dialectical schools, nor entirely without a substantive position.' In this view, 'Ultimate theological truth is, however, limited to what can be *imagined* on the basis of human *conjecture* concerning custom and the meaning of Scriptures.'[22]

THE REFORMATION CONTEXT

One of the more hotly contested historiographical controversies concerns the formation of late medieval 'schools of thought' and the relationship of those schools of thought to the Reformation in general and Luther in particular. Luther's challenge to the Church's practices regarding justification, including the roles of baptism, confession, penance, and works, necessarily included a challenge to the late medieval theology of justification.[23] In this way, any discussion of Reformation-era perspectives on justification, and the corollary subjects of grace and free will, rests on how much the early modern debates about these issues actually deviated from medieval theological and practical perspectives.

Alister McGrath argues that efforts to link the theological developments of the early modern period in general, and the Reformation in particular, to medieval concepts of free will and justification lie in the concern that 'if it can be shown that the central teaching of the Lutheran Reformation, the fulcrum about which the early Reformation turned, the *articulus stantis et cadentis ecclesiae*, constituted a theological *novum*, unknown within the previous fifteen centuries of catholic thought, it will be clear that the Reformers' claim to catholicity would be seriously prejudiced, if not totally discredited.'[24] This assertion also has serious implications for the study of Erasmus, since Erasmus conceived of his theological views as being within the bounds of Catholic tradition, despite his evolving views on free will and justification. Saak notes the complicated arguments surrounding the appearance of a unique late-medieval Augustinianism and its influence on the Reformation debate about free will.[25] He, too, notes that the debate about the role of Augustine in late medieval theology is complicated by the implications of that debate for Reformation history, since 'not only is it of primary importance for conceptions and interpretations of the Reformation, but it also carries implicit – and at times explicit – overtones of how history should be done in the first place.'[26] That is to say, how historians view Augustine's theology in the Reformation context and how theologians view the history of Augustinianism in the formation of Reformation theology influences the very understanding of Luther and Lutheran theology. By extension, and in the context of this study, it also influences the interpretation of Erasmus's contributions to the Reformation debate on free will. For the broader interpretation of Luther's theological antecedents and influences, however, the debate is particularly significant.

The debate was important for Luther and Erasmus, but probably was just as important for others who had a stake in the reform of the Church. Although Erasmus had initially been interested in Luther's attacks on monasticism and ecclesiastical and papal corruption, it increasingly became clear that they stood at quite a distance on important theological matters. Nevertheless, Erasmus was reluctant to write against Luther. But by 1524 Luther's attacks against Rome took on new weight. The Peasant's War had begun that summer, and though Luther eventually publicly condemned the peasants, many associated their uprising with Luther's ideas. Furthermore, Luther had made it clear that he intended to break with Rome, not just reform the existing Church. As a result, key figures throughout Christendom felt a renewed urgency to convince Erasmus, the leading intellectual of his age, to write against Luther.[27] Both the pope, Clement VII, and Henry VIII, alarmed at Luther's attacks on the Church and its doctrine, made it known that they hoped Erasmus would end his ambiguous responses to Luther and write convincingly against him. He finally did so in 1524 in *De libero arbitrio* (On the Free Will).[28] In that work, he challenged Luther's view of the pervasiveness of original sin and defended the human role in the process of salvation. Luther defended justification by faith alone and rejected free will a year later in *De servo arbitrio* (On the Bondage of the Will), a work that he later viewed as one of his two most important theological tracts.[29]

Given Erasmus's interest in the relationship between theological truth and the freedom of the will, it is not surprising that he picked this topic on which to debate Luther. It offered him a great deal of security in a contentious religious and political environment: doctrinal flexibility, a wide range of patristic sources on which to draw, and established medieval and Renaissance opinions upon which to build. Moreover, the topic struck at the very heart of Luther's reform agenda. Well versed in the medieval theological tradition and heir to and promoter of the Renaissance recapitulation of theology in pastoral and rhetorical terms, Erasmus understood the doctrinal flexibility of the issue of justification and, by extension, free will in the Church. Erasmus's choice not only defined the subject of his personal debate with Luther, but also prefigured the trajectory that the conflict between reformers and Catholics took as Luther's split with Rome became irreparable.

Indeed, the extent of human freedom in the process of salvation proved to be *a*, if not *the*, sticking point in the Lutheran split from Rome. Although the issue came to the forefront beginning in 1524 with Erasmus's attack on Luther's stance on justification, it remained a focus in efforts to resolve the rift in the Church and bring the Lutherans back into the fold.[30] The Confutation of 1530, for example – the response of the Roman Church to the *Confessio Augustana* and Melanchthon's letter to the papal legate, Campeggio – asserted: 'it is Pelagian error to say that one can merit grace by one's own powers alone … On the other hand,' it continued, 'it is a Manichaean error to deny that one can merit with the help of grace.'[31] The Protestants rejected the confutation.[32]

As it turned out, the *Confessio Augustana* and its confutation found many points of agreement, but not on the role of free will in justification. Despite the recognition of common ground in the theological and ecclesiastical disputes between the reformers and the Church, the issue of justification remained an obstacle. Both sides feared that the conflict would come to war, however, and they continued to work for a resolution. Cardinal Contarini, a papal delegate, and Melanchthon, Luther's spokesperson in the process, made additional efforts to formulate a view of justification acceptable to Protestants and Catholics at the Colloquy of Regensburg in 1541. After considerable work by Contarini and Melanchthon to create a statement of 'double justification' tolerable to both sides, both Luther and the pope rejected the formulation. The Catholics convened the Council of Trent 1545, and the Protestants chose not to participate. When the council made its final pronouncement on justification in 1547, it became clear that 'there was little hope any more of any kind of agreement on doctrine.'[33]

Yet there was an additional effort to find a *via media*, at least in the German lands. In 1548, after the Schmalcald War, renewed efforts to find a solution took place, but 'the voices of the Roman Catholics grew harsher, while those of the Lutherans indicate[d] both their awareness of their weakened situation and their determination not to yield on their central doctrine of justification.' Despite final attempts at doctrinal rapprochement by Melanchthon, no official progress was made, and by 1555 'western Christendom was permanently divided.'[34] The issue of justification, and the corollary issues of grace and free will, proved the insurmountable theological obstacles to unity.

In the post-Tridentine period, a clear distinction between a 're-formed' and a 'Catholic' stance emerged. Yet it is important to recognize that throughout the Reformation, the issue underwent serious discussion and revision on both sides of the divide. Luther, for example, began with a position very close to the positions of the anti-Pelagian Augustine, though, as McGrath points out, even the early Luther's stance on justification can be distinguished from that of Augustine, primarily in his rejection of Augustine's neo-Platonist anthropology in favour of a theological discussion based on Paul. Later, according to McGrath, Luther moved 'increasingly away from Augustine' and adopted a strong necessitarian stance, which asserted that 'all things happen by absolute necessity.'[35]

Other reformers also revisited the subject throughout the Reformation and post-Tridentine period. As noted earlier, Melanchthon's understanding of justification underwent serious revision when he worked to find unity with Catholics on the issue. John Calvin, meanwhile, embraced 'an important aspect of Luther's understanding of justification which Melanchthon abandoned – the personal union of Christ and the believer in justification.'[36] Werner Elert asserts, 'Finally, however, the doctrine of justification asserted itself as the definitive expression for the evangelical relationship between God and man, and it remained lastingly effective as the fundamental impetus for the whole church.'[37] In the light of this fluidity in the debate, it is unsurprising that just as the reformers, Catholic and Protestant alike, worked to understand and articulate the issue of justification during this period, so did Erasmus.

DE SERVO ARBITRIO, DE LIBERO ARBITRIO

The story of Erasmus's theological journey neither begins nor ends with his association with Luther. In the thick of his theologically most productive years,[38] however, Erasmus found himself embroiled in the greatest controversy of his age with that most dangerous type of thinker: a popular one. Unlike the imagining of heaven and hell, the daily routines of monks and priests, or the ceremonies and observances practised or not practised by the Christians of Europe, the arena of this debate and the consequences of its resolution were immediate and highly tangible. Moreover, the debate was channelled through that most vexing of historical figures, Martin Luther. To avoid him in writing about Erasmus's emerging theology of grace would be to tell an incomplete story. At the same time, to use either man as a mere foil for the other would be to empty both of their individual significance.

The central experience of contention between the two men remains their well-known debate on the freedom of the will. Erasmus's position in this debate has been portrayed as a feeble attempt to muffle the increasingly vocal suspicions of his critics regarding his commitment to the Church and to re-establish his role as the defender of the faith.[39] Many historians have depicted Luther's response as a decisive theological victory for the true theologian of the pair, whose sincere and convincing response proved Erasmus to be a mere dabbler in theologically important issues.

De servo arbitrio is considered by many important scholars to be Luther's most significant theological treatise. It is one of the most succinct and impassioned articulations of his theological program, and it holds a place as one of the most enduring pieces of his theological legacy. Luther wrote the treatise in response to Erasmus's *De libero arbitrio* and, in doing so, effectively ended any speculation that a secret theological alliance or private bond of agreement in the Reformation debate existed between the two men. This was by design, of course, and Erasmus knew that in writing *De libero arbitrio* he would take a step towards silencing those who had questioned his orthodoxy and allegiance to the Church during the preceding few years.

De servo arbitrio outlines what Luther considered the very heart of the gospel and therefore of the reform of theology and the Church: the freedom of the will. He wrote to Erasmus: 'You alone

... have attacked the real thing, that is the essential issue. You have not worried me with those extraneous issues about the Papacy, purgatory, indulgences and such like – trifles, rather than issues – in respect of which almost all to date have sought my blood ... you, and you alone, have seen the hinge on which all turns, and aimed for the vital spot. For that I heartily thank you; for it is more gratifying to me to deal with this issue.'[40] For Luther, then, the Reformation hinged on the subject that Erasmus had purposefully addressed: the very crux of the painful rending of the One True Church and the most important of all the myriad issues that the Reformation had brought to a head.

Luther's response to Erasmus's attack represented a fundamental defence of his own program, demonstrating that the bondage of the will and the essential lack of human freedom comprised the intrinsic characteristics of the human relationship to God. The doctrine of the bondage of the will fit neatly into Luther's own understanding of true Christianity. As George Anderson, Austin Murphy, and Joseph Burgess note, 'Thus for Luther the answer to the question "How do I get a gracious God?" must be "by faith alone," by trust in nothing but God's promises of mercy and forgiveness in Jesus Christ. Here Luther went beyond the Augustinian primacy of grace (*sola gratia*) to that of faith (*sola fide*).'[41] In *De servo arbitrio*, Luther responded to Erasmus in a way that clearly and succinctly articulated his view on free will and justification.[42] Ernst Winter describes the contest in this way:

The two protagonists become symbolic for two camps, unable to meet. Erasmus defines free will: 'By freedom of the will we understand in this connection the power of the human will whereby man can apply to or turn away from that which leads unto eternal salvation.' Luther says that man is unable to do anything but continue to sin, except for God's grace. The whole work of man's salvation, first to last, is God's. Both proceed from different vantage points. Erasmus dismisses both the excessive confidence in man's moral strength, held by the Pelagians, and what he believed to be St. Augustine's view, the excessive hopelessness of a final condemnation passed on by man. He identified Luther with the latter. Erasmus calls on Scripture to help in outlining his reasonable and conciliatory middle way, really a philosophical and pragmatic statement of man's essential freedom. Luther interprets this to mean assigning free will to divine things, because his interest lies in practical implementation of a classical Christian paradox, which he thought solved. His solution is 'faith alone sets us free.'[43]

In these ways, then, Luther and Erasmus confronted a central issue of their age – at least one made central by Luther's insistence on its importance. In so doing, each theologian used his formidable linguistic, theological, and humanistic resources to defend a position, the belief in which would secure the salvation of those who held it as truth.

For Luther, salvation was an immediate issue because every human inevitably faced the impending certainty of divine judgment. As Heiko Oberman summarizes: 'What Luther saw on the horizon were the dark clouds of divine judgment gathering over a world nearing its end, a world fettered and enslaved in a thousand ways, that insisted on self-determination before God, that dared to speculate about the "meaning of history" and to speak of freedom of the will without being able to free itself from the paralyzing primeval fear of being trapped helplessly in the cage of an impenetrable world history.'[44] The absolutely pressing nature of divine judgment made salvation a question of pressing importance. As a result, it became the issue around which Luther structured his program of reform and the theology upon which he built a new faith. McGrath argues that Luther built this theology 'upon his insight that man cannot initiate the process of justification, and his conviction that the church of his day had, by affirming the direct opposite, fallen into the Pelagian error.' Luther contended that 'the gospel destroys all human righteousness, in that man is forced to recognize that he is totally devoid of soteriological resources, and thus turns to receive these resources *ab extra*.' McGrath elaborates Luther's position: 'Man is justified by laying hold of a righteousness which is not, and can never be, his own – the *iustitia Christi aliena*, which God mercifully "reckons" to man.'[45] While Luther concentrated on one aspect of medieval Catholic theology that underscored good works in the economy of salvation, Erasmus took advantage of his own understanding that Catholic tradition held a variety of positions on free will and justification. Again, the very doctrinal fluidity of this issue is most likely precisely why he selected it for his attack against Luther. It was, essentially, the safest theological issue he could find.[46]

Both Luther and Erasmus deployed vast arsenals of scriptural evidence to support their seemingly opposing positions. The two divergent arguments hinged on differing, and often very finely manipulated, interpretations of scripture in general, and Pauline scripture in particular. Since both men understood that this battle was one that could be fought – and certainly won – only on the basis of New Testament support, they deployed Paul as the primary weapon.

Like Erasmus, and other humanists for that matter, Luther shared the conviction that all interpretations of holy scripture must be based on the original text, or as close to such a text as one was likely to get.[47] Luther, however, was also convinced that the scriptures constituted the guide to understanding God's will and the truth about salvation. Paul was central to this conviction, though not simply in the manner in which he had been interpreted, processed, and explained through the Church Fathers and the authority of a thousand years of tradition. Rather, the Paul of the scriptures was, like the scriptures themselves, radically transcendent. Apart from language and context, across time, and apart from and despite tradition, Luther believed that Paul led to the truth. Thus, for Luther, the link between Paul (i.e., scripture) and salvation was both experiential and spiritual.[48]

For Erasmus, on the other hand, truth was formed through the marriage of scripture and tradition, especially the tradition of the Church as interpreted by the Fathers. Erasmus relied on Romans extensively in *De libero arbitrio* precisely because he knew that this Pauline epistle held the most problematic scriptural evidence against free will. He boldly declared that Paul could be used to support his position: 'Let us see whether support for free will can be found in Paul, the vigorous champion of grace, who lays unremitting siege to the works of the Law.'[49]

In the diatribe, Erasmus first argued that to use Paul's words as evidence of the enslavement of the human will is nonsensical; God would not require actions from the sinner if those actions would not produce spiritual fruit: 'First of all we come across the passage in the Epistle to the Romans, chapter 2[:4]: "Do you despise his wealth of goodness and patience and forbearance? Are you not aware that God's goodness leads you to repentance?" How can the accusation of contempt for God's commandment be made if the will is not free? How can God invite us to repentance if he is the cause of impenitence? How can the accused be justly condemned when the judge compels him to crime?'[50] Erasmus employed Romans 13:12 in a similar way: '"Let us cast off the works of darkness," says Paul; and "sloughing off the old man and all his acts": how can we be ordered to "throw off" and "strip off" if we cannot do anything?'[51] Erasmus also used Romans to contend that what appears as Paul's attack on the freedom of the will is actually an attack on the role of Old Testament Law in justification. He argues on the basis of Romans 1:18–22 and Romans 2:17–23: 'The Jews gloried in the temple, in circumcision, in sacrifices; the Greeks gloried in their wisdom: but now that the wrath of God has been revealed from heaven by the gospel, all that glory has withered.'[52]

For his part, Luther often referred to Romans in *De servo arbitrio* to bolster his arguments against Erasmus. Luther used the Epistle to the Romans to caution Erasmus, to warn him against presuming to know too much and giving too much to the intellect in matters of faith: 'But those who wished to seem wise argued themselves out of it till their hearts grew dark and they became fools, as Rom. I says (vv.21–22), and denied, or pretended not to know, things which the poets, and the common people, and even their own consciences held as being most familiar, most certain, and most true.'[53] Luther understood Romans 9 to underscore divine foreknowledge[54] and asserted that Paul emphasizes that humans have no free will:

> The apostle, therefore, is bridling the ungodly who take offence at his plain speaking, telling them they should realize that the Divine will is fulfilled by what to us is necessity, and that it is definitely established that no freedom or 'free-will' is left them, but all things depend on the will of God alone. And he bridles them by commanding them to be silent, and to revere the majesty of God's power and will, against which we have no rights, but which has full rights against us to do what It pleases. No injustice is done to us, for God owes us nothing, He has received nothing from us, and He has promised us nothing but what He pleased and willed.[55]

Again and again, Luther turned to Paul to establish his determination that the will is fundamentally unfree and that Erasmus had misinterpreted, if not misused, the apostle's words.

For Luther, the question of the bondage or freedom of the will was particularly important because of its connection to the central doctrine of justification by faith alone. Elizabeth Galbraith explains:

For Luther, divine grace and human freedom are contradictory concepts, in the sense that, when grace is given, human freedom is ruled out. However, one might ask why it is that grace rules out freedom and works in preparation for salvation? The answer for Luther is quite clear, since 'what need is there of the Spirit or of Christ or of God if free choice can overcome the motions of the mind towards evil.' What Luther means is that to suggest that human effort is necessary to overcome evil and gain righteousness cheapens grace by implicitly neglecting the significance of the life and death of Jesus. The reconciliation of persons with God is made possible only by the atonement of Jesus. That is God's gift to humans, given at the immeasurable cost to God of the death of the Son. Hence the idea that people can merit salvation by exercising freedom of choice is nothing short of blasphemous. The exercise of freedom is irrelevant to salvation since for those saved through Jesus Christ, salvation is a certainty apart from works.[56]

McGrath, however, warns against viewing 'Luther's doctrine of justification and of the *servum arbitrium* ... as two sides of a coin.' He sees the issue as complicated by Luther's understanding of *iustitia Christi aliena* and notes that the connection between justification and the unfree will was challenged by Lutheran theologians 'at a comparatively early stage.'[57] For Luther, nevertheless, this link between human bondage of the will and his underlying theological principle of justification by faith alone made Erasmus's defence of free will an attack on the central tenet of his theological program.

What doubt can there be, then, that Luther and Erasmus became locked in a fierce battle, playing out their roles as theological foes whose fundamental interpretations of scripture differ so greatly as to be irreconcilable and essentially antithetical? What doubt is there, then, that Erasmus was a dilettante, playing at theology, defending what would later be defined as Church orthodoxy on the will and setting himself up as the 'anti-Luther'?

But who wrote these words?

> Not the grace for which this world is accustomed to pray in its usual way, but a true and a new grace, that is the free gift of the truly justifying faith of the gospel. And I also wish that as a result of the complete absolution through grace of the sins of your former life, you may have the peace of a conscience now free from anxiety and a steadfast friendship with God. These two things neither the strength of human wisdom affords, nor the observance of the Mosaic Law, instead they originate for all from the unique generosity of God the Father and of his Son, our Lord Jesus Christ.[58]

Or these words?

> By the gospel I mean justification through faith in Jesus Christ, the Son of God, whom the Law promised and prefigured.[59]

What about these?

> Would that even all the Jews might abandon their Moses and be converted to Christ. The Jews now persuade themselves that it is sufficient for gaining salvation if they are sons of Abraham and possess the Law once given to them by God. However, none of this will profit them unless they show themselves worthy through faith of being drawn and cherished by God.[60]

And these as well?

> But Christ is a man in such a way that at the same time he is also God, not the God peculiar to this or that nation, but the God of the whole world, and a God who is one with the Father. He is in command of all, and all these things are carried out by his inscrutable wisdom. Because of such an unusual love for the human race, praise and thanksgiving are owed to him alone for all eternity. Amen.[61]

These are not Luther's words but those of Erasmus, the reputed defender of free will, the spokesman for Roman Catholic unity, the humanist biblical scholar. They posed a problem for Erasmus in his lifetime, as his controversy with Alberto Pio, the Prince of Carpi, demonstrates, and they pose a problem in our current time for those who wish to know and understand Erasmus's role in the Reformation debate.

Erasmus's Pauline annotations and exegesis show us that his Pauline journey did not end with his role as the anti-Luther and defender of free will. Erasmus was not merely the humanist sceptic, the voice of reason in a time of prophetic and sometimes alarming faith, as some historians of Erasmus, the Reformation, and Luther have depicted him. Erasmus, we have believed, was the humanist who looked at problems much as we expect modern scientists to approach disease: clinical, sceptical, remote, accurate, and above all transparent. He created the *philosophia Christi*, a 'reasonable' faith, a faith almost prophetic in its very modernity.[62] Yet Erasmus, at least in his dealings with Paul, did not steadfastly adhere to any of the positions upon which much of his reputation rests. Like an adolescent whose thoughts and experiences evolve, only to solidify later, Erasmus was not theologically stagnant, and his development was not complete – probably not even at his death. A man of his learning and determination could only continue to find more in a text so rich with uncertainty and certainty, so full of import and pressing impact.

Erasmus's journey in the footsteps of Paul and his efforts to show us and his contemporaries the true Paul are really the story of a problem. The passages just quoted concern the core of the Reformation debate and mean, for the historian of Erasmus and of the Reformation, that we are no longer able to fall back on the neat and discrete division between Luther and Erasmus as a way to delineate and define the Reformation conflict. Erasmus no longer can be viewed as the defender of an as yet undefined Roman Catholic orthodoxy, nor can he be used as the litmus test of the anti-Lutheran. This problem is further complicated by its implications for the historical understanding of the relationship between humanism and the Reformation. Nevertheless, it has its root in evidence left by Erasmus on the very subjects that formed the backbone of the Reformation debate: faith, justification, grace, the freedom of the will, and the role of Paul and his Epistle to the Romans in establishing the proper theology of the will for Christians.

Erasmus both reconsidered and reworked his own understandings of Paul and justification while endeavouring to comprehend and assess the scriptural perspective on the freedom of the will that Luther so vigorously articulated. In a lengthy letter to his close friend Thomas More in 1527, Erasmus fretted over the implications of the freedom or servitude of the will in the process of salvation and pledged to continue his investigation:

> If I treat the subject from the point of view of the monks and theologians, who attribute too much to man's merits because it is to their advantage to hold this opinion, clearly I speak against my conscience and knowingly obscure the glory of Christ. But if I govern my pen in such a way as to attribute some power to free will, but great efficacy to grace, I offend both sides, which was my experience with the *Diatribe*. If I follow Paul and Augustine, very little is left to free will. Augustine, in fact, in the two books he wrote in his old age against Valentine, does indeed affirm the existence of free will; but he makes such a case for the power of grace that I do not see what is left to free will. He admits that works performed before the action of grace are dead; he attributes to grace our ability to repent, our will to do good, the good we have done, our perseverance in doing good. He admits that grace works all these things in us. Then where is merit? Confronted by this dilemma Augustine had recourse to saying that God imputes his good works to us as merits and crowns his own gifts in us. Is that not a clever defence of free will? For myself, I should not be averse to the opinion according to which we can of our own natural powers and without particular grace acquire congruent grace, as they say, except that Paul opposed this view. For that matter not even the schoolmen accept this opinion.[63]

The concerns Erasmus articulated to More informed the changes he made to the early published versions of his *Annotations* and *Paraphrases* on Paul's Epistle to the Romans.

Thus, there was a difference between Erasmus and Luther in their initial contest over the interpretation of free will, but Erasmus continued to consider his initial position and his interpretation of Paul's writings after 1524. On the issue of justification, Erasmus eventually articulated a view that could be identified (as it often was by his contemporary critics) as Protestant. By his own account,

Erasmus's interpretation of Paul's understanding of justification remained in flux after his initial polemic on the subject with Luther.

The next chapter will examine Erasmus's ongoing engagement with Paul through his scriptural studies, the *Annotations* and *Paraphrases* on the New Testament, and his polemical works, *De libero aribtiro* and the *Hyperaspistes I* and *II*. Erasmus readdressed the relationship between grace and salvation as he strove to understand Paul's message to believers about justification.

TWO

Erasmus on Romans: Texts and Authorities

૪૧

Erasmus began his journey with Paul in earnest after returning from a trip to England.[1] As early as 1501 he wrote that he was preparing a commentary on Paul. He then dedicated himself to studying Greek in order to facilitate his engagement with Pauline scripture. By 1514 he made it known that he was working on some sort of commentary or paraphrase of Paul. Yet the *Paraphrases on Romans* remained unpublished until 1517 and likely did not contain the commentaries he had originally planned. Erasmus believed 'that the function of paraphrase is to improve the text by making it clearer,' and he worked on many editions of the *Paraphrases on Romans* in order to capture the voice of Paul himself and to present his readers with as clear a picture of the epistle as possible.[2] The *Paraphrases* formed an essential part of Erasmus's reform program and his desire to bring the faithful closer to Paul's intention in his letter to the Romans. As Rudolf Padberg writes, 'His reform program found a kerygmatic and pastoral realization in the *Paraphrases* of the New Testament.'[3] The *Paraphrases* also appeared when the theological environment was particularly preoccupied with the message of Paul and his interpretation. After all, Erasmus was finishing this work at just about the same time that Luther went public with his famous theses.[4]

Erasmus's work on Paul underwent serious and often contradictory changes during the late 1520s and early 1530s. Examining four of Erasmus's published encounters with Pauline text in communication with one another brings these contradictions into sharp relief (see table 2.1). As the following three chapters will show, the *Paraphrases on Romans*, the *Annotations on Romans*, the *De libero arbitrio*, and the *Hyperaspistes I* and *II* demonstrate a

Table 2.1
Partial Publication History of Erasmus's *Annotations* and *Paraphrases* of
the Book of Romans during His Lifetime

Paraphrases	Annotations	De libero arbitrio	Hyperaspistes I	Hyperaspistes II
1517, Martens, Louvain	1516, Froben, Basel			
January 1518, Froben, Basel				
November 1518, Froben, Basel				
April 1519, Froben, Basel	1519, Froben, Basel			
October 1519, Strasbourg				
1520, Froben, Basel				
1521, Froben, Basel				
1522, Froben, Basel	1522, Froben, Basel	September 1524, Froben, Basel		
1523, Froben, Basel	1527, Froben, Basel		Winter/Summer 1526, Froben, Basel	Summer/Fall 1527, Froben, Basel
1532, Froben, Basel				
1534, Froben, Basel				
	1535, Froben, Basel			

Sources: For the *Paraphrases*: CWE, Vol. 42, xx–xxiii. For the *Annotations*: Rummel, *Erasmus' Annotations*, vii. For *De libero arbitrio* and *Hyperaspistes I*, see CWE, Vol. 76. For the *Hyperaspistes II*, see CWE, Vol. 77.

migration through various understandings, interpretations, and articulations of Paul that was a nuanced and experimental journey made all the more urgent by the pivotal role of Paul's epistles and the issue of justification in the Reformation theological debates. First, however, this chapter will provide a brief overview of these four texts' engagement with Romans and of the Church Fathers on whom Erasmus relied in his interpretations of scripture.

THE *ANNOTATIONS*

The *Annotations* is the best place to begin to understand Erasmus's development as a theological scholar. Here, with scripture itself, Erasmus started to question and work with the accepted and received version of the Bible, St Jerome's Vulgate. In 1516 Erasmus's *Annotations* on the New Testament was issued by the Basel publisher Johannes Froben, along with his new and revised Latin translation and his Greek version of the New Testament.[5] Erika Rummel describes the *Annotations*: 'In their original form, the *Annotations* were predominantly a philological commentary, recording and discussing variant readings and commenting on passages in the Vulgate that were in Erasmus' opinion either obscurely or incorrectly rendered. Material added to the notes in subsequent editions (1519, 1522, 1527, 1535) broadened their scope considerably. They became a mixture of textual and literary criticism, theological exegesis, spiritual counsel, and polemical asides.'[6] The 1527 *Annotations on Romans*, in particular, reflects Erasmus's search for Paul's intent. In this edition of the *Annotations*, also published by Froben, Erasmus expanded upon his philological and theological understanding of Paul's Epistle to the Romans. The edition details Erasmus's interaction with the text and highlights his commitment to reworking, reviewing, and recasting Paul's theological message by means of extended philological explanations and the inclusion of additional theological input from the Church Fathers. In particular, Erasmus increasingly incorporated Chrysostom's interpretation of Romans.

THE *PARAPHRASES*

Evidence of Erasmus's changing interpretation of Paul can also be found in his *Paraphrases on Romans*, which he designed primarily as a study tool to provide students of scripture with an approachable commentary. Erasmus spent an enormous amount of time in his most productive years working on his Pauline exegesis. Indeed, as John Bateman notes, 'There were twenty-eight editions of the *Paraphrases on the Epistles*, directly or indirectly authorized by Erasmus, between the first publication in November 1517 and the posthumous *Opera omnia* of 1540.'[7]

To make the paraphrases more accessible, the *Paraphrases* was printed in a variety of sizes, and beginning in 1519 the octavo edition appeared 'in the italic type commonly found in such books-for-the-hand (*enchiridia*).' In using this format, Erasmus and Froben made available an easily transportable version of the *Paraphrases* for those interested in better understanding scripture. Beginning in 1522, the *Paraphrases* also appeared in a folio edition, which enabled the reading public to examine Erasmus's theological works as a whole body (i.e., the revised New Testament, the Greek New Testament, and the *Paraphrases*). The goal of publishing in this format was 'to provide a more lucid and readable exposition of the meaning of the biblical text.' As a result, by 1523 the public could enjoy the *Paraphrases* 'in two different formats, a folio edition matching the folio edition of the *Novum Testamentum*, intended, presumably, for theologians and other students of the Bible, and an octavo edition for private reading, though the numerous side notes allowed it, too, to be read alongside the biblical text.'[8]

The early paraphrases were fine tuned over the remainder of Erasmus's life, and not all of the major changes to the text can be attributed to correctors and press workers.[9] The *Paraphrases on Romans* (1517) was the first to be published.[10] Over time, Erasmus introduced not only grammatical and typographical corrections but also substantive and theologically important changes, particularly in 1532. In that year, the Froben edition of his *Paraphrases on Romans* evidenced Erasmus's affirmation of a unique and not fully orthodox position – in the sense that orthodoxy would later come to be defined by the Council of Trent – on theological principles fundamental to the Reformation debate. It is here that Erasmus solidified what his search for understanding Paul brought to him.[11] At the same time, he continued his exegetical efforts on the works of Paul's Epistle to the Romans in the *Annotations*, and the two efforts – one exegetical, one grammatical, and both theological – often but not always reflected the same concerns and changes in Erasmus's interpretation of the apostle.

DE LIBERO ARBITRIO

De libero arbitrio, Erasmus's polemic on the freedom of the will, discussed in some detail in chapter 1, constitutes what most historians of the Reformation have regarded as the only articulation of his thoughts on the freedom of the will. Naturally, Erasmus hoped that the work would also serve to silence those who associated his theological, exegetical, and humanistic work with Luther's theological program and rebellion against the papacy.[12] In *De libero arbitrio*, Erasmus affirmed the role and authority of scripture as well as the place of Church tradition in his defence of human freedom in the process of justification.[13]

HYPERASPISTES I AND II

Erasmus's debate with Luther continued beyond *De libero arbitrio* in the *Hyperaspistes I* and *II*, published in 1526 and 1527, respectively. In these works, Erasmus responded to Luther's criticisms in *De servo arbitrio*. The *Hyperaspistes I* primarily dealt with Luther's concerns about the non-scriptural portions of Erasmus's arguments in *De libero arbitrio*, which Erasmus addressed more fully in *Hyperaspistes II*.[14]

In the first part of the work, as Cornelius Augustijn notes, Erasmus responded to Luther and the problem of the connection between scripture and the Church. To that end, Erasmus focused on the concept of the *claritas scripturae*.[15] In both texts, he sought to clarify and refine his argument against Luther's stance on the enslavement of the will. In some ways Erasmus retreated to safer ground, at least given his position in the Church, by concentrating on the grammatical meaning of central terms as well as the historical contours of the debate on Church tradition.[16] In the *Hyperaspistes II*, in particular, Erasmus addressed the perspectives of Augustine and Paul and relied heavily on Romans as support for his attacks against the servitude of the will. Charles Trinkaus notes in the introduction to *Hyperaspistes II*: 'Erasmus will rely heavily on Augustine to support the minimalist position he chooses to take. He is thus able to cite Augustine as at least recognizing the existence of free-will, as over against Luther, and will use him as a foil against Luther, the self-affirmed follower of Augustine. Erasmus will have more difficulty with Paul, arguing that he is being wrongly interpreted, but will find this hard to sustain.'[17]

While Erasmus had hoped that these efforts would silence his critics and clarify his theological differences from Luther and thus his distance from the Protestant camp, quite the opposite occurred. As a result, he felt defeated, undermined, and unable to please either side in the debate.[18] However, the debate did not mark the cessation of his efforts to discern the role of free will in Christian salvation. If anything, it prompted him to look deeper into the works of Paul, especially the Epistles to Romans and

Galatians, and at the contributions of the Church Fathers, particularly Augustine and Chrysostom.

AUGUSTINE

The Fathers themselves differed in their interpretation of the freedom of the will, and by Erasmus's time the Church had reached no defined orthodoxy on the matter. In some ways, the Church defined what was 'not orthodoxy' more clearly – especially through its proclamations of heresy, which proscribed heretical beliefs on a case-by-case basis. On the issue of the will, the most important item was the proscription of the fifth-century Pelagian heresy. Alister McGrath outlines the key point of the Pelagian heresy: 'The fundamental doctrine of Pelagius' theological system is the unequivocal assertion of the autonomous and sovereign character of the human *liberum arbitrium*: in creating man, God gave him the unique privilege of being able to accomplish the divine will by his own choice, setting before him life and death, and bidding him choose the former – but permitting the final decision to rest with man himself.'[19]

It was against this heresy that Augustine, the Father central to the Reformation debate on the freedom of the will, wrote his most emphatic works on the subject: *On Nature and Grace* and *On the Proceedings of Pelagius*. Augustine's reaction to the Pelagian heresy, set within the context of his own struggles with personal sin, ultimately 'set the terms in which medieval (and, indeed, post medieval) debates on the relationship between nature and grace were subsequently conducted,' according to Francis Oakley.[20] Augustine's understanding of justification had initially developed before his work specifically targeted Pelagianism. His opposition to Pelagianism, however, forced him to clearly articulate a doctrine of justification in opposition to the Pelagian confidence in human freedom. Augustine did so primarily because he 'opposed Pelagian rigorism which, if it had had its way, would have transformed the whole Christian Church into a vast monastery.' Moreover, Augustine, like Erasmus eleven centuries later, worried about the unity of the Church. Pelagius's views, and regional Christian reactions to them, challenged that unity.[21] Augustine's position on free will and grace changed in the light of the Pelagian controversy and of his reassessment of Paul's Epistle to the Romans, in particular Romans 9. McGrath neatly summarizes

Augustine's position on free will and justification. Augustine, he argues, abandoned 'his earlier teaching that man's response to God depends solely upon his unaided free will' and instead asserted that 'man's response of faith to God's offer of grace is ... in itself a gift of God.' Furthermore, Augustine came to insist that man's free will 'is compromised by sin, and incapable of leading to man's justification unless it is first liberated by grace.'[22]

Although a series of councils condemned Pelagius's belief that man was capable through 'the freedom of his will and by his own natural powers to avoid sin and attain perfection in this life,' the Church allowed that 'it clearly lay within man's power, therefore, to spurn the divine advances,' and it also 'suggested ... that man retained some power freely to cooperate with God's grace and by such cooperation to do at least something to further his own salvation.'[23] The Council of Orange in 529 formulated the most important statement regarding the matter. McGrath explains: 'The Council declared that to teach that the "freedom of the soul" remained unaffected by the Fall was Pelagian. The Faustian doctrine of the *initium fidei* – i.e., that man can take the initiative in his own salvation – was explicitly rejected: not only the *beginning*, but also the *increase* of faith, are alike gifts of grace. While the Council declared that man's *liberum arbitrium* is injured, weakened and diminished, its existence was not questioned.' Yet the council's decisions seem to have been largely unknown to medieval and early sixteenth-century theologians.[24] Thus, Augustine's was not the last word on the matter of the freedom of the will, and the theological latitude offered by the Church's councils was vigorously utilized in countless debates on the will throughout the medieval and early modern periods.

While the medieval scholastic tradition, in which Erasmus was well versed, surely influenced his practice, Erasmus turned to the Church Fathers for answers to questions of text and interpretation. He supported each change in the *Annotations* and *Paraphrases*, most often with direct or indirect reference to patristic sources. In doing so, he was able to experiment with a stance on justification brought to the fore by Luther without abandoning the Roman Catholic patristic tradition. Erasmus asserted that the Church Fathers could and would lead to proper theological interpretations of the New Testament, especially those texts most contested in the Reformation. He relied most often on Latin Fathers Jerome, Hilary, and Ambrose and on Greek Fathers Chrysostom, Origen, and Cyril. In his later development, the Greek Fathers appeared increasingly often, and his dependence on Chrysostom in particular rose steadily after 1527.[25] As McSorley puts it, 'Erasmus made no secret of the fact that he preferred Origen and St John Chrysostum to Augustine.'[26]

Although his critics consistently complained that he neglected Augustine, Erasmus's annotations to the gospels contain more than 200 references to Augustine alone.[27] His exegesis of Paul's Epistle to the Romans shows his dependence on and utilization of a variety of Fathers, but over the years his editions of the *Annotations* and *Paraphrases* reflected a growing engagement with Augustine's perspective. Although in 1525 the Catholic theologian Noël Beda accused Erasmus of repudiating Augustine's ideas, Erasmus, in fact, cited Augustine in his work on Romans, and he did editorial work on a ten-volume edition of Augustine published by the Froben press between 1528 and 1529.[28] Beda's accusation stung all the more, given Erasmus's devotion to elevating the religious authority of the Fathers over the medieval schoolmen.[29] Erasmus's growing familiarity with and dependence on Augustine is evident in his work on Romans around the same time, for his use of Augustine to bolster his opinions increased dramatically.[30]

Augustine left two works on Paul's Epistle to the Romans, *Exposito quarundam Propositionum ex Epistula ad Romanos* and *Epistulae ad Romanos inchoata expositio*,[31] both of which influenced Erasmus greatly. In these and in other works in which he interpreted the meaning of Paul's Epistle to the Romans, Augustine demonstrated 'that the issue of works of the law as over against works based on grace was the key to the whole.'[32] Following Augustine, Erasmus focused ever more closely on this aspect of Romans in his later editions of the *Annotations* and the *Paraphrases*. Augustine also 'recognized the existence of a debate within primitive Christianity, a struggle between those believers of Jewish background and those of Gentile origins.'[33] Exegetes also took hold of this debate and turned their attention to circumcision, and in the 1532 *Paraphrases on Romans* Erasmus likewise highlighted Paul's need to differentiate between the two groups.[34]

Luther's use of Augustine was both real and imagined. That is to say, Luther's theology sometimes quite closely reflected Augustine's formulation of justification and human freedom, while at other times his theology departed significantly from that of Augustine. McGrath points out, for example: 'Luther and

Augustine both interpret *iustitia Dei* as the righteousness by which God justifies sinners, rather than as the abstract divine attribute which stands over and against mankind, judging on the basis of merit.' Nevertheless, while Augustine saw this *iustitia Dei* as corresponding to human understandings of *iustitia*, Luther viewed *iustitia Dei* as 'revealed only in the cross of Christ,' a concept that 'if anything contradicts human conceptions of *iustitia*.' Furthermore: 'Whereas Luther's doctrine of justification is based on the concept of *servum arbitrium*, Augustine's is based upon that of *liberum arbitrium captivatum*, which becomes *liberum arbitrium liberatum* through the action of *gratia sanans*.'[35]

ORIGEN

Although few scholars have closely examined Erasmus's uses of patristic sources, the existing scholarship tends to focus on his relationship to three Fathers: Augustine, Jerome, and Origen. Origen has drawn particular attention. André Godin, for example, has asserted that of the Church Fathers with whom Erasmus preoccupied himself, Origen was the most important and exerted the greatest influence on Erasmus's theological work. Godin has noted Erasmus's dependence on Origen's Neoplatonic theology and allegorical exegesis, particularly in the *Enchiridion militis* (1503–4). Moreover, Godin sees Origen's influence in Erasmus's promotion of an interior and personal religion and points to his stamp on the *Annotations*, especially on Romans,[36] as well as in *De libero arbitrio* in Erasmus's defence of human freedom. Other scholars, including Jan den Boeft, Jean-Claude Margolin, and J. Chomarat, have also noted the prevalence of Origen in Erasmus's theological work.[37]

CHRYSOSTOM

A thorough investigation into Erasmus's later editions of the *Paraphrases* and *Annotations* on Romans, however, indicates that, while Origen played an essential role in his theological development, he depended on Chrysostom for the most significant changes to his work on Romans between 1527 and 1535. The fourth-century Greek bishop and theologian became increasingly important to the development of Erasmus's theology during the Reformation. Erasmus's 1527 *Annotations* and 1532 *Paraphrases* on

Romans reflect a thorough reconsideration of Chrysostom and contain a considerable number of references to his work. Erasmus referred to Chrysostom particularly in many of the most controversial changes he made to his interpretation of Romans and often for verses wherein he discussed the will, grace, and justification. And, when considering Chrysostom and Augustine as sources, he made no secret of whom he more greatly revered. In 1527 he wrote to John III of Portugal in the hope that the young king would become a patron: 'Our Augustine, who can perhaps compete in the number of his writings, devoted much of his energies to grammar, logic, music, and problems of secular philosophy. Although Chrysostom was well trained in these disciplines ... he nowhere parades his learning but makes all his secular knowledge serve the Christian faith, bringing the two into harmony. It is like diluting fine wine with a little water: there is no evidence of the taste or colour of water, but you are aware that the wine is sweeter.'[38]

Scholars have most likely overlooked Chrysostom's influence because they have concentrated on Erasmus's early theology (i.e., prior to *De libero arbitrio*) and neglected the significant changes Erasmus made to his Pauline theology during the height of the Reformation. However, it is clear that Chrysostom played a central role in his theological development. Indeed, there is both chronological and theological support for this conclusion.

The chronological evidence is straightforward. In 1525 Erasmus began publication of Chrysostom's work, concluding with a five-volume edition in 1530.[39] Concurrently, Erasmus made significant, sometimes even 'Lutheranizing' changes to his *Annotations* and *Paraphrases on Romans*. Chrysostom's homilies on Romans were accessible to Erasmus, and several of Erasmus's surviving letters indicate his continued interest in locating manuscripts and editing Chrysostom's work for publication. In a 1526 letter to Germain de Brie, only a year before his new edition of the *Annotations on Romans* appeared, Erasmus wrote that he had acquired Chrysostom's commentary on Romans.[40]

Theologically, Erasmus frequently cited Chrysostom in general, and in particular he often cited Chrysostom when he made a change to his work on Romans regarding grace, works, or justification. These 'Lutheranizing' changes, which I have found most clearly reflect Erasmus's Reformation theological trajectory after 1527, demonstrate the mark of Chrysostom's influence. Erasmus's new 'theology of the will' sometimes approximated Luther's even while it endeavoured to incorporate into its expression the Church tradition Erasmus held so dear.

Erasmus valued Chrysostom's exegesis highly, and the latter's impact on Erasmus's theology in general, and on his interpretation of Paul more specifically, is evident in the additions he made to the *Annotations* of 1527 and the *Paraphrases* of 1532. The very changes evident in his interpretation of Pauline theology in Romans, those that evince parallels with Luther's own theology, may also have been due to Chrysostom's influence.[41] Additionally, as we have seen, Erasmus published some of Chrysostom's 'treatises and homilies ... in the Greek text or in a Latin translation between 1525 and 1529,' and he presented an edition of his complete works in a five-volume set in 1530.[42]

Chrysostom's primary concern in his explication of Paul was to demonstrate that Paul was eager to provide his Roman readers with 'a moral and spiritual correction.' Furthermore, Chrysostom's work fell into a period (roughly 386–97) when two strains of influence dominated Greek biblical exegesis. One strain, the 'Origenist line,' left only fragmented aspects of Origen's exegesis of Romans available to his late fourth-century counterparts. Of more importance for Chrysostom's development was the second, 'Antiochene strain,' represented especially by Diodore of Tarsus. This tradition emphasized in Paul the 'progress from the old to the new covenant of salvation and a strong focus on the problem of predestination and free will.' Also characteristic of Antiochene exegesis, and present in Chrysostom's work as well, was an emphasis on the 'objective salvation/history contained in Scripture which unfolds in stages – creation, fall, history of Israel – which climax in the event of the Incarnation of Christ.' While the belief in human free will is maintained in this theology, an individual's salvation 'is obtained through identifying with Christ in his earthly and human life of obedience, wherein grace is received, and the hopeless web of fruitless human speculation about God cut asunder.'[43]

For Erasmus, Chrysostom's exegesis offered a unique and complex understanding of the relationship between divine power and human freedom. Chrysostom believed that faith was the central issue of concern for Paul in his Letter to the Romans, a 'faith by which a man clings to God in Christ as the ultimate and only source of salvation.' Significantly, considering the importance of Chrysostom's interpretation to Erasmus's later Pauline interpretation, Chrysostom believed, according to Peter Gorday, that

'Paul's desire to inculcate holiness in his readers must involve some instruction in right doctrine without which true holiness would be impossible.' Gorday continues:

> And in one place Chrysostom indicates what this right doc-
> trine in Romans might be: he says that in Romans Paul 'dis-
> cusses at length the fact that those who are hostile to God and
> sinners, who were not justified by law or works, were sud-
> denly by faith alone advanced to the highest favor.' If Paul's
> intent in writing Romans is to move his readers to lives of
> great virtue, then the substance of his argument consists of
> the teaching that salvation is by faith, faith which ... is a quiet
> and humble submission to the divine sovereignty resulting in
> all manner of good works. Chrysostom, in a way which re-
> sembles the Protestant Reformers and which endeared him to
> some of them, seems to be primarily concerned in exegeting
> Romans with the *fides qua creditur*. His actual exegesis bears
> this contention out.

This preoccupation with the centrality of salvation also reflects Chrysostom's concern for 'the pursuit by individual Christians of spiritual and moral perfection,'[44] a theme, as we will see, that was reflected as well in Erasmus's own theological program.

Erasmus's engagement with Paul's letter to the Romans was ongoing, iterative, and evolutionary. As he attempted to under-stand the fundamental issues of his time through Paul's eyes, his thoughts were shaped by these Fathers who had been down their own paths with Paul. Erasmus's work on Chrysostom after the appearance of *De libero arbitrio* provided him with a touchstone as he addressed the hotly contested issues of free will, grace, and justification.

THREE

Reconsideration

Between 1527 and 1532, while the Reformation debate intensified, Erasmus made some of the more significant changes to his *Annotations* and *Paraphrases* – changes that addressed free will, justification by faith, grace, and works. For the 1532 Froben edition of his *Paraphrases on Romans*, Erasmus made more than thirty-four major changes to the 1523 version. The revisions constitute the most significant changes to the text made in all editions since the *Paraphrases on Romans* was first published in 1517. The changes often, but not always, reflect noteworthy additions, of which the 1527 and 1535 editions most closely approximate the corresponding text of the 1532 *Paraphrases*. Erasmus's alterations to these two works demonstrate that the 1524 *De libero arbitrio* and the *Hyperaspistes I* and *II* did not fully – or accurately – embody his maturing theology of the economy of salvation.

This chapter and the following two chapters demonstrate how Erasmus's theology of the freedom of the will developed into a theology of grace. My method examines the content of his amendments to the 1532 *Paraphrases on Romans* and the 1527 *Annotations on Romans*, the theological and philological roots of the changes, and their significance within the context of the Protestant Reformation and Catholic Reformation debates over justification. In the 1527 and 1535 *Annotations* and in the 1532 *Paraphrases on Romans*, grace, justification, and the will came to occupy a more important and prominent place in Erasmus's theology. Through the descriptive and interpretive exegetical structure of the *Paraphrases*, he emphasized and de-emphasized theological elements according to his understanding of scripture. In reconsidering Paul's Epistle to the Romans, he undertook his most thorough revision of his exegesis at the very height of the Reformation debate on the profoundly divisive and ultimately destructive issue of free will, on which he had expressed a very different position just a few years earlier in his polemic with Luther.[1] The examples in this chapter and the two that follow confirm the presence in Erasmus's later work of elements that James Tracy has also noted, such as the attack on the *praesidia humana*, a renewed commitment to 'saving faith,' an affirmation of *fiducia* as 'faith' rather than merely 'trust,' and an emphasis on the gratuitousness of divine grace. These elements reveal the extent to which Erasmus's understanding of Paul's emphasis on the need for faith rather than knowledge in the Pauline epistles changed in the late 1520s and early 1530s.[2]

THE CHANGES

In what follows, more than thirty-four changes to verse and commentary are presented and discussed. These changes demonstrate Erasmus's recasting of his understanding of Paul in the *Paraphrases* and *Annotations*. The principal changes to his 1527 *Annotations on Romans* and the 1532 *Paraphrases on Romans* demonstrate his theological metamorphosis and give evidence of an increasing conviction of Paul's belief in the bondage of the human will. Each example includes Erasmus's New Testament version of the verse and how it differs from the Vulgate (if it does so), explains how Erasmus justified any changes to the Vulgate in his *Annotations*, shows how those changes were altered in succeeding versions of his *Annotations*, and, when pertinent, discusses how the *Paraphrases* of relevant verses reflected Erasmus's new understanding of Paul's view of the role of the human will in the economy of salvation.

The changes to these texts fall into four broad categories. First, there are alterations to the 1532 *Paraphrases* that treat the will and related issues and are also reflected in either the 1527 or the 1535 *Annotations*. These verses are treated together to demonstrate the links between Erasmus's grammatical concerns in the *Annotations* and the theological changes he sometimes made based on those grammatical challenges. These changes are presented in the present chapter. Second, there are changes that appear only in the *Paraphrases* or only in the *Annotations*. These two categories are considered together in chapter 4. Finally, there are alterations to·

verses that Erasmus used differently in *De libero arbitrio* and the *Hyperaspistes* than in subsequent versions of the *Annotations* and the *Paraphrases* on Romans. This category most clearly demonstrates the distance between Erasmus's early theological foray in the polemic with Luther and his later, maturing theology of the will. It is treated separately in chapter 5.

CONTEMPORARY PERSPECTIVES

The amendments to the *Annotations* and *Paraphrases* between 1527 and 1535 are discussed briefly and contextualized in reference to the mainly patristic sources Erasmus used when preparing them, as well as in the light of other Reformation thinkers (Catholic and Protestant) when possible, in order to familiarize the reader with contemporary perspectives. The perspectives of Melanchthon and Luther are sometimes given on a particular verse in order to provide the evangelical context for Erasmus's exegesis. Melanchthon's 1532 *Commentary on Romans*, in particular, provides an important insight into evangelical perspectives on free will and justification at the same time as Erasmus's changes to his *Paraphrases on Romans* appeared. Timothy Wengert notes that the 1532 version of Melanchthon's *Commentary on Romans* indicated that 'small, subtle shifts had taken place in Melanchthon's position on justification and the free will.' Wengert warns us that we should not make too much of these changes, but he notes that, although in the 1532 commentary Melanchthon 'criticized scholastic theologians for imagining that human beings could satisfy the law by their own powers, an error that arose from the blindness of human reason,' he 'made more room in his theology for the notion of reward.' Wengert continues: 'He still strongly rejected the arguments of some "Epicureans" who imagined that the word "flesh" did not imply the entire human being. Yet for the first time he put Rom. 9–11 under the commonplace *de ecclesia*. Here the issue for Melanchthon had become one of comfort, not curiosity, and he now placed some cause for the election in the recipients of God's mercy, insofar as they did not repudiate the offered promise.'[3] The 1540 version of Melanchthon's Romans commentary is radically different from the 1532 version.[4] In fact, the two versions hold very few of the same comments. Overall, however, the tenor of the comments remained the same, excluding, of course, those 'subtle shifts' Wengert identifies.

Georg Witzel's (1501–73) Reformation-era writing offers the perspective of what might be termed the 'mediating Catholic,' while Johannes Cochlaeus (1479–1552) offers the anti-Lutheran Catholic perspective. Witzel emerged as what John Patrick Dolan refers to as an 'Erasmian irenicist,' who attempted to address the theological disputes of the Reformation era through 'practical solution.'[5] Born in Vacha in Thuringia, Witzel attended the University of Wittenberg but eventually left to become a priest. He nevertheless married and had eight children with his wife.[6] He remained a priest despite his marriage, and, although attracted to aspects of Lutheranism, he eventually rejected it on the grounds of incongruities he found in his investigation into Luther's ideas in the context of his own studies and observations.[7] As one of the most influential '*Vermittlung*' theologians,[8] Witzel attempted through his many works to articulate a mediating, middle path through the theological strife of the Reformation.[9] He participated in the Leipzig discussion in 1539 as well as in the efforts of the Duchy of Cleves to 'maintain a position of neutrality respecting religion and imperial policies of Charles V.'[10] Most interesting for our purposes, Witzel proposed a conciliatory treatment of justification, in which he proposed that 'the preacher should teach, with a little circumspection and not abruptly, that "sola fide" justifies without indicating what kind of faith this is.' The passage continues: 'Otherwise certain hearers will take the occasion to think that good works are of no avail and are not necessary. The preacher is therefore admonished to tell the people that we are justified through faith (inert faith) but a faith that is made operative through charity. And just as a good tree bears good fruit, so there can be no doubt that true faith will produce good works. However, where there are no good works there can be no living faith regardless of verbal protestations.' This position, as Dolan notes, reflects the language used in the Regensburg book, a product of efforts to articulate a possible path to union for Catholics and Protestants.[11] Interestingly, the majority of Witzel's publications appeared at about the same time as Erasmus made significant changes to his own theology of grace.[12] Indeed, Erika Rummel notes that 'Witzel was no slavish imitator of Erasmus, but he greatly admired him, placing him "next to the apostles and heroic theologians of old."'[13]

Johannes Cochlaeus, an early and attentive Catholic critic of Luther and the Protestant movement, rejected the mediating efforts of Witzel and others like him. Ralph Keen asserts that

Cochlaeus's importance and impact on the Reformation era mainly concerned two qualities: 'the volume of his work and the rhetorical ferocity of his reaction to the beginnings of Protestantism.'
Born in humble circumstances outside Nuremberg, Cochlaeus
made remarkable progress in life on the basis of his intellectual
merits. At the University of Cologne, he studied theology. Later
he travelled to Italy and earned a doctorate in theology in Ferrara;
in 1518 he became a priest. Although it is unclear precisely how
Cochlaeus became involved in the Lutheran controversy, his commitment to attacking Luther emerged in several published tracts
and verbal disputations.[14] In addition to his *Commentaria Joannis
Cochlaei, de actis et scriptis Martini Lutheri Saxonis*,[15] Cochlaeus published a fierce attack in perhaps his most well-known work, *The
Seven-Headed Luther*. Keen notes: 'The seven "heads" are the various personalities Luther appears to have exhibited in his works:
Doctor, fanatic, fool, church visitor, churchman, criminal, and
Barabbas.'[16] Here, I draw primarily upon *Adversus cucullatum minotaurum wittenbergensem: de gratia sacramentorum iterum* from
1523, the *Philippicae I–VII* (1534), and the *Commentaria Ioannis
Cochlaei, de actis et scriptis Martini Lutheri Saxonis* (1549). In the latter, Cochlaeus sums up his position with humour:

> The Catholics did not want to admit that 'We are justified by
> faith alone,' since the Apostle James also does not admit it, it
> was agreed that the article should indeed say 'We are justified
> by faith,' but not 'by faith alone' – since no scripture has it so,
> but rather the opposite. And Dr Johannes Eck added a joke,
> that this word 'sola' should be sent to the shoemakers, who
> well know what 'sola' means in German and know how to use
> 'sola' properly. Therefore, when that word 'sola' was omitted,
> it was agreed that Justification or Remission of sins is accom-
> plished formally through grace, accepting favor, and faith, and
> instrumentally through the word and the Sacraments.[17]

These and other contemporaries of Erasmus (including Johannes
Mensing, Contarini, Johannes Dietenberger, Melanchthon, and
Cajetan) demonstrate the many perspectives and interpretations of-
fered on grace, free will, and justification and their meaning in
Paul's Epistle to the Romans during the Reformation.

For the purposes of this study, the significant aspect of the uses
of scripture in Erasmus's *Annotations* and *Paraphrases* is the way in

which he altered them in his later years, subsequent to the publication of his polemic with Luther. The *Annotations* and *Paraphrases* on Romans rarely reflect the incorporation of significant terms that formed the backbone of much of late medieval and early modern debate about the freedom of the will. Instead, Erasmus's tone and lexicon reflects the genre in which he was engaged. For example, he uses the first person in the *Paraphrases*, that is, the voice of Paul speaking to the Romans. In the *Annotations*, he explains the grammatical changes he makes to the Vulgate text. Even when these changes to the Vulgate resulted in significant theological ramifications, Erasmus's concern was to justify the grammatical changes with support from the Church Fathers and, occasionally, from Aquinas and scholastic theologians. The exclusion of scholastic terms does not mean that Erasmus was unconcerned with or ignorant of the theological implications of his interpretations. To the contrary, he simply rarely utilized the scholastic vocabulary that others had employed to describe the theological principles he discussed. While Luther spoke in terms of *iustitia imputata*, generally accepted *fides informis* over *fides formata cum charitate*, and attacked conceptions of merit both *de congruo* and *de condigno*,[18] Erasmus's positions on such concepts are much harder to pin down precisely because his *Paraphrases* and *Annotations* only hint at the ideas behind the terms and only rarely utilize the terms themselves to express his theology. As a result, his exact stance on such terms and their theological merit can only be approximated, given the interpretation he presents of the verses in question.

PHILOLOGICAL CHANGES, EXEGETICAL RECASTING: CHANGES MADE TO BOTH THE *ANNOTATIONS* AND THE *PARAPHRASES*

In order to trace Erasmus's changes to the *Annotations* and the *Paraphrases*, I first created a collation of seven editions of the *Paraphrases* published by Froben in Basel between 1518 and 1532 (1518, 1519, 1520, 1521, 1522, 1523, and 1532). These texts were produced in Erasmus's lifetime. A 1534 version of the *Tomus secundus*, which contained the *Paraphrases* of the Epistles, was 'essentially a reprint of the text of the 1532 edition.'[19] Other versions of the *Paraphrases* appeared after his death, but I have not included them here because I cannot determine whether any changes would have been made by Erasmus. Between 1523 and 1532 Erasmus appears to have been busy revising the *Paraphrases*. In those years, it had received a great deal of attention from his detractors.[20] I have compared this collation with the notes in the critical edition of the Collected Works of Erasmus and have found that our notes on changes to the text correspond.[21] I also compared it with the Leiden edition.[22] In order to see how Erasmus's changes to the *Paraphrases* corresponded with changes he made to *Annotations* during the same period, I used the annotated collation by Reeve and Screech.[23] To contextualize Erasmus's changes to and explanations in the *Paraphrases* and *Annotations*, I have provided, when possible and relevant, examples from the *Glossa ordinaria*, the Church Fathers, and contemporary theologians.

Romans 1:7

Erasmus: *Omnibus qui **Romae estis**, dilectis Dei, vocatis sanctis, Gratia vobis & pax à Deo patre **nostro & Domino Iesu Christo**.*

Vulgate: *Omnibus qui sunt Romae, dilectis Dei, vocatis sanctis, Gratia vobis & pax à Deo patre & Domino nostro Iesu Christo.*

Before 1532 Erasmus's paraphrase of this verse was to the point and not much longer than the verse itself:

For all of you at Rome who are beloved of God and have been called from your former wickedness to holiness of life, I wish grace and peace. Not the grace for which this world is accustomed to pray in its usual way, but a true and a new grace.

In this sense, then, Erasmus is very close to a 'neutral' interpretation of the verse. There is nothing theologically questionable here. As Karl Hermann Schelkle points out in his study of the interpretation of Romans by the Church Fathers, this verse defines a biblical Christology, and through their commentaries on it the Fathers most often attempted to both elucidate its meaning and, most important, 'to protect against heretical interpretations.'[24]

In 1532, however, Erasmus substantially revised his paraphrase of the verse, almost tripled its length, and added an important sentence in Paul's voice. His initial interpretation of the verse remained unaltered, but he addended it as follows:

that is, the free gift of the truly justifying faith of the gospel. And I also wish that as a result of the complete absolution through grace of the sins of your former life, you may
have the peace of a conscience now free from anxiety and a
steadfast friendship with God. These two things neither
the strength of human wisdom affords nor the observance
of the Mosaic law; instead, they originate for all from the
unique generosity of God the Father and of his Son, our
Lord Jesus Christ.[25]

In this significant addition to the paraphrase, Erasmus chose to
emphasize the role of God and the sacrifice of the son in salvation
while simultaneously minimizing the efficacy of the Law (and
therefore the works that support it) and the potential of human
wisdom in the quest for salvation. He chose not to undermine
merely ceremonial law but the entire 'observance of the Mosaic
law.'[26] The paraphrase of 1532 shows that Erasmus repudiated the
efficacy of all forms of the Mosaic Law, not just the ceremonial
aspects. Throughout previous editions a grace he consistently
termed merely 'new,' he here clarifies as gifted by the 'truly justifying faith of the gospel.' Faith, and faith alone, offers to justify,
and the locus of this faith is found in the gospel. This same faith,
grounded in the gospel, not only promises to justify but also
promises 'complete absolution through grace of the sins of your
former life.'[27] Erasmus decided to expand a relatively harmless
paraphrase into controverted ground. Padberg argues that
Erasmus moved to an evangelical understanding of justification
and an emphasis on the salvatory nature of faith and the power of
justification through faith, unmitigated by human works.[28]

The same verse underwent significant reconsideration in the
1527 *Annotations*, demonstrating that the shift evidenced in the
1532 *Paraphrases* was already under way in 1527. To this verse
alone Erasmus made four significant annotations, two of which
underwent modification in 1527, the first modification since the
last publication of the work in 1522. Although Erasmus annotated
this verse thoroughly and added to the *Annotations* many times,
the changes he made reflected a different tenor from that of the
changes he made to the *Paraphrases* of the same verse. (However,
it should be noted that the *Annotations* sometimes reflected both
theological and philological ideas.) The changes to this verse in
the *Paraphrases* of 1532 seem to be based largely on similar changes

made to the *Annotations* of 1527. More interesting for this study, however, is the passage Erasmus added in 1527 on the relationship between grace and peace to a section that originally had nothing to do with either term. The original 1516 annotation clarifies the meaning of *vocatis sanctis*, found in the Vulgate and unchanged in Erasmus's Latin New Testament. In this, Erasmus follows the *Glossa ordinaria*, the medieval commentary on the Vulgate with references to patristic sources to which Erasmus had access. The *Glossa ordinaria* focuses exclusively on *vocatis sanctis* in the explication of Romans 1:7: '*Vocatis sanctis*. Non ideo vocati quia sancti, sed ideo sancti effecti quia vocati: et ideo vocati, quia dilecti.'[29]

The second half of the annotation deals not at all with saints, but rather with the relationship between grace and peace in Pauline scripture:

What he calls 'grace,' however, is spontaneous generosity. First he said ἀγαπητοῖς [beloved], then κλητοῖς [called], but since someone can be called and loved on his own merit he adds 'grace.' Grace given brings forth forgiveness of sins, which in his customary way he calls 'peace.' For sin puts hostility between God and men. He called us, it was not we who sought him; he loved us first when we were hostile [to him]; he bestowed the gift of the Spirit upon those who deserved punishment; through the Spirit, however, he bestowed forgiveness of sins and an abundance of gifts.[30]

John Payne argues that in this instance, as well as in Romans 9:32 and Galatians 3:9, Erasmus hoped to 'broaden the range of works which are to be branded as legalistic beyond those that are merely ceremonial: and in doing so he betrays the possible influence of Luther and/or Melanchthon.' While Payne sees 'Lutheranizing changes' as much more obvious in the 1532 paraphrases on Galatians, he adds that the 1532 paraphrase of Romans 1:7 'connects grace with forgiveness of sins and the peace of a secure conscience' and thus reflects the 'Lutheranizing sentiments' conspicuous particularly in Erasmus's 1527 annotations and 1532 paraphrases of Romans.[31] At the same time, Erasmus's thoughts on this verse also reflect the influence of Origen, who confirmed that 'Paul aligns grace with peace,' and of Chrysostom, who viewed grace as bringing peace.[32] More directly, they also reflect the influence of Augustine, who argued in his *Rudimentary Exposition of the Epistle to the Romans* that in this verse, 'Paul has emphasized God's grace rather than the saints' merit, for he does not say "to those loving God" but rather "to God's beloved."'[33]

Erasmus's 1527 changes to the annotation and 1532 changes to the paraphrase of Romans 1:7 also reflect remarkable similarities to Melanchthon's 1532 explication of the verse. Melanchthon's commentary notes: '"Grace" means the favor of God in relationship to his mercy. "Peace" means in the Hebrew more generally happiness, or rather, as we say, well-being. Together, therefore, peace of conscience is the gift left behind, which is works.'[34] Even Luther did not focus as much as Erasmus did on grace in the glossa in his *Lecture on Romans* (1515–16): '*To all who are*, in Greek: "you who are," *in Rome, the beloved of God*, because His love is the beginning of all good things in us. *Called to be saints*, sanctified through Christ. *Grace*, which bestows the remission of sins, *to you and peace*, which removes the torment of the conscience, *from God the Father*, from whom we have everything, *and from our Lord*, not from men and the world, because "not as the world gives peace, do I give to you" (John 14:27), *Jesus Christ*.' Luther's marginal gloss for this verse emphasizes that 'the call comes before justification.' Moreover, 'he wants his listeners to know that they are saints not on the basis of their merits, but on the basis of the love and call of God, so that everything is centered in God.'[35] Like Erasmus, Luther took great pains to demonstrate that the origin of grace is found not in merit, but in God.

Romans 1:13

Erasmus: *Nolo autem vos ignorare fratres: quia saepe proposui venire ad vos (& **licet praepeditus fuerim usque adhuc**) ut aliquem fructum **haberem inter vos quoque**, sicut & in ceteris gentibus.*

Vulgate: *Nolo autem vos ignorare fratres: quia saepe proposui venire ad vos, (& prohibitus sum usque adhuc) ut aliquem fructum habeam & in vobis, sicut & in ceteris gentibus.*

Erasmus's New Testament version of this verse differs substantially in two places from Jerome's Vulgate, and he comments in the *Annotations* on one additional aspect of the verse that appears in his Latin New Testament exactly as it does in the Vulgate. The

first of Erasmus's alterations to the verse is relevant to his understanding of Paul's intent regarding the will. Instead of the Vulgate's
version of the phrase '& prohibitus sum usque adhuc,' Erasmus asserts that this portion of the verse should read '& licet praepeditus
fuerim usque adhuc.' Erasmus's annotation of his translation of the
verse directly reflects the influence of Chrysostom. (That influence
is attributed in 1535 [changes in boldface], while the segment was
edited also in 1527, although to a lesser extent, and those changes
are not referenced to Chrysostom.) Erasmus explained the reason
for the change in this annotation most relevant to the will:

> ἐκωλύθην which means 'I was prevented' rather than 'I was
> prohibited,' no doubt by affairs that stood in the way – the
> Greek for the latter is ἐμποδίζειν. Strictly speaking, one 'pro-
> hibits' who forbids you to do something; **unless we are to
> understand that Paul was prohibited by the Holy Spirit, as
> in Acts 16, when he wanted to go to Bithynia, but the Holy
> Spirit did not permit him to do so. For Chrysostom suggests
> something like this when he says, τῷ μὲν θελήματι τοῦ θεοῦ
> οὐκ ἀντιπίπτων, τὴν δὲ ἀγάπην διατηρῶν [not resisting the
> will of God, but maintaining love]. For Paul, when he is not
> given the opportunity to go to Rome, interprets this devout-
> ly as the will of God.**[36]

Erasmus takes pains here to distinguish between 'prohibition'
and 'prevention.' Prohibition is predicated on the option of dis-
obedience: one is told not to do something and then makes the
decision to either follow or reject the prohibition. Prevention does
not involve choice: one is prevented from engaging in an activity
(in this case, a journey) by some outside force, not by one's own
will. In this annotation, Erasmus stressed, following Chrysostom,
that Paul was detained not by choice but by the action of the Holy
Spirit. It was not his will at play in his delay but rather the om-
nipotence of the Lord. Chrysostom interpreted this verse as indicating Paul's 'yielding to Providence' and maintained that the
uncertainty that may come from obedience to God's providence is
'a main feature of faith.'[37]

Erasmus's treatment of Romans 1:13 in the *Paraphrases* reveals a
pattern similar to that of Romans 1:7. Here, too, Erasmus made
substantial changes to his earlier paraphrases. What Erasmus
chose to add to the paraphrase of this verse in 1532 is not directly

related to the content and emphasis of the annotation of the verse.
Nor is the addition particularly related to the verse content. Until
1532 the paraphrase read:

> It has been by no means my own fault that this has not yet
> come about. On the contrary, I would not wish to hide from
> you, my brothers, that I have often intended to make a visit to
> you but have been unable to do so up to the present time due
> to obstacles which have fallen in my path. I was especially
> eager to visit you for this reason, that I might reap some har-
> vest among you also, just as I have previously done among
> other nations. This task of preaching the gospel has been en-
> trusted to me by God, nor am I obligated to any particular
> nation, but just as God is equally God of all, so the gospel of
> Christ extends equally to all.[38]

Erasmus stressed what he viewed as Paul's emphasis on three aspects of his message. First, Paul emphasizes a message that should
appeal to all, a commitment to visiting the Romans even though
he had previously been unable to do so. Second, Paul informs the
Romans of his experience: what he wishes for the Romans he has
done in other places. Third, Paul emphasizes that he is God's mes-
senger and that God is available to all believers.

In 1532 Erasmus departed radically from these three elements
to focus instead on justifying faith, that which is not merely promised by the gospel but *is* the gospel. The Law both promised and
prefigured Christ, and Christ's gospel is in itself the justification
provided by faith in him. Erasmus added the following phrase in
1532:

> **By the gospel I mean justification through faith in Jesus Christ,
> the son of God, whom the Law promised and prefigured.[39]**

With this addition, Erasmus deviated not only from the scriptural
text but also from his own previous emphases in the *Paraphrases*.
Furthermore, while both the 1527 additions to the *Annotations* and
this 1532 addition to the *Paraphrases* mark a departure from his
previous explanation of the text, they do so in different ways. The
Annotations focus on the will, and the *Paraphrases* focus on faith
and justification. Both, however, represent an invigorated preoccupation with issues central to the Reformation debate.

Because Erasmus did not attribute anything directly to a patristic influence in the *Paraphrases* and made direct references to the Church Fathers or commentators only in the *Annotations*, the *Paraphrases* lend merely clues as to what influences might have worked on his own developing exegesis. In the case of Romans 1:13, it may be that Erasmus had clung to Chrysostom's insistence, through his student Theodoret: 'The Grace of God, said Paul, leads me.'[40] This particular addition to the paraphrase appears to have been somewhat haphazardly placed, and the verse does not seem to call for this additional comment. However, it could be that Erasmus was trying to define the 'fruits' of Paul's efforts, mentioned in the verse itself, in which case he may have been following Ambrose, who argued that Paul's aim was to bring the Romans to the faith by the fruit of his labours.[41] If this is the case, Erasmus took it upon himself in the 1532 *Paraphrases* to define for his readers the fruit of belief as the gospel, through his addition: 'By the gospel I mean justification through faith in Jesus Christ, the son of God, whom the law promised and prefigured.'[42]

Even if Erasmus decided to define the fruit of Paul's labours as the bringing of the gospel, it is nevertheless a remarkable place to emphasize justification by faith alone. Erasmus may have been inspired to change the 1532 paraphrase of the verse by his previous change to the verse in the *Annotations* of 1527, but, given the long span of time between the publication dates, it is impossible to tell whether the influence of Chrysostom, which inspired the 1535 addition to the annotation, was also responsible for the addition to the paraphrase in 1532. Yet, if one assumes, as Protestant interpreters often, if not always, did, that 'gospel' always indicates and includes justification by faith alone, Erasmus's paraphrase here makes a great deal of sense, given the Reformation context.[43]

Romans 3:30

Erasmus: *Quoniam quidem unus est Deus qui **justificabit** circumcisionem ex fide, & praeputium per fidem.*

Vulgate: *Quoniam quidem unus est Deus, qui justificat circumcisionem ex fide, & praeputium per fidem.*

The annotation for this verse is grammatical in basis and focuses on the tense of the verb *justificat*. In the 1516 edition Erasmus changed this verb from the Vulgate's present tense, 'justifies,' to the future tense, *justificabit*, that is, 'who will justify.' In explaining the change, Erasmus asserted that God will justify, in the future, those 'who were still in Judaism or paganism.' Elsewhere, he explained that 'the future tense implied a distinction between the time before and the time since evangelical grace.'[44]

The paraphrase ignores this change in tense and leaves 'justifies' in the present tense. The purpose of the paraphrase is not grammatical but rather explanatory, and Erasmus used the opportunity to clarify the two groups of the justified:

Moreover, since God is one and the same for all, it is proper also that the gift of God be common to all. And so it is not the case that there is one God who justifies the circumcised leading him from faith in the law **which promised a Saviour**, to faith in the gospel **which exhibited the promise**, and another God who justifies the uncircumcised, calling him from the worship of idols to a common faith.

Here, Erasmus emphasized that the faith is the promised faith, that God 'justifies the circumcised leading him from faith in the law which promised a Saviour, to the faith in the gospel which exhibited the promise.'[45] Again, Erasmus drew attention to the futility of outward manifestations of the law, in this case circumcision, and to the universality of the common faith available to all through the gospel. Erasmus followed the lead of the early Fathers in their emphasis on the achievement of justification through belief and faith, not through works. The specific phrases added in 1532 were designed to emphasize the revocation of the law by the coming of the saviour. The *Glossa ordinaria*, like Melanchthon's 1532 *Commentary on Romans*, has no specific comment on this verse. In 1540, however, Melanchthon wrote in his commentary on it, 'From this it can readily be understood that Paul is speaking about the entire Law, not only about ceremonies, as he shows also below, where he confirms that justification is taken away from the entire Law.'[46]

Erasmus's changes to the *Paraphrases* and *Annotations* of Romans discussed above demonstrate two trends in his theological work of the late 1520s and early 1530s. First, the changes to the *Annotations* incorporated Erasmus's desire to demonstrate his reliance on not only the Greek New Testament but also the Greek

Church Fathers, particularly Chrysostom, after 1527. Second, they revealed a shift in the emphasis of his scholarship. As Jerry Bentley notes, 'The goals of personal transformation, social reform, and religious renewal – which Erasmus so passionately advocated in the *Paraclesis* and other works – thus stood behind his technical scholarship on the New Testament.'[47] Erasmus's *Annotations* and *Paraphrases* had always reflected those goals. By 1527, however, the pressing concerns of the Reformation had changed the focus of those goals to reflect Erasmus's preoccupation with the themes of free will, grace, and justification. The *Paraphrases* extended his philological studies into exegesis and commentary. By 1532 they, too, exposed Erasmus's preoccupation with the central theological debates of the Reformation.

FOUR

Reassessment

The verses explored in the previous chapter underwent significant changes regarding free will, grace, and justification in both the 1532 edition of the *Paraphrases* and either the 1527 edition or the 1535 edition of the *Annotations*. This chapter contains verses for which Erasmus altered only the *Paraphrases* or only the *Annotations*. I have treated them separately not only for convenience, but also to show that Erasmus's changes sometimes demonstrated more grammatical concerns (evidenced in the *Annotations*) and sometimes illustrated more exegetical preoccupations (in the *Paraphrases*). In both cases, however, the changes demonstrate his ongoing reassessment of Pauline scripture.

CHANGES TO THE *PARAPHRASES*

Romans 3:2

Erasmus: *Multum per omnem modum. Primum quidem, quia credita sunt illis* **oracula** *Dei.*

Vulgate: *Multum per omnem modum. Primum quidem, quia credita sunt illis eloquia Dei.*

In revising his paraphrase of Romans 3:2, Erasmus took the opportunity to emphasize that the grace of the gospel is the gift of God's message. It supersedes the Law and challenges the position of the Jews. His addition to the paraphrase is a fascinating negation of his original intent for the verse:

> As far as the grace of the gospel is concerned, the position
> of the Jews is not at all better than that of the gentiles. But
> yet in some respects, it is indeed an advantage to belong to
> the Jewish race. For first on this count they may justly boast,
> whether because to them especially the words of God have
> been entrusted or because to them in particular the law and
> the prophets were handed down or because to them only
> God saw fit to speak. In the first place it is a wonderful thing
> for this nation to have been given this honor by God. Secondly,
> he who holds the promises of the law appears to be much
> more prepared for the faith of the gospel, and he who holds
> the image of the truth is the nearer to it; for the law of Moses
> and the oracles of the prophets are indeed a step toward the
> evangelical teaching of Christ.[1]

Again, Erasmus chose to emphasize the role of the Law in preparing for the grace of gospel. In doing so, he demonstrated that the
promise of the gospel and its justifying elements are not as easily
available to the Jews because of their dependence on and adher-
ence to the Law. While the original intent of the paraphrase was to
underscore the preparatory nature of the Law for the grace freely
given in the gospel, Erasmus's 1532 prefatory addition indicates
that, on the contrary, dependence on the Law is in some ways a
barrier to the true meaning and gift of the gospel. His addition,
therefore, serves to discredit the rest of the paraphrase. Payne
concurs with this assessment of the impact of this addition to the
meaning of the paraphrase: 'Erasmus modifies his interpretation
to stress somewhat more the unmerited character of grace.
However, while seeming to reject the view that divine grace can
be, strictly speaking, merited, he does not deny the appropriate-
ness of human preparation for the gospel.'[2]

Melanchthon's 1540 commentary offered a slightly different version but reflected the same distinction: 'Praestant igitur Iudaei
gentibus, non quod per cultus et alia opera legis meriti sint iustificationem, sed quod inter ipsos fuerunt revelatae promissiones.
Norant igitur verbum et promissionem misericordiae, quod aliqui
apprehenderunt et salvati sunt.'[3] Like Erasmus, Melanchthon asserted: 'Jews are superior to the Gentiles and that they have this
advantage: they have the promises.' He continued: 'Therefore they
are superior not on account of the Law, not because they can merit
justification by the law, but because they have the promises.'[4]

Romans 3:26

Erasmus and Vulgate: *In sustentatione Dei, ad ostensionem justitiae ejus in hoc tempore: ut sit ipse justus, & justificans eum, qui
est ex fide Iesu Christi.*

Erasmus's original paraphrase focused on the path of righteousness through faith in the gospel (1517 to 1523). In 1532, however,
he audaciously added that merits are irrelevant to forgiveness
and thus to the status of righteousness as well (boldface text added in 1532):

> **He does not forgive because they have merited it, but be-
> cause he himself has promised [forgiveness].** Nor did he
> endure sinners until then because he was ignorant of their
> sins or approved them, but to make known his righteousness
> at this appointed time, so that it might be clear that he is by
> nature and of himself truly righteous, and he is the one and
> only author of human righteousness. And this he is without
> respect of persons for all who have faith in the gospel of Jesus
> Christ. Tell me, therefore, you Jew, where is your boasting?[5]

While it is true, as Tracy argues, that 'Erasmus always maintained
that saving faith was not complete without charity, or obedience
to the new and spiritual law revealed in Christ,'[6] this addition to
the paraphrase seeks to discredit the notion that the gospel of
Christ and the forgiveness it offers is in any way obtainable
through meritorious action. (However, charitable and obedient
action, as Erasmus makes clear in other paraphrases, may flow
from righteous persons.)

The editors of the Collected Works of Erasmus note the possible
influence of Ambrosiaster here, who similarly 'stresses the divine
promise.'[7] Yet Chrysostom's authority may also be at work, as
Chrysostom interpreted this verse in his *Homily on the Epistle to the
Romans*, along with Romans 3:24–5, as a reminder of the omnipo-
tence of God. Worthiness for righteousness cannot spring from
man; rather, 'it is to God, he says, that the righteousness belongs.'[8]
In addition, the end of Erasmus's paraphrase actually references
Romans 3:27: 'Then what becomes of our boasting? It is excluded.
By what law? By that of works? No, but by the law of faith.'[9]
Chrysostom was much more interested in that verse in his homily.

He asserted: 'Thus now the sentence being henceforth passed, and all being upon the point of perishing and He being at hand who by grace would break these terrors, they had no longer the season for making a plea of amelioration wrought by the Law. For if it were right to strengthen themselves upon these things, it should have been before His coming.'[10]

Cochlaeus understood this verse quite differently; his interpretation shows how distant Erasmus was from at least some of his Catholic contemporaries. In his fiery polemic against Luther, *Ein Nötig und Christlich Bedenken auf des Luthers Artikeln* (1538), Cochlaeus argued that, though Luther stated that 'das allein der glaube an Christum uns gerecht mache,' in part on the basis of Romans 3:23–6 and 3:28, he was mistaken. To be sure, Cochlaeus asserted, good works come not from believers but from Christ. It does not follow, according to Cochlaeus, that belief alone justifies. Faith and Christ are not one thing, he insisted. Rather, faith is a gift of Christ.[11] In a similar vein, Witzel maintained, also in 1538, that Romans 3 should not be taken to mean that Paul intended to undermine all works done in faith when he disputed the worth of the Mosaic Law.[12]

Erasmus's addition, 'He does not forgive because they have merited it, but because he himself has promised [forgiveness],' to his paraphrases of Romans 3:26 would likely not have given either Cochlaeus or Witzel pause. Nevertheless, it did deviate from the thrust of his original paraphrase, which followed the sense of the *Glossa ordinaria* quite closely: '*In sustentatione. Patienter sustinuit Deus peccata eorum qui fuerunt ante legem, et sub lege: non punivit, neque remisit, ita ut gloriam haberent, donec venit qui delicta tam praecedentium, quam subsequentium precio sui sanguinis absolveret.*'[13]

Romans 4:25

Erasmus and Vulgate: *Qui traditus est propter delicta nostra, & resurrexit propter justifcationem nostram.*

Erasmus's paraphrase of this verse is as follows (boldface text added in 1532):

We ought therefore to attribute the righteousness and innocence we have received not to Moses, but to Christ, who voluntarily surrended [sic] himself to death so that **through faith** he might as a pure favour wash away our sins. And likewise he rose from the dead and lived again in order that we might refrain from deeds belonging to the dead and that we might not sin hereafter, doing the same deeds again on account of which Christ had met death. He died, I say, in order that he might slay sin in us, and he rose from the dead so that we who once died through him to our former sins, and were then raised again along with him and through him to a new life, might live henceforth for righteousness, a righteousness we have received through his kindness.[14]

Again, without prompting from the original text, Erasmus has added a reference to justification 'through faith' into his exegesis of Romans.[15] Although the verse claims that Jesus was carried away for our sins and resurrected for our justification, the verse itself does not mention that the justification comes through faith.

Like Erasmus, Chrysostom viewed this last verse of Romans 4 as arguing that 'Christ's death and resurrection come as a further confirmation of the power of faith for salvation.'[16] Likewise, Melanchthon's 1532 *Commentary on Romans* emphasized the role of faith in the remission of sins and the imputation of justice: 'Deinde iterum clare testatur nos fide consequi remissionem peccatorum et imputationem iustitiae, et diserte addit mediatorem, ne cogitemus aliquos ignaros promissionis et mediatoris christi tamen fiducia misericordia. Ideo in hac fiducia necesse est simul apprehendi promissionem et mediatorem Christum.'[17] Cochlaeus, however, insisted that Romans 4:25 supported his case against Luther. He employed it, along with Romans 3:23–6 and John 1:29, to assert that Luther was mistaken in arguing that faith in Christ alone saves. Instead, Cochlaeus stated, Romans 4:25 and other verses attest that Christ and the gift of grace from Christ saved. Later in the same anti-Luther work, Cochlaeus used Romans 4:25 to insist that 'non in sola fide aut operatione nostra est spes et fiducia nostra.'[18]

Erasmus's addition of 'through faith' in this verse may have been prompted by the new weightiness of the term at the height of the Reformation. It should be noted, however, that he also introduced the term in 1521 to his paraphrase of Romans 9:1, where, just as he did in his 1532 paraphrase of Romans 4:25, he inserted 'through faith':

Would that even all the Jews might abandon their Moses and be converted to Christ. The Jews now persuade themselves that it is sufficient for gaining salvation if they are sons of Abraham and possess the law once given to them by God. However, none of this will profit them unless they show themselves worthy **through faith** of being drawn and cherished by God. But Christ, even though promised by the law and received by the gentiles, is stubbornly rejected by them. And I would not say this out of hatred of my people, even though they are everywhere hostile to me. Christ (who knows all things) is my witness that what I say is true; my conscience (whose counsellor and examiner is the Holy Spirit) is my witness that I tell no lies.[19]

In 1521 Erasmus changed 'by faith' to 'through faith,' but the emphasis on the subplantation of the law and the call for faith was already present before the grammatical shift from *'fide'* to *'per fidem.'* From its first publication in 1517 Erasmus decided to retain the focus of this verse on the act of demonstrable faith as the indicator of the acceptability of acts within the law. He was not following Chrysostom's homilies here, and even Augustine seems to have been less than interested in this particular introductory verse. The addition to this paraphrase is a rare case: before 1532 Erasmus seldom introduced such significant changes regarding faith and grace.

Romans 8:25

Erasmus and Vulgate: *Si autem quod non videmus, speramus, id per patientiam expectamus.*

This verse represents another addition to the 1532 *Paraphrase on Romans* that is concerned with faith. That is to say, Erasmus's paraphrase before the addition of the 1532 phrase sufficed to explain the verse (boldface text added in 1532):

Here we would not be praised for our faith or hope if all the things which Christ has promised to us were now visible. **But precisely in this way are we rendered acceptable to God by our faith** if we discern with the eyes of faith things which cannot be seen with the eyes of the body, and if we meanwhile persevere in our sorrows and wait with the persistent hope for what has been promised.[20]

Before 1532 Erasmus used this paraphrase to define 'hope.' Faith and hope make it possible for humans to believe in the promises of Christ. After 1532 Erasmus added that that same faith makes sinners acceptable to God. Paul Althaus notes that for the Protestant reformers in general, and for Luther in particular, 'the two effects of faith in Christ are: It receives the forgiveness of sins and therewith the imputation of righteousness; it also establishes a new being and makes a man righteous in himself.' Justification, in turn, involves two aspects: 'the righteousness imputed for Christ's sake, and man's transformation to a new obedience.' Althaus continues: '"Justification" in the full sense of the word consists in both of these together. The basic and decisive factor is that man is forgiven and receives new worth before God.'[21] Erasmus defined this process as becoming 'rendered acceptable to God by our faith.'[22]

Melanchthon, for his part, cast this as the precise definition of 'justification' in the *Loci Communes* (1555): 'As the words *are justified* mean 'to be pleasing to God,' so *righteousness* must be understood as the imputed righteousness of which Paul speaks.'[23] However, Melanchthon did not refer to Romans 8:25 to support his definition. Erasmus's interpretation also echoed Augustine, who used Romans 8:24ff to demonstrate 'that the posture of faithful and patient waiting is the only one possible for the believer who yearns for the vision of God.'[24] In contrast, the *Glossa ordinaria* emphasizes the merit of hope: '*Spe enim*. Ideo dicit ut majus meritum spei videatur et ideo debeat salvare.'[25]

Romans 9:28

Erasmus: ***Sermonem enim perficiens***, *& apprevians in aquitate: quia verbum breviarum faciet Dominus super terram.*

Vulgate: *Verbum enim consummans, & apprevians in aquitate: quia verbum breviarum faciet Dominus super terram.*

Erasmus paraphrased the verse in this way (boldface text added in 1532):

Because of this Isaiah likewise said [28:22]: 'The Lord will

execute his sentence upon the earth with vigour and dispatch.' Shadows seem to have an element of deception and the law speaks at great length; it promises, foreshadows, instructs, warns, and consoles. But Christ has been sent and has fulfilled once and for all what was promised, has embodied what was foreshadowed and has reduced the lengthy list of instructions to the single precept of evangelical love. He scattered the seed of heavenly doctrine which, though it has borne no fruit among many in the nation, nevertheless has borne fruit in some men.[26]

In the 1532 addition to this paraphrase, Erasmus emphasized that the new doctrine is one of 'evangelical love.' The overly complicated Law has been reduced to the simplicity of grace, a concept also found in Chrysostom: 'What this means is that salvation will come quickly, and it depends on very few words. There is no need to make a big palaver of it or get involved with the vexation of the works of the law.'[27] It is likely that Erasmus followed Chrysostom's lead in his interpretation of this verse, as he often did in the additions made to the paraphrases on Romans in 1532. Augustine, too, emphasized that Romans 9:28 'referred to the new way of righteousness in Christ by grace.'[28] In addition, Erasmus's use of 'shadows' as a tool to explain the verse is echoed in Luther's scholium of the verse:

For before this Word of faith, the Word of the Spirit, was revealed, everything was in shadow and figure because of the slowness of the Jews: the Word was unfinished and incomplete and therefore easily understood by all, because it spoke in figures about things that could be perceived by the senses. But when the figures and the things perceived by the senses were excluded, then God began to speak the hidden Word of the Spirit, which is the Word of faith, and thus He began to bring forth the finished and complete Word, which at the same time must of necessity be also cut off from figures and signs and symbols.[29]

Romans 10:15

Erasmus and Vulgate: *Quomodo vero praedicabunt nisi mittantur? Sicut scripturam est: Quam speciosi pedes euangelizanium pacem, euangelizantium bona!*

The paraphrase follows (boldface text added in 1532):

> Moreover, how will they hear unless there should be one to proclaim him who is unknown? And how will the apostles preach unless they have been sent by he whose gospel they are preaching? Isaiah calls them to mind when he says [52:7]: 'How beautiful are the feet of those who preach the gospel of peace, the gospel of good things.' You hear what the heralds of Christ are ordered to preach: not circumcision and the keeping of the sabbath, but 'peace,' **which through faith, after our sins have been abolished**, welds us together by mutual love in Christ; and those 'good things' which are always good because they are good by their own nature.[30]

Erasmus greatly changed the meaning of the paraphrase in 1532 when he emphasized that peace is ultimately achievable through faith and therefore is a product of grace. Peace that is brought with grace is available after the abolition of sin – or justification – which Erasmus stressed is available only through faith with his addition to the text: '*Auditis quid jubeantur praedicare Christi praecones, non circumcisionem & sabbatismos, sed pacem, **quae per fidem abolitis peccatis.**'*[31] Furthermore, Erasmus juxtaposed the law ('circumcision and the keeping of the sabbath') to 'peace,' which he saw as ushered in 'through faith' and thus likened to salvation.

Melanchthon's 1540 commentary on Romans 10:15 likewise defined peace as 'health and salvation' and contrasted it to the Law: 'It reminds us that the kingdom must be administered through the Word, and indeed through the preaching of a new Word, namely, the Gospel, in which there will be proclaimed peace, that is, health and salvation which is divinely given. The contrast is opposed to the Law and sin and the miseries of mankind, as though he said, "Then will sin be taken away and the other ills which the Law could not take away, and there will be true comfort and the gift of righteousness and eternal life."'[32] The *Glossa ordinaria*, by contrast, focused on that which Erasmus's original paraphrase of the verse highlighted, that is, peace, which 'welds us together by mutual love in Christ; and those "good things" which are always good because they are good by their own nature.'[33] While the *Glossa* punctuated peace, however, it also emphasized justification by faith: '*Pacem.* Reconcilitationem inter populum et populum diruta maceria legalis ritus in Judaeis, et idolatriae in gentibus. Et inter Deum ipios per fidem justificantem, et homines in eum credentes.'[34]

CHANGES TO THE *ANNOTATIONS*

The following verses underwent significant changes regarding the will and justification in the 1527 edition of the *Annotations*. However, these changes do not correspond directly to changes in the paraphrases of these verses.

Romans 1:1

Erasmus: *Paulus, servus Iesu Christi, **vocatus ad munus apostolicum**, segregatus in Euangelium Dei.*

Vulgate: *Paulus, servus Iesu Christi, vocatus Apostolus, segregatus in Euangelium Dei.*

This particular verse is heavily glossed, as if Erasmus wanted to begin his annotations of Romans with a bang. Although he changed only one phrase in the verse itself, he wrote three extensive annotations on it, even on aspects of the verse to which he had made no grammatical alteration. Of particular interest are the additions he made in 1527 and 1535 (underlined text added in 1519, boldface in 1527). The entire annotation demonstrates the evolution of Erasmus's interpretation and its increasingly audacious character:

> The apostles have certain special words of their own – grace, calling, election, foreknowledge, destination, and predestination – and these are virtually always opposed to trust in the Law, a danger, paramount at that particular time, that seemed to threaten. I am not unaware that Origen, using the opportunity afforded by this word, discourses – with shrewdness and erudition, no doubt – concerning those who are indeed called, but who fall short of the reward of their service. It is not my intention to reject such an interpretation; but in divine literature the simplest and the least forced interpretations are more satisfactory. Yet I would certainly not deny that this word κλητός [called] is sometimes used in a way not much different from a participle, as in Matthew: 'Many are called, but

few are chosen' [22:14], where ἐκλεκτοί [chosen] and κλητοί [called] are read. **This word belongs especially to Paul, who is eager to remove from everyone trust in human works, and to transfer all the glory to the God who calls. Whoever heeds God when he calls is saved. Thus Paul soon obeyed after he had been called from heaven.**[35]

The 1527 addition to the annotation underscores the inefficacy of works and the centrality of the 'call' to salvation. It does, however, leave room for the human will to respond to God's call, though Erasmus emphasizes that 'human works' should not be relied upon. A similar interpretation can be found in Augustine, who used the same verse to highlight that 'Paul distinguishes the Church's dignity from the desuetude of the synagogue.'[36] Chrysostom, in his homilies on Romans I, likewise uses the term to demonstrate God's power and to undermine trust in the human will. Paul says that he has been 'called' in order to demonstrate 'that it was not because he sought that he found but that when he was called, he came near and obeyed.'[37]

Another of Erasmus's annotations on this verse (boldface text added in 1527) clarified his alteration of the phrase 'segregatus in evangelium dei.' The annotation reads:

ἀΦωρισμένος. With an admirably increasing emphasis he commends his own position as one who not only has been called to perform the service of an apostle, but **as a chosen vessel,** has also been selected and separated for the duty of preaching the gospel. For ἀΦωρίζειν [aphorizein] not only means 'to separate' but also 'to distinguish and select with judgement.' Thus physicians call rules stated briefly and complete in themselves ἀΦορισμοί [aphorismoi 'aphorisms'], as the ἀποΦθέγματα [apophthegmata] of the wise are called.

This expression does not have a simple significance. For in the first place, he seeks to avert the charge of inconstancy, because he appeared to be deserting the law of Moses. He says 'called' and 'set apart,' as though he were some chosen and special instrument; Christ himself bears witness 'He is my chosen vessel, to bear my name before the gentiles.' Second, he makes an allusion to the party to which he adhered in Judaism, playing on its name. For the Jewish people, although they embraced the same Law, were divided into various schools: Josephus, in the second chapter of the eighteenth book of Antiquities, mentions the chief of these – Essenes, Sadducees, and Pharisees. Paul belonged to the Pharisaic sect, which receives its name from the Hebrew word ... *pharas* [separate], because they wanted to appear separated and removed from the common people due to their noteworthy holiness of life and their superior doctrine. Paul therefore began to be in the gospel what he had been in Judaism, but in a different way. Under Judaism his title was one of pride; in the gospel he had been marvellously separated from Moses unto Christ, from the letter unto the spirit, from trust in works unto grace.[38]

Melanchthon's 1540 *Commentary on Romans* emphasized similar elements: 'However Paul in the beginning at once sets forth the definition, in order that we might know what is being taught, and might diligently distinguish the Law from the Gospel, as though he were saying: Paul, divinely called for teaching the Gospel about Christ, not for teaching the law or philosophy.'[39] This annotation again underscores the idea of being 'chosen' in the sense of being called, but more important, from 1516 onward it had emphasized the dichotomies between 'old' and 'new' highlighted in Paul: Moses versus Christ, the letter versus the spirit, and, most significant in the context of Reformation theology, works versus grace.

Romans 1:5

Erasmus: *Per quem acceptimus gratiam, & apostolatum **ut obediatur fidei** in omnibus Gentibus **super ipsius nomine**.*

Vulgate: *Per quem acceptimus gratiam, & apostolatum ad obediendum fidei in omnibus Gentibus pro nomine ejus.*

Regarding his correction of the Vulgate's '*ad obediendum fidei*' to '*ut obediatur fidei*,' Erasmus wrote (underlined text added in 1519, boldface in 1527):

In Greek this is a noun, not an infinitive, εἰς ὑπακοὴν πίστεως, that is, *ad obedientiam fidei* [to the obedience of faith]. But since this expression is ambiguous in Latin, the Translator has clarified it with a gerund, I with a verb: 'that the faith might be obeyed.' By 'obedience of faith' he means, **as Chrysostom explains**, that [faith] is not obtained by a painstaking process of logical reasoning, but by simple obedience and quiet compliance. And this applies to both peoples: to the Jews who sought for signs, and to the gentiles who demanded philosophical arguments; and perhaps today it applies to the convoluted labyrinths of the questions of the scholastics concerning those matters of which it is pious to be ignorant.

Here, Erasmus explained from 1516 onward – only in 1527 attributing the explanation to the influence of Chrysostom – that Paul means that 'obedience of faith' is achieved not 'by a painstaking process of logical reasoning, but by simple obedience and quiet compliance.' He clarified this most probably to exclude the scholastic metaphysical interpretations of the verse. In 1519 he added a piece to the annotation regarding the 'convoluted labyrinths of the questions of the scholastics concerning those matters of which it is pious to be ignorant.'[40] This portion of the annotation is flavoured with Erasmus's ongoing reconsideration of Paul's message and his desire to contextualize it: the scholastics are those who came to mind when Erasmus heard Paul reminding the Romans of God's call for 'the obedience of faith.'[41] There is no process in faith, no act, but rather a quiet acceptance. In this, Erasmus followed Chrysostom, as he says in the annotation.

In yet another annotation to this verse (underlined text added in 1519, boldface in 1527), Erasmus argued, 'Grace,' too is a Pauline word, a word Paul repeatedly emphasizes, desiring to 'exclude carnal reliance on the Mosaic law.' He continued:

> In Greek, however, χάρις sometimes means 'a kindness' that is conferred without recompense – whence also the verb χαρίζεσθαι 'bestow' or 'give freely'; sometimes 'favour,' for example, 'you have found *gratiam* [favour] with God'; sometimes 'an obligation for an act of kindness,' for example, ἔχω χάριν [I owe thanks, am grateful], οἶδα χάριν [I am grateful], καὶ [and] μεμνήσομαι χάριν [I will show gratitude] ... **By grace here he means that he was called back from error; and not only called back, but also chosen to call, with authority, others to the grace of the gospel.**[42]

In 1527 Erasmus also chose to emphasize grace as independent of the 'carnal' law and the fact that God conveys grace as the antidote to error, and thus to sin. Significantly, Rolf Schäfer notes that it was Erasmus's interpretation of Romans 1:5 that cemented Melanchthon's 'understanding of the Pauline concept of grace as *favor*.'[43] The *Glossa ordinaria*, incidentally, also uses the verse to juxtapose grace and the Law: '*In omnibus*. Gentibus non solum Judaeis, in quibus quia sine lege vocati: non debent sub lege agere.'[44]

Romans 7:25

Erasmus: ***Gratias ago deo*** *per Iesum Christum dominum nostrum Igitur ego ipse mente servo legi Dei; carne autem, legi peccati.*

Vulgate: *Gratia Dei per Iesum Christum dominum nostrum Igitur ego ipse mente servo legi Dei; carne autem, legi peccati.*

The annotation reads as follows (small caps text added in 1519, boldface in 1527, and underlined in 1535):

BUT THE REPLY TO THE EXCLAMATORY QUESTION IS SPOKEN UNDER A DIFFERENT PERSONA, NAMELY, OF ONE WHO HAS BEEN FREED FROM THAT MOST WRETCHED SERVITUDE NOT THROUGH THE LAW, BUT THROUGH THE GRACE OF CHRIST. Accordingly, he gives to one persona the exclamation 'Wretched man that I am, who,' etc. to another, the speech of him who gives thanks to God. In the same way, Origen would also have the many things Paul mentioned above – about 'the law of death' and 'of the members' and about the necessity of sin – spoken under the persona of the former.

IN HIS INTERPRETATION, AMBROSE LIKEWISE SAYS THAT FROM THESE WORDS WE MUST UNDERSTAND THAT THE MAN *HAS BEEN* FREED BY THE GRACE OF GOD FROM THE BODY OF HIS DEATH; HE IS NOT *TO BE* FREED. THE WORDS THAT SOON FOLLOW SUPPORT THIS: 'FOR THE LAW OF THE SPIRIT OF LIFE IN CHRIST JESUS HAS FREED ME FROM THE LAW OF SIN AND DEATH' [8:2]. **But if he had followed the reading 'the grace of God,' this phrase would not be suited to Paul, who did not have to be freed, but was freed, and Ambrose's argument is inconsistent. Therefore we must read either 'thanks be to God' or 'I give thanks.' With these words, he gives thanks – now freed – to**

God, through whose grace he has attained what neither the law, nor the law of Moses, nor conscience, nor works could offer him ...

It is not the point that certain interpreters, citing this passage, call to mind the phrase 'the grace of God,' and suggest that here is shown the one who frees from the body of death, since whoever gives thanks to God for his freedom, by this very act indicates the means through which others can also be freed. But all apply to the person of Paul [the words] wherein he gives thanks as one who has been freed; they differ on the exclamatory question. The ancient commentators are unwilling to have it applied to the Apostle; Jerome believes it is said under the persona of 'Everyman.' **And yet if we take 'body of death' as a tendency to sin – as though to say 'a dying body' – nothing prevents all this from also fitting Paul, in accordance with the Latin reading.** Certainly Augustine, in the first book *Against the Two Letters of the Pelagians*, the eighth and following chapters, contends that this whole passage is appropriate to Paul either as a boy, or under the law of sin, or under grace – sensing the stir of the affections, but not assenting. But he twists many things so harshly that it is more suitable [to say] that Paul assumes the persona of the whole human race: as a pagan, he is outside the Law; as a Jew he is carnal under the Law; and as spiritual he has been freed through grace.[45]

Erasmus employed the Church Fathers in his explication of the verse primarily because of the importance of Romans 7 in the Reformation debate. Erasmus approached this verse, as he did many verses in Romans 7, through several additions, and the result is a multilayered assessment of Paul's view of the Law and the believer's relationship to it. On one level, Erasmus's interpretation reveals a preoccupation with this central theme of the Law and its role in the righteousness of the Christian. On another level, Erasmus demonstrated his interest in sin and its connection to the Law. In both cases, as Jaroslav Pelikan shows, Erasmus held a position similar to that of not only Augustine but also Luther, who argued that 'there is the one man Paul, who recognizes himself to be in two different situations: under grace he is spiritual, but under the law carnal. It is one and the same Paul who is under both.'

Indeed, Erasmus's language in the portion of the annotation added in 1535 is almost identical to Luther's in *Against Latomus*.[46]

To be sure, Erasmus's explication also mirrored Melanchthon's in his 1540 commentary on the verse. Melanchthon, too, explained the verse by differentiating between the inner and the outer selves:

> The reader should also be reminded of the distinction between the inner and the outer man, about the mind and about the flesh. The inner man signifies a person insofar as he has been renewed by the Holy Spirit, that is, insofar as he has true fear and true trust. Here the mind does not signify only the part which knows, but both parts; knowing and laying hold of, as far as it has been renewed by the Holy Spirit, as he says: 'With my mind I serve the Law of God' [7:25]. By contrast, the outer man or the flesh signifies the entire man insofar as he has not been renewed by the Holy Spirit. They signify not only the appetites of these senses or the external members, but also the higher powers, reason and will, insofar as they have not been renewed, as will have to be said again below.[47]

The timing of each set of changes reveals a great deal about Erasmus's preoccupations and interests. The sections added to the annotation of the verse in 1519, for example, demonstrate his interest in Ambrose, whose works were published under his supervision in a four-volume set in Basel in 1527. The 1527 additions to the annotation reflect Erasmus's growing concern with grace and, incidentally, evidence the same preoccupation about which he wrote to Thomas More that year.[48] Likewise, his 1535 additions reflect a remarkable boldness. Published just one year before his death, this annotation includes language remarkably similar to that of both Luther and Melanchthon.

Romans 8:28

Erasmus: *Scimus autem quoniam deligentibus Deum omnia simul adiumento sunt in bonum, iis, qui iuxta propositum vocati sunt.*

Vulgate: *Scimus autem quoniam deligentibus Deum omnia cooperamur in bonum, iis, qui secundum propositum vocati sint sancti.*

The annotation to this passage first appeared in 1519 (boldface text added in 1527, underlined word in 1535):

> That is, 'according to a determining judgment,' so that the 'purpose' does not refer to 'saints,' or to a 'person with a good resolution,' but refers to 'the predestination of God.' So Origen and Thomas, though Ambrose seems to refer to both senses. And yet Origen, too, a little further on, when he distinguishes those who are said to be called and not chosen from those who are called and chosen, varies his position somewhat, for he explains that those are said to be 'called according to the purpose' who, before they were called, were already inclined in heart to the worship of the divine, [and] whose will, even then ready, needed only the call. This is to say that the 'purpose' belongs not to the God who destines, but the person who makes a mental resolution, **unless perhaps [Origen's] translator [Rufinus] added these words on his own. In his book *On Rebuke and Grace*, the seventh chapter, Augustine follows Ambrose: 'They were chosen,' he says, 'because they were called according to a purpose, not, however, their own but God's.' For in the next chapter of this Epistle Paul has spoken of the 'purpose of God' in a similar sense; and again in the first chapter [of the Epistle] of the Ephesians.**
>
> In the Greek, 'saints' is not added; there is only 'the called.' It is clear from Origen's exposition that he so reads, when he says: 'One must consider whether perhaps from the fact that he says "to those who have been called according to the purpose and whom he foreknew and whom he predestined" etc.' Ambrose reads likewise, for in his discussion he says: 'But these are called according to the purpose, who, as believers, God foreknew would be suitable to him, so that they were known before they believed.' **Augustine reads the same in his book *On Rebuke and Grace*. Chrysostom and** Theophylact follow both this reading and this understanding, though Thomas and <u>many</u> old Latin codices resist it. But it appears that 'saints' was added from other passages in which these two words, 'called saints,' are often joined.[49]

Interestingly, Erasmus draws upon the writings of Aquinas in this annotation. While not unprecedented in his *Annotations on Romans,* it was not common for Erasmus to have done so. Certainly, this passage posed difficulties for Erasmus. His initial interpretation seems to support the notion of the human will contributing to preparations for salvation. His addition to the text in 1527 questioned this initial interpretation, which he attributed to Origen, and argued that the verse could indicate the opposite. That is to say, Erasmus left the reader with Origen's assertion that 'the "purpose" belongs not to the God who destines, but the person who makes a mental resolution' until 1527, when he indicated that it was possible that Ambrose and Augustine had it right when they argued, '"They were chosen," he says, "because they were called according to a purpose, not, however, their own but God's."'

Cochlaeus, conversely, used this verse to deny the evangelical position that Christians are saved by faith alone and used Romans 8:28 to underscore that a loving God plays a role in salvation. His point provides perspective on the distance between Erasmus and at least some contemporary Catholic interpreters:

Wie nu nicht gebürt su sagen, das die werck allein gerecht machen, ob sie schon von Christo herkommen, also gebürt auch nicht su sagen, das der glaub allein gerecht mache. Denn Christus ist das heubt, der uns fürnemlich durch die gnad und andere mittel (die er zur vergebung der sünde und rechtfertigung verordnet) gerecht macht und vonn sünden erledigt. Solcher mittel seind viel, nicht der glaub allein, nemlich die heligen sacrament, durch welcher gebrauch wir die gnad erlangen, item die liebe, die forcht Gottes, der glaub, die hoffnung, die guten werd, die demut und alle tügende, die uns zur gnad dienstlich seind, dadurch wir, von Got der sünden entledigt und los gemacht, gerecht werden, welchs uns unmüglich were aus uns selbs, ist aber müglich worden durch Christus sterben und ausserstehen vom tod.[50]

This verse played an important part in the evangelical landscape, as well. Erasmus's annotation demonstrates that he understood the pivotal nature of the verse and that which followed it in the question of human freedom in general and predestination in particular. Luther intensively explicated the verse in the *Scholia* and used it to assert that Paul 'from this point on begins to discuss the matter of predestination and election, which is not as deep a subject as is commonly thought, but rather is a wonderfully sweet thing for those who have the Spirit, but a bitter thing and harsh above all things for the prudence of the flesh.' Luther went on to say that the 'theologians, however, brilliant as they are, think that they have accomplished something great when they bring in their concept of "the contingent," saying that the elect are saved necessarily, namely, by the necessity of consequence, but not by the necessity of the consequent. These are only empty words.'[51] Luther rejected the scholastic interpretation and terminology and favoured his own simpler interpretation of predestination, which rested on his view of the enslaved will. Thus, Erasmus's addition in 1527 regarding God's purpose, which denies a role for free will in justification, fits nicely with Luther's view, articulated in *De servo arbitrio*: 'For if we believe it to be true that God foreknows and predestines all things, that he can neither be mistaken in his foreknowledge nor hindered in his predestination, and that nothing takes place but as he will it (as reason itself is forced to admit), then on the testimony of reason itself there cannot be any free choice in man or angel or any creature.'[52]

Romans 8.29

Erasmus: *Nam **quos praesciverat**, & praedestinavit conformes fieri imaginis Filii sui, ut sit ipse primogenitus in multis fratribus.*

Vulgate: *Nam quos praescivit, & praedestinavit conformes fieri imaginis Filii sui, ut sit ipse primogenitus in multis fratribus.*

The annotation to this passage is a long one, but quoting it in its entirety demonstrates the many layers of interpretation Erasmus accumulated throughout the various editions. The annotation first appeared in 1516 (small caps text added in 1519, boldface in 1527).

οὓς προέγνωκεν [whom he had foreknown], OR AS SOME READ, προέγνω [FOREKNEW]. I have already noted above that in Greek this verb is sometimes understood in the sense of 'decide' or 'determine,' because coming to a resolution implies knowing.

These words seem not so much to stand apart from one another through some fundamental incompatibility, as to belong together, distinguished from one another in a sort of sequence of time and logic. In this way, PAUL CAN SET THE

MATTER FORTH more vividly: προγνῶναι is used of one deliberating and deciding; deciding, however, what could in some
way be changed – to speak in a manner appropriate to the
human sphere; next, προορίζειν [mark out beforehand] or
ὁρίζειν [mark out] is used of one who now openly proclaims
what he has decided, and this usually occurs when something has been determined in such a way that it cannot be
changed. Moreover, when you have proclaimed your resolution it remains that you must deliver and fulfil what you have
promised. Now he who calls and invites is beginning to fulfil
[his promise]. Then, lest he seem to have called in vain, he
also justifies the called, without which we are not capable of
receiving the promise. Finally a reward is given to the justified. Therefore God προέγνωκεν [foreknew] from eternity
those whom he decided and determined were to be called to
immortality; he προώρισεν [marked out beforehand] those
concerning whom he proclaimed, making known his decision already through his prophets, and even more through
his Son. Now, he has called through the preaching of Jesus, he
has justified through his death, he has glorified through the
resurrection and the reward of immortality. **Or he has called
through the teaching of the gospel, he has justified through
baptism, he has glorified through the gifts of the Spirit.** In
this way Paul arrives in a sort of sequence from what is primary to the culminating point so that the matter might be
more firmly grounded and more definitive.

But if anyone judges too harshly that in this passage I do
away with foreknowledge, he should know that such is the
interpretation of Theophylact, the Greek interpreter, and a recent one (for some will more willingly believe a modern),
who thinks that the difference between πρόγνωσις [foreknowledge] and προορισμός [predetermination] (or ὁρισμός
[determination]) is this, that the former is less firmly, that latter more firmly established. In fact, one can go further: where
Peter writes προεγνωσμένους γὰρ πρὸ τῆς καταβολῆς τοῦ
κόσμου, which, on this view, should be translated 'foreknown
[before the foundation of the world],' Lyra does not scruple
to expound as 'foreordained.' And Thomas points out that
there were some who interpreted foreknowledge in this passage in a different sense, namely, as the preparation for grace,

which God manifests – temporally – in the saints; their intent, no doubt, was to make a distinction between foreknowledge and predestination. But Thomas justly rejects their fabrication. Origen thinks that in this passage we should not take πϱόγυωσις (that is, foreknowledge) in the usual sense, according to which God 'foreknew' even those who were to perish – so that the statement that 'all whom he foreknew he had predestined' then becomes false. But just as divine Scripture says, by a customary idiom, that those are 'known' whom God embraces with affection ('I do not know you'; 'THE LORD KNOWS THE PATH OF THE RIGHTEOUS'), so here they are called 'foreknown.'

I am well aware, however, that some have sought from this passage a field for EXERCISING their ingenuity, in which they philosophize about God's foreknowledge and predestination – namely Origen, St. Augustine, Thomas Aquinas, and subsequently all the theological schools. I do not criticize their industry, but here the sense I have established seems to me simpler and more genuine. If anyone prefers something different, as far as I am concerned, let each use his own judgement. I am only advising, not dictating; AND I AM PRESENTING MY OWN OPINION, WITHOUT PREJUDICING ANYONE ELSE AT ALL.[53]

In this annotation, Erasmus may support a position of 'predestination based upon foreknowledge.'[54] Nevertheless, he ultimately qualifies the notion by asserting that there is no easy understanding of this, and the best course of action is to 'let each use his own judgement.' In this, he is consistent with Melanchthon's early view, which fundamentally 'opposed speculations about God's will behind God's predestination, especially about the causes of God's predestinating will.'[55] Just as Erasmus's view on this very important matter underwent significant revision, however, so did Melanchthon's. As Meijering points out, Melanchthon argued in 1559 (twenty-three years after Erasmus's death): 'Free will cannot obey and love God completely,' because 'these spiritual acts man cannot do without (the help of) the Holy Spirit.' Meijering identifies the 'most important shift in Melanchthon's views of free will' in the realization that 'these spiritual acts are not *the work of* the Holy Spirit, but they are done *with the help of* the Holy Spirit. The Holy Spirit, when it is at work in man, needs the Word of God through which it speaks and it needs the consent of human will.'[56] This position stood some distance from Luther's assertion that 'moral autonomy' is destroyed – that there is no free will in the process of human salvation.[57]

One last aspect of this lengthy annotation is worthy of additional attention. Erasmus wrote: 'Therefore God ... [foreknew] from eternity those whom he had decided and determined were to be called to immortality; he ... [marked out beforehand] those concerning whom he proclaimed, making known his decision already through his prophets, and even more through his Son. Now, he has called through the preaching of Jesus, he has justified through his death, he has glorified through the resurrection and the reward of immortality. Or he has called through the teaching of the gospel, he has justified through baptism, he has glorified through the gifts of the Spirit.' The last sentence was added in 1527 and seems a departure from the 1516 sense of the annotation. It is possible that Erasmus inserted the last paragraph as a safeguard against his critics, who would have been on the lookout for his support of predestination. Indeed, at the end of the annotation, Erasmus wrote a defensive appeal to his critics in 1519: 'And I am presenting my own opinion, without prejudicing anyone else at all.'[58]

Romans 11:6

Erasmus: **Quod si per gratiam**, *jam non ex operibus:* **quandoquidem gratia jam non est gratia.**

Vulgate: *Si autem gratia, jam non ex operibus: alioqui gratia jam non est gratia.*

There are three annotations for this verse; the second two are relevant to this study (small caps text added in 1519, double underlining in 1522, boldface in 1527, and underlined in 1535.)

ἐπεί, that is, 'since' or 'inasmuch as.' And yet the translator's version is correct and clear, for in Greek εἰ δὲ μή [otherwise] is understood, as I shall soon show.

... THE GREEK CODICES HAVE SOMEWHAT MORE HERE THAN DO THE LATIN. FOR THEY PROVIDE A REPETITION IN THE 'WORKS THAT ARE NOT WORKS' EXPRESSION IN THE FOLLOWING MANNER

– FOR THE LATIN EXPRESSES THE FORM ONLY IN RELATION TO
GRACE: εἰ δὲ χάριτι, οὐκέτι ἐξ ἔργων, ἐπεί ἡ χάρις οὐκέτι
γίνεται χάρις. εἰ δὲ ἐξ ἔργων, οὐκέτι ἐστί χάρις, ἐπεί τό ἔργον
οὐκέτι ἐστίν ἔργον, THAT IS, 'BUT IF THROUGH GRACE, NO LON-
GER FROM WORKS, INASMUCH AS GRACE IS NO LONGER GRACE;
BUT IF FROM WORKS, IT IS NO LONGER GRACE, INASMUCH AS
WORK IS NO LONGER WORK.' AND THIS IS HOW THEOPHYLACT
READS AND ALSO INTERPRETS. BUT SINCE I DO NOT FIND THIS
ADDITION IN ORIGEN, I AM SOMEWHAT DOUBTFUL THAT IT IS
THE TRUE READING, **especially since Chrysostom in ex-
pounding this passage reads only** εἰ δὲ χάριτι, οὐκέτι ἐξ
ἔργων, ἐπεί ἡ χάρις οὐκέτι γίνεται χάρις. **He adds nothing to
these words.** MOREOVER, THE PARTS OF THE SENTENCE SEEM
INVERTED, AND SHOULD BE ARRANGED RATHER IN THIS ORDER:
'BUT IF THROUGH GRACE, NO LONGER FROM WORKS, INASMUCH
AS WORK IS NO LONGER WORK; BUT IF FROM WORKS, NO LONGER
FROM GRACE, INASMUCH AS GRACE IS NO LONGER GRACE' – UN-
LESS IN ἐπεί THERE IS LATENT AN IMPLIED EXCEPTION, AS ELSE-
WHERE IN PAUL'S USE OF THE WORD. THEN THE SENSE WOULD BE
'IF BY GRACE, NO LONGER FROM WORKS; IF THIS WERE NOT SO,
GRACE WOULD NOT BE GRACE,' THAT IS, IT WOULD BE FALSELY
CALLED GRACE. I INCLINE TO THE LATIN READING, IN VIEW OF
THE FACT THAT PAUL IS NOT DISCUSSING HERE WHETHER WORK
IS A WORK, BUT IS SUPPORTING GRACE, WHICH THE JEWS WERE
TRYING TO DRIVE OUT. And yet, the Aldine edition, **and even
the Spanish edition,** agree with what I have found in the
Greek copies.[59]

Erasmus offered here a defence of grace over works, citing several
Fathers. Most important, however, is his purposeful dismissal of
Chrysostom's interpretation of the verse. In his homilies,
Chrysostom spent a great deal of time on this particular verse,
and his interpretation does not stand in opposition to Erasmus's
interpretation.[60] The complex layers of additions to explain the
verse and the changes Erasmus made to the Latin reflect primarily
grammatical concerns. Nevertheless, Erasmus's preoccupation
with the subject of grace and works is evident in his thorough
explication and frequent revisiting of the text.

Like Erasmus, Melanchthon used the text to illuminate Paul's
promotion of grace over works in the 1540 *Commentary on Romans*:

'He adds the teaching that the church has not been elected on account of the Law, on account of the form of government, but that the people of God which accepts the Gospel by faith has been elected. He adds that the cause of election is mercy, not the Law, not the form of government, as was said above about the distinction between the two peoples.'[61]

More interesting, perhaps, is Luther's gloss on the verse, which quite closely reflects Erasmus's language in the annotation: *'But if it is by grace*, that is, out of grace or through grace, *it is no longer on the basis of works*, that is, one's own righteousness. He adds that of necessity this is impossible, for, *otherwise*, if this does not stand; but it does stand; therefore that cannot stand, *grace*, if it is bestowed because of the merits of our own righteousness and because of works, *would no longer be grace*, which ought according to its name be given freely – which is a false and ridiculous idea.'[62]

However, Catholic critics of Luther's interpretation viewed the verse quite differently. Johannes Dietenberger, for example, argued on the basis of Romans 11:6 that, though grace must always precede works that follow grace, works can also play a role in salvation: 'Die Gnade wird, wenn sie zuerst gegeben wird, durchaus umsonst gegeben und keinesfalls aus unseren Werken, die etwa der Gnade in verienstlicher Weise nach Erlangung der Gnade aus der Gnade oder wegen der Gnade gegeben wird, kann auch aus oder wegen der Werke, die der Gnade folgen, gegeben werden und nichtsdestoweniger aus Gnade sein, und zwar deshalb, weil es der Gnade keineswegs widerstrebt (durch Vermittlung anderer Tugenden), Ursprung der guten Werke zu sein, deren Ziel das ewige Leben ist.'[63]

Romans 4:3

Erasmus: *Quid enim dicit Scriptura?* **Credidit autem Abraham** Deo: **et imputatum est** *illis ad justitiam.*

Vulgate: *Quid enim dicit Scriptura? Credidit Abraham Deo: & reputatum est illis ad justitiam.*

The annotation is as follows (underlined text added in 1535):

ἐλογίσθη, that is, 'it was imputed,' at least in this passage. For the Greek word is ambiguous. But *reputare* means something quite different from *imputare*. *Reputare* means to consider, *imputare* means to count to one's credit, or to add to the account, generally with no pejorative connotation. *Deputare* has the meaning of *supputare* [to count, calculate], or of *existimare* [to suppose] or *aestimare* [to judge, esteem]; while the Greek word corresponds variously to 'consider,' 'impute,' 'reckon.' Strictly speaking, *imputare* corresponds to ἐλλογεῖσθαι [rather than λογίζεσθαι], and this word, too, the Apostle has used elsewhere.[64]

Erasmus asserted that the word *imputare* is better than *reputare* for this verse. As a result, the verse alludes to the idea that righteousness is given, not deserved. As Erasmus observed, *reputare* gives the sense of something that is considered, so that in this verse Abraham's belief was 'reckoned to him as righteousness.'[65] Erasmus's use of *imputare* gives the opposite sense, that Abraham's belief was given to him *for* his righteousness.

The use of the word *imputare* for the process through which righteousness emerges in a person formed an important part of the Reformation debate on faith and grace. It became an important part of Lutheran thought quite early on. According to Werner Elert, Luther's doctrine of justification depended on a concept of 'alien righteousness' that is 'infused' from outside. Luther's use of the word 'to infuse' (*infundere*) 'was definitely supplanted by the word "to impute" (*imputare*).' Indeed, Elert states that, for Luther 'the expressions "to account" (*reputare*) and "to impute" (*imputare*) deny in the strongest way all synergism as well as the scholastic teaching that there is a disposition (*Habituslehre*).' Elert continues: 'For him they characterize in the sharpest way God's attitude in justification. God speaks the word of forgiveness of sins, and by doing so He declares that He does not debit sins and that He accounts faith in Christ as righteousness. Justification is no psychic change; it is a word of God spoken to the sinner.' In this way, *imputare* was an essential part of the early articulation of Luther's program.[66]

Melanchthon, like Erasmus, moved from the word *reputare* to *imputare*. In his 1521 *Loci*, Melanchthon used the word *to infuse* in his discussion of justification by faith. He wrote, 'Iam et fidem infusam et acquisitam ac generalem et specialem et nescio quae portenta verborum finxerunt.'[67] In his 1532 commentary on Romans 4:3, however, Melanchthon used 'imputatum est' in the verse but described it this way (using *reputare*): 'Secundum argumentum sumptum est ex testimonio Genesis, ubi textus clare definit iustificationem: Dicit Abraham reputari iustum, quia credidit. Igitur iustifcatio contigit non propter nostras virtutes aut qualitates aut opera, sed fide, h. e. fiducia misericordiae.'[68] In the 1540 commentary on the verse, Melanchthon argued, 'Secundum ex definitione. Iustificatio est gratuita imputatio iusticiae, Ergo non iustificamur propter nostram qualitatem aut dignitatem etc.'[69] Susi Hausammann notes that Romans 4:3 was also central to the Swiss reformer Heinrich Bullinger's 1525 understanding of *sola gratia*. He, too, pointed to the importance of using *imputare*, which intimates that 'justification relies on the benevolent generosity of God "without works added."'[70]

For Catholics, too, the perceived importance of the use and defence of the term during the Reformation counted for a great deal. Gasparo Contarini, for example, argued in *Epistola de iustificatione* (1541) that 'insuper donat nobis cum Spiritu Christi Christum ipsum et omnem iustitiam eius gratis ex ipsius misericordia nostram facit, nobis imputat, qui induimus Christum' in his defence of 'duplicem iustitiam,'[71] an argument, incidentally, that was later rejected by the Council of Trent.[72] The *Glossa ordinaria* of the verse reinforces the role of belief but also emphasizes the place of works and avoids the use of *imputare* and *reputare*: 'Credere, suffíciens causa fuit ei justitiae, et est aliis, sed tamen qui habet tempus operandi, ei non dábitur merces secundum gratiam tantum, sed secundum debitum operationis suae; sed ei qui non habet tempus operandi, si credit, sola fides sufficit ad justitiam, et ita ad salutem secundum gratiam propositam omnibus, vel secundum quod Deus legem ante posuit.'[73] Thus, Erasmus's use of *imputare* echoed Luther's use of it to explain justification by faith, later Protestant uses of it by Melanchthon and even Bullinger to reinforce justification without works, and the later Catholic employment of the term by Contarini in his articulation of a (failed) plan that he hoped would appease both Catholics and Protestants.[74]

Romans 5:1

Erasmus: *Iustificatio igitur ex fide,* **pacem habemus erga Deum** *per Dominum nostrum Iesum Christum:*

Vulgate: *Iustificatio igitur ex fide, pacem habeamus ad Deum per Dominum nostrum Iesum Christum:*

Almost all of the annotation to this verse first appeared in this form in 1535.[75] Note that the second paragraph takes on a pastoral tone:

In most of the Greek codices the reading is ἔχομεν [we have], in others the reading varies; for example in Theophylact the [biblical] text [cited] has ἔχομεν 'we have,' but the exposition ἔχωμεν 'let us have.' In Chrysostom the text [cited] has ἔχωμεν 'let us have,' and likewise the commentary; but that this is a mistake made through the carelessness of copyists is implied by what follows, τοῦτ᾽ ἔστιν, οὐκ ἔτι ἁμαρτάνομεν, that is, 'we sin no more,' where [the copyist] has not changed the omicron [to omega]. I do not know whether the first person of τὰ αὐτοπαθητικά has the same form as the indicative, as the second [person] has ἔχομεν, ἔχετε [we have, you have].

Granted that it does, the sense here does not allow the imperative mood. For the Apostle is speaking here about those who, justified through faith, now have a peace with God; if he wished to deter them from sinning, so that they would not lose the peace they had received, he would have said more fittingly τηρῶμεν [let us keep] rather than ἔχωμεν. For here he is not warning those who are justified, but he is expressing joy in their felicity, because as a result not of their own merits but of the freely offered kindness of God they have been freed from their sins and reconciled to him with whom formerly they were at enmity. This sense is reflected in the words that follow about the assurance of access to God, about the hope of the glory of the sons of God – a hope that perseveres even in the afflictions of this world – and about the love of God who reconciled the world to himself by the death of the Only-Begotten.

It is clear that Ambrose read 'we have,' not 'let us have,' as is shown by these words: 'Faith, not law, makes [us] have peace with God. For this reconciles us to God – the sins taken away that had made us enemies to God; and because the Lord Jesus is the minister of this grace, through him we have made peace with God.' And his exposition reflects this reading. He says, 'Through these things that he has perceived – what it is to be justified by faith and not through works – [Paul] very clearly invites to the peace of God that passes all understanding, and in which also consists of the fullness of perfection.' So far Origen. In the same way one who extols the tranquility of the monastic life proclaims the praises of virginity [and] invites to this manner of life those who have not yet embraced it. There follows at that point in Origen: 'When we were enemies of God we were reconciled to God' etc. But Origen shows the consequence, that one who has been freely reconciled to God thinks no more those things that are hostile to God. It is not strange if thereupon Origen, using [Paul's] words to express his own thought, changes the indicative mood into the imperative, 'let us have peace': 'let there not be in us yes and no.'

There is no need, then, of a verb in the imperative for this exhortation, but the situation itself exhorts us, once freed from our sins and reconciled to God, not to fall back again into those things that sever the friendship between God and men. What Chrysostom writes agrees with this account, and Theophylact, too, who borrowed his material from him. And this kind of admonishing suits better the modesty and civility of Paul. It is a familiar figure of speech: we say something is being done that (we wish to have understood) ought to be done. For example, 'one who is born of God does not sin,' and 'a mother cannot hate her son,' and 'a ruler measures everything by the good of the state.' I have argued my case without, however, absolutely condemning the other reading. For this statement can apply to those baptized who are still weak in spirit, and from time to time fall back into sin, so that the Apostle, to soften his admonition, included his own person.[76]

Erasmus used this verse to emphasize that it is not through any type of merit but rather solely through faith that sinners are justified. He wrote that righteousness is given 'as a result not of their own merits but of the freely offered kindness of God by which they have been freed from their sins and reconciled to him with whom formerly they were at enmity.' To support this perspective, he called on the writings of a wide range of Fathers, including Chrysostom, Origen, Ambrose, and Theophylact. He argued on behalf of the imperative form of the verb, that is, *habeamus*, because, he says, the intention of Paul is to speak to the justified, not to those who seek justification.

This verse figured predominantly in Melanchthon's discussion of the forgiveness of sin in the *Loci Communes* of 1555. Melanchthon argued: 'Romans 5:1: "Since we are justified by faith, we have peace with God through our Lord Jesus Christ. Through him we have obtained access to this grace in which we stand." This sentence is clear and comforting, for Paul unambiguously says we are justified through *faith*; and that we may know how this happens, and what this faith is, he says, "through this faith the heart has peace before God" [*cf.* Rom. 5:1].'[77] Likewise, Melanchthon's 1540 commentary on the verse reflected Erasmus's emphasis on the 'joy' intended in the verse for those who are justified – 'joy in their felicity, because as a result not of their own merits but of the freely offered kindness of God they have been freed from their sins and reconciled to him with whom formerly they were at enmity.' Melanchthon articulated this joy as comfort: 'Second, this statement should be used to teach and comfort pious consciences which acknowledge their weakness in order that they may be recalled to Christ, the mediator, and may learn that they are accounted righteous by faith on account of Christ – not on account of their own beginning and imperfect obedience, but by faith on account of Christ.'[78]

Not surprisingly, the verse figured prominently in the *Augsburg Confession* to clarify: '"Rechtferigen aber heisst an dieser Stelle nach richterlicher Gewohnheit (forensi consuetudine) eine Angeklagten (reum) freisprechen und für gerct erklären, aber um einer fremden Gerechtigkeit willen, nämlich Christi. Diese fremde Gerechtigkeit wird uns zuteil durch den Glauben. Da also an dieser Stelle unsere Gerechtikeit die Anrechnung einer fremden Gerechtigkeit ist, ist hier anders von Gerechtigkeit zu reden, als wie wenn wir in der Philosophie oder im Gericht nach der Gerechtikeit des eigenen Werkes fragen, welche sicher im Willen begründet ist."'[79]

Catholic critics of Lutheran theology used the verse, as well. Cajetan, for example, used Romans 5:1, along with other verses, to argue: 'Die Sündenvergebung werde dem Glauben und der Liebe zugleich zugerechnet.' As Vinzenz Pfnür notes, Cajetan used this verse in his efforts to demonstrate 'in what ways God's gift is realized in Men.'[80]

CONCLUSION

By 1535 Erasmus had significantly changed a number of aspects of his *Paraphrases* and *Annotations* of Romans. Several themes emerge in those changes. First, after 1527 Erasmus began to high-light salvation through faith alone and to challenge the efficacy of not only ceremonial works but also all human efforts. He noted in the 1532 revision of his paraphrase of Romans 1:7, for example, that grace is granted neither through 'the observance of the Mosaic law' nor through 'human wisdom' but completely through the generosity of God.[81] The 1527 addition to the annotation of Romans 1:1 likewise emphasized that Paul aimed to 'remove from everyone trust in human works.' There remained no room for any kind of human works, not only works related to the observance of the Law, in Erasmus's new formulation of Pauline salvation. The annotation of Romans 5:1, almost all of which was added in 1535, again demonstrated this emphasis.

Second, after 1527 Erasmus's theology exhibited an emphasis on *fiducia*, trust. He illuminated the connection between *fiducia* and faith without works in several places in the revisions he made to the *Paraphrases* and *Annotations* after 1527. Erasmus inserted 'and trust' into his 1532 paraphrase of Romans 3:22 in order to argue that righteousness came not through ceremonies and cir-cumcision, as practised by the Jews, 'but through faith and trust in Jesus Christ, through whom alone true righteousness is conferred … upon each and every one who has faith in him.' The same em-phasis appeared in Romans 1:16–17 and, as James Tracy has point-ed out, also in 1 Corinthians 1:21.[82]

Third, Erasmus increasingly rejected a connection between righteousness and human works. In the 1532 edition of the *Paraphrases on Romans*, he emphasized the futility of any works of merit in the process of salvation. In Romans 2:10, he changed the meaning of the paraphrase by inserting 'through faith.' Until 1532, he argued that 'glory, honor, and peace' would be the re-wards of those who 'have lived well.' After 1532 he stated that those rewards would be given 'equally to all who, through faith, have lived well.' Likewise, in Romans 3:26, Erasmus asserted first in the 1532 edition: 'He does not forgive because they have mer-ited it, but because he himself has promised [forgiveness].'[83] In Romans 4:25, as well, Erasmus changed the meaning of his para-phrase with the 1532 addition of 'through faith' to his paraphrase. Instead of Christ surrendering 'himself to death so that he might as a pure favour wash away our sins,' Erasmus asserted that Christ's favour comes 'through faith.'[84]

Again and again, Erasmus changed the meaning of his *Annotations* and *Paraphrases* to reflect his evolving understanding of the centrality of faith in salvation. In Romans 8:25, 9:1, and 10:15, he continued his reassessment of the connection between faith and meritorious action for the sinner. Nevertheless, as Tracy points out, 'if the notion that God reveals his justice in the reprobate sounds unmistakably Lutheran, it is still Erasmus who holds out the possibility that all men will at some time be called by God. He has not abandoned free will, but he has learned that Paul makes life difficult for its defenders.'[85]

All of these changes, not only those to Erasmus's *Annotations* and *Paraphrases* (1527, 1532, 1535) but also the changes and declarations and offers evident in the works of, for example, Melanchthon (1540) and Contarini (1541) make sense if one keeps in mind something very important about the chronology of the Reformation: the permanent split between Catholics and Protestants did not take place until probably 1547, 'when the Tridentine decree on justification with its anathemas was published,'[86] and certainly by 1555 at the Peace of Augsburg, when all efforts at theological rapprochement had failed. One of the major sticking points for both sides had been justification, and after 1555 it became a permanent barrier between the two camps.[87] Erasmus recognized early on the seriousness of the debates around justification, grace, and free will. I submit that his movements on these matters reflect not only his inherent irenicism but also his attempts to grapple with evangelical interpretations of the central debates of the Reformation.

The examples in the following chapter demonstrate that in other verses, too, Erasmus exhibited an increased concern for these three elements of Pauline theology. They also demonstrate the distance that Erasmus's theology of grace travelled after the publication of *De libero arbitrio*.

FIVE

Controversy

By 1527, as the previous two chapters have shown, Erasmus had
developed a renewed interest in the will, grace, and justification. In
1535, the year before his death, he was still making changes to the
annotations of Romans as he clarified his thoughts about these
ideas, all fundamental to the Reformation debate. This is under-
standable, given the enormity of the repercussions during the past
ten years of Luther's intended split with Rome and Erasmus's increasingly shaky position in the world of theological discourse.
How do we reconcile this picture of the later Erasmus with what he
had written just a few years before in his polemic against Luther?
Part of the answer is to acknowledge *De libero arbitrio* and the
Hyperaspistes for what they were: defensive gestures to satisfy his
critics that amounted to hastily drawn-up documents making use
of sometimes flimsy, if not deliberately misleading, scholarship.[1]

Many historians, including Charles Trinkaus, have regarded
Erasmus's confrontation with Luther as both planned and 'inevitable'[2] and have viewed Erasmus's theological views in *De libero
arbitrio* as representative of the opinions he would develop over
the remaining years of his life. Yet, as the examples in chapters 3
and 4 have demonstrated, his interpretation of Paul developed
and changed after the publication of *De libero arbitrio* and continued to develop distinctly from his polemical work even while he
worked on the *Hyperaspistes*. *De libero arbitrio* and the *Hyperaspistes*,
moreover, represented only one manifestation of his theological
work and ideas in the 1520s. This chapter will demonstrate the
ways in which Erasmus's use of Romans in *De libero arbitrio*
and the *Hyperaspistes* were neither representative of the sum of
his biblical scholarship between 1524 and 1527, when they were

published, nor an accurate foretaste of his exegesis of Romans in the later editions of the *Annotations* and *Paraphrases*.

THE CONFLICT

De libero arbitrio, written in 1524, came to signify to Erasmus's contemporaries one of two duelling theological interpretations in the Reformation debate. Erasmus defended the freedom of the will and, seemingly by extension, the unity of the Church and the peace of Christendom, while Luther, with *De servo arbitrio*,[3] responded to Erasmus's attack on the central theme of his theological program: the bondage of the will.

De libero arbitrio is structured as a casual conversation about the freedom of the will. To explain his position and defend the freedom of the human will from Luther's assertion of the utter lack of human freedom in the process of justification, Erasmus carefully selected Old and New Testament verses. He agreed that 'salvation is by faith alone,' but he also 'wished to do justice to the passages in Scripture which offer rewards for good deeds.' Many view Erasmus's efforts to defend the not yet official Catholic teachings as not only inaccurate but misguided. Harry McSorley and others insist that Erasmus misunderstood the central issues at stake in this controversy. Not only did Erasmus fail to grasp the nature of this particular theological debate, suggests McSorley, but Luther also misunderstood Catholic dogma on the issue. This misunderstanding, argues McSorley, was a reflection of the larger late medieval 'theological unclarity' surrounding the issue of the bondage or freedom of the will.[4] Earlier, Roland Bainton argued: 'The debate as to the will was made needlessly sharp by misunderstanding on the part of Erasmus and exaggeration on the part of Luther. Erasmus supposed that his opponent made man into an automaton. But Luther granted freedom to the natural man in all of the normal affairs of life.'[5] Erasmus's misunderstanding of the debate, as many see it, doomed his diatribe to failure. Its glaring inadequacy in the face of Luther's skill and conviction made the polemic an unfortunate defeat for the Dutch humanist. A more recent assessment by Erika Rummel notes that 'his belated contributions to the anti-Lutheran campaign, *De libero arbitrio* and *Hyperaspistes*, were considered by many traditionalists a purposely feeble defense of the Catholic position and did not vindicate Erasmus as he expected.'[6]

James Tracy, conversely, explains the delicacy of the opinions Erasmus expressed in these polemics as testimony that he 'was conscious of the ambiguity of his position, and was capable of entertaining two divergent opinions, albeit for different reasons and in different ways.' Tracy elaborates:

> On the one hand, as a student of the New Testament he rec-
> ognized that the letters of St. Paul, particularly as understood
> by St. Augustine, envisioned a human will enslaved by sin
> until liberated by grace, so that it might consent to the grace
> of divine forgiveness. On the other hand, as a student of
> Origen and the Greek Fathers, and an admirer of the pagan
> sages of antiquity, he had some sympathy for the view, taught
> by late scholastic theologians and never to Erasmus' knowl-
> edge condemned by the Church, that the human will unaid-
> ed by grace might perform morally good actions that could
> fittingly (*de congruo*) be rewarded by divine grace.[7]

Heiko Oberman views the situation more as the natural result of two theologians calling upon elements of a diverse tradition of interpretation, not as a consequence of a lack of theological clarity in the early modern period. The medieval Church, Oberman pos-its, while simultaneously keeper of both text and tradition, had formulated an economy of salvation in which 'the Church distrib-utes Christ's righteousness like the talent that can be increased by hard work and good investment.' In this view, 'Christ's justice does not make a man righteous before God; it puts him in the position to become righteous.'[8] Alongside this pastoral and hier-archical formulation, Erasmus was able to draw on a multitude of interpretations ranging from Augustine's virulent anti-Pelagian configuration of justification to Thomas Aquinas's more pastoral 'faith active in love,' in addition to independently re-approaching the text itself for a fresh look at Paul's intent.[9]

Jaroslav Pelikan also believes that justification and its role in salvation were central issues in the reformations of the sixteenth century. Erasmus's conflict with Luther was an outgrowth of this debate. Pelikan notes that the 'presupposition for the doctrine of justification was a vigorous reassertion of Augustinian anthropol-ogy.' For his part, Luther aligned himself with the anti-Pelagianism of Augustinian theology and drew it into his debate against those whose views he saw as reproducing the Pelagian errors. Erasmus called upon tradition in his defence of *De libero arbitrio* and chose to put 'himself on the side of those "who ascribed something to free will, but the most to grace."'[10]

Whether the debate took its form from a misunderstanding or because both theologians were able to draw upon a plethora of doctrinal options and the freedom provided by a fluid sense of orthodoxy on the issues of faith, grace, and justification, it subsequently yielded norms by which later generations evaluated the theological positions and skills of both men. Unfortunately for Erasmus, almost never are his efforts seen as successful. The result of Erasmus's efforts to do justice to Catholic tradition appeared to many to be a waffling not unlike that of a politician eager to make all of his constituents happy by supporting both sides of a given political issue. Even his continued efforts to respond to Luther in the *Hyperaspistes* failed to silence his critics and re-establish his credibility.[11] History has been unkind in assessing Erasmus's failure in his tangle with Luther.

Yet history has offered a view of Erasmus's polemic that is in some respects incomplete, in others incorrect. If the ambiguity in his work was the product of a theological misunderstanding of sorts, one could conclude that the entire Reformation had its roots in a gross misreading of the basic principles at stake. If Erasmus misconstrued the those principles, it was deliberately so. He was not the only one to 'misunderstand' Luther in such a way.[12] The Church hierarchy had its own problems with Luther's theology, and Rome's judgment on Luther in no way depended upon Erasmus's formulation of the economy of salvation. Still, it is incorrect to view his understanding of the debate as based on a fundamental failure to perceive the issues and the theological principles in which they were grounded, particularly since, by Luther's own admission, no one understood the debate and its enormous theological and pastoral consequences better than Erasmus.[13]

Finally, Erasmus's *De libero arbitrio* and *Hyperaspistes* and the subsequent changes he made to his interpretations of Romans cannot be deemed the result of misunderstanding. The nature and content of these two works resulted from both Erasmus's context and his own intellectual struggle with the theological stakes on which the Reformation turned. The context was this: Erasmus attempted to shape his own theology to mollify his critics, and, in a process that would continue for the remaining twelve years of his life, he was brought by the debate to reconsider his own understanding of Paul and justification. Luther may have sensed the pressures under which *De libero arbitrio* had been written. He wrote in his introduction to *De servo arbitrio* that Erasmus's reluctance to write *De libero arbitrio* was evidence of his knowledge of the weakness of his arguments:

> Your book, by comparison struck me as so worthless and poor that my heart went out to you for having defiled your lovely, brilliant flow of language with such vile stuff. I thought it outrageous to convey material of so low a quality in the trappings of such rare eloquence; it is like using gold or silver dishes to carry garden rubbish or dung. You seem to have had more than an inkling of this yourself, for you were reluctant to undertake the task of writing because, I suppose, your conscience warned you that, whatever literary resources you might bring with you into the fray, you would not be able to impose on me, but I should see through all of your meretricious verbiage to the vile stuff beneath.[14]

As regards Erasmus's reconsideration of Reformation theology, *De libero arbitrio* was not the only or even the most important or well-articulated expression of his theological program. The *Annotations*, the *Paraphrases*, *De ratione fidei*, and other works form a corpus of theological experimentation and expression quite distinct from the polemical format and public debate that formed the context for the diatribe on the freedom of the will. As Manfred Hoffmann has pointed out, Erasmus had a complex theological rubric from which he operated, one based on the gospel, faith, and 'the believer's commitment, both intellectual and moral, to the truth and its consequences.'[15]

Moreover, *De libero arbitrio* and the *Hyperaspistes* bear the marks of the circumstances in which Erasmus wrote them. He wrote against Luther under pressure from authorities, particularly the pope, Clement VII, and Henry VIII of England. He nevertheless hoped to 'oppose Luther in such a way as not to satisfy the Pharisees.'[16] Finally, Erasmus could have chosen to address any of Luther's 'errors' in order to satisfy those who wanted him to publicly refute Luther, but he chose to address the freedom of the will.[17] The doctrinal plurality and the incomparable complexity of the issue, as well as the many ways it had been interpreted by the Fathers and the scholastics, provided suitable elasticity for Erasmus's subject matter.

Yet the issue Erasmus chose was, for Luther and others, the most important one of the Reformation debate. Approaching it carefully, Erasmus displayed a rather generous view of human depravity and a moderate opinion of original sin's effects. He argued for prevenient grace, that 'man can, before the advent of sanctifying grace, but with the help of God, prepare himself for the divine favor by works that are morally good.'[18]

De libero arbitrio has traditionally been viewed as a humanist's attempt to discredit Luther's ideas. In the process, Erasmus's 'obvious desire to preserve what he regarded as truly evangelical in Luther's teaching' has been neglected. As Tracy argues, although Erasmus outright rejected aspects of Luther's thought, especially 'Luther's doctrine of predestination,' owing to its potentially 'disastrous moral consequences and because the question itself is a matter of vain speculation and produces nothing but hatred among Christians,'[19] he always maintained that excessive trust in human works was antithetical to the message of Paul.

The following examples demonstrate that although Erasmus did write against Luther in De libero arbitrio and Hyperaspistes, the opinions he expressed in those works did not necessarily reflect a perspective that would remain static. His treatments of Paul's Epistle to the Romans changed over time, and by the eve of his death (1536) he had significantly altered his interpretation of many of the verses he had used in his defence of the freedom of the will. In this chapter, I examine twelve verses of Romans that Erasmus used in his polemics with Luther and compare them with his treatment of those verses in his Annotations and Paraphrases. The verses are sometimes contextualized with the interpretations offered by Erasmus's contemporaries. They demonstrate the considerable distance Erasmus's interpretation of Romans travelled in the years following the appearance De libero arbitrio (1524). They are presented not in the order they appear in Romans but instead in an order that enables a clear progression through the theological themes they examine.

Romans 4:12

Erasmus: *Et sit pater circumcisionis, **iis qui non solum genus ducerent a circumcisis**, non iis tantum qui sunt ex circumcisione,* *sed & iis qui sectantur vestigia quae est in praeputio fidei patris nostri Abrahae.*

Vulgate: *Et sit pater circumcisionis, non iis tantum qui sunt ex circumcisione, non iis tantum qui sunt ex circumcisione, sed & iis qui sectantur vestigia quae est in praeputio fidei patris nostri Abrahae.*

The annotation of Romans 4:12 demonstrates the many layers of thought present in Erasmus's exegesis and also highlights the way in which he had already begun in 1519 to reassess his interpretation of certain Pauline verses (small caps text appeared in 1519, boldface in 1527, and underlining in 1535):

The Greek is quite different τοῖς οὐκ ἐκ περιτομῆς μόνον, ἀλλὰ καὶ τοῖς στοιχοῦσι, that is, 'who not only are of the circumcision, but also walk in the footsteps' etc. From this, you understand that to be a son of Abraham it is not enough to have been born a Jew, unless you follow in his footsteps, which is the characteristic of sons. AMBROSE AGREES WITH ME, READING AS FOLLOWS: 'THAT HE MIGHT BE THE FATHER OF THE CIRCUMCISION – OF THOSE WHO NOT ONLY ARE OF THE CIRCUMCISION, BUT ALSO OF THOSE WHO FOLLOW IN THE FOOTSTEPS OF FAITH.' ORIGEN'S INTERPRETATION IS NOT INCONSISTENT WITH THIS READING, INDICATING THAT THE JEWS WOULD THEN INDEED HAVE ABRAHAM AS A FATHER IF THEY HELD TO THE FAITH WHICH HAD GAINED FOR HIM THE EPITHET 'RIGHTEOUS' WHEN HE WAS NOT YET CIRCUMCISED. **Certainly Chrysostom agrees with me, though the passage is somewhat different in Theophylact's exposition. In the codex that I used, the scribe had carelessly omitted οὐ [not]. Someone has added this particle, but not in its proper place, οὐ τοῖς μόνον [not to those only who], whereas Chrysostom reads τοῖς οὐ μόνον [to those who not only],** and his exposition reflects **this order. For [Paul] means** by these words **not that Abraham is the father of both the Jews and the gentiles, but that he is not the father of the Jews unless they follow in his footsteps.** For he said before that he is the father of all races, not of all indiscriminately, but of those who believe. Here he says that he is likewise father of the Jews, and, lest they should think it enough to have sprung from the stock of Abraham, he shows that the relation by blood is useless unless, by imitating his faith, they show themselves his true sons. The conjunction καί repeated unusually soon, ἀλλὰ καὶ τοῖς [but *also* to those], is something of an obstacle, but some scribe could possibly have added that syllable.

I obtained again the Greek codex of Theophylact, and checked the passage more carefully. In his commentary he repeats the same reading clearly, as I have indicated, with οὐ [not] added above the line, and he even points out how it must be read, although he does not differ in his view from Chrysostom. The translator of Theophylact rendered the Greek in such a way that I doubt if he fully understood it; consequently, I shall not hesitate to render this passage faithfully: 'He removes an objection that arises. For perhaps someone would say: If Abraham was justified when he was uncircumcised, why was he circumcised? To this he answers that he received the sign of circumcision as a seal, which pledged and proclaimed that he had been justified by faith, the faith he had shown before when he was uncircumcised. And so since these two things are observed in Abraham, uncircumcision and circumcision, he is indeed shown through uncircumcision [to be] the father of the uncircumcised. But of which [of the uncircumscised]? Of those who believed as he himself had believed, so that to them also faith might be imputed for righteousness, that is, [imputed] to this end, that they might become righteous. On the other hand, through circumcision he is shown [to be] father of the circumcision, that is, of the circumcised. But he is father not to those only who have circumcision, but also to those who walk in the footsteps of his faith, the faith that he had in uncircumcision. It should be read, then, in this manner: "And that he might be father of the circumcision, not to those who resemble him in circumcision only, but also to those who walk in the footsteps of faith," that is, who believe, as he did, in the resurrection of dead bodies' etc. The translator has omitted some words and added one. But I suspect that this passage in Theophylact is not free from error. For since he points óut how it should be read, it is probable that he had adopted the same reading Chrysostom followed, inasmuch as the rest of his comments show that he held the same view [as Chrysostom].

I think, however, that I see a way out of this difficulty, so that neither repetition of the conjunction nor the transposition of the negative will be an obstacle. That is that μόνον [only] modify not the negative, as Chrysostom understands, but ἐκ περιτομῆς [of the circumcision], so that we recognize two groups among the Jews: on the one hand [are] those who have nothing in common with Abraham except that they have been circumcised – it is denied that Abraham is the father of these; on the other hand are those who, in addition to circumcision, imitate also his faith – of these only will [Paul] have Abraham be father. This is the sense, and this the reading Theophylact followed, nor did he diverge from Chrysostom's opinion. Here, however, the conjunction καί [also] raises an obstacle, since it is not the proper position – ἀλλὰ καί τοῖς [but also to those who]; but if we read ἀλλὰ τοῖς καί [but to those who also] not the slightest difficulty remains. This is probably a mistake made through the carelessness of the scribes.

Either reading has almost the same – and a Catholic – sense. Yet in each there is a difficulty: in the first, the repetition of [the article] τοῖς; in the second, the transposition of καί. If we remove the article, the first reads as follows: τοῖς οὐκ ἐκ περιτομῆς μόνον, ἀλλὰ καί στοιχοῦσι τοῖς ἴχνεσι πίστεως, τῆς ἐν τῇ ἀκροβυστίᾳ, that is, 'to those who not only have been circumcised, but who follow also in the footsteps of faith, the faith [Abraham] had in the time of uncircumcision.' The second reads οὐ τοῖς ἐκ περιτομῆς μόνον, ἀλλὰ τοῖς καὶ στοιχοῦσι τοῖς ἴχνεσι πίστεωςα, that is, 'not to those who are nothing other than circumcised, but to those who also walk in the footsteps of faith,' so that the word 'also' recalls the circumcision. I prefer the second reading. But the Translator has given us neither reading, though I suspect the passage was corrupted by copyists.[20]

In the annotation, Erasmus moves away from the literal meaning of the text and relies on the Greek Fathers to provide, interestingly enough, a reading he defines as 'Catholic.' He insists, as he did in the annotation of Romans 4:3, on using the term *imputare* to describe the process through which Abraham achieved salvation. He writes, 'Of those who believed as he himself had believed, so that to them also faith might be imputed for righteousness, that is, [imputed] to this end, that they might become righteous.'

In the *Hyperaspistes II*, however, Erasmus took this verse to mean that Abraham 'earned through faith the praise of being called just, even when he was not yet circumcised.'[21] Cochlaeus, in a similar vein, used Romans 4:9f to argue against Luther's *sola fide* assertions: 'Quinto ait: "Denique hoc confirmat potentissimo exemplo Abrahae, qui iustificatus est non ex circuncisione, sed fide ante circuncisionem." Sequiturne hinc, Nesene, aut bona opera fidelium nihil esse coram Deo aut sola fide iustificari nos christianos?'[22]

Romans 9:6

Erasmus: *Non autem haec loquor quod exciderit sermo dei. Non enim omnes qui ex Israel hii sunt Israelitae.*

Vulgate: *Non autem quod exciderit verbum Dei. Non enim omnes qui ex Israel, hii sunt Israelitae.*

The paraphrase of this verse first appeared in 1521. The boldface sections were added in 1532:

All the more must the impiety of certain Jews be denounced. For in slandering the Son they are also insulting the Father who wished to be exemplified through the Son. And yet their impiety is not so strong that God fails to fulfill what he promised he would fulfill by the oracles of the prophets. This happiness was promised to the Israelites and to the posterity of Abraham. However, it was not promised indiscriminately but only to those who were truly the descendants of those men. For not all who are descended from Israel are true Israelites. **Only those who through firmness of faith are strong and unconquered in their struggles against the troubles of this world (troubles which God uses to test our piety of mind) truly fit the name of Israelite, that is, of one powerful with God.**[23]

The second addition (1532) is noteworthy, as it was, for the most part, made before the appearance of Erasmus's work against Luther, *De libero arbitrio*. It sets 'firmness of faith' as the prerequisite for being a true Israelite. Thus, the true Israelites are Christians.

Chrysostom has a long section dedicated to this verse in his homily on Romans. Rather than emphasize the pre-eminence of faith, he focuses on grace and the Law together: 'For the adoption came of His grace, and so too the glory, and the promises, and the Law.'[24] Most interestingly, Erasmus emphasizes faith in his interpretation of this verse even more strongly than Augustine. The latter, according to Gorday, 'seemed never to have focused on the issue of the faithfulness of God and his promises; rather he argued that from the first Israel was divided into two groups, the wheat and the chaff, those saved by grace and those not.'[25]

In the *Hyperaspistes II*, Erasmus used Romans 9:6 to defend the freedom to assent to the fulfilment of God's promise:

> For, though men are deceived because they are ignorant of the future and so they often promise their gifts to the unworthy, God sees both the present and the future and knows them with full certainty. Was it because they showed themselves to be unworthy of the promises and for that reason were not to receive what was promised? But why promise it? How does Paul resolve this difficulty? He does it by showing who that Israel is to whom the promise was made. After this was shown, the other point could also be shown, namely, that all the promises were fulfilled. Therefore, to make this clear, he says: 'For not everyone born of Israel is an Israelite.' And that is why he does not even use the word 'Jacob,' but rather 'Israel,' because it recalled the strength of a just man and the gift given from heaven and the fact that God was seen by him.
>
> Certainly he said that 'all have sinned and lack the glory of God.' But if all have sinned, how does it happen that some are saved, some are destroyed? Because not everyone wished to give their assent.[26]

In this assertion, Erasmus stood quite within what Hubert Jedin defines as 'the embodiment of the Council[of Trent]'s 'answer' to the new doctrine of salvation,' which took many more months to articulate in a formal decree.[27] Both Luther (in the *Scholia*) and Melanchthon (in the *Commentary*) used the verse to support grace and denounce works. Erasmus did not clearly do this in his paraphrase, but he did, once again, use the verse to highlight the importance of faith in making the believer acceptable to God.

Romans 2:10

Erasmus: *Gloria autem, & honor, & pax omni operanti bonum, Iudaeo primum, & Graeco.*

Vulgate: *Gloria autem, & honor, & pax omni operanti bonum, Iudaeo primum, & Graeco.*

The paraphrase of Romans 2:10 underwent only two small changes in 1532, but one is a very significant change (changes in boldface):

On the other hand, glory, honour, and peace will be repaid equally to all who, **through faith**, have lived well, but in the first place to the Jew, then to the Greek, **finally to all the barbarians**.[28]

The first change moves the emphasis of the verse from those who 'have lived well,' or 'done good,' to those who have done so 'through faith.' The verse indicates that those rewards are for *omni operanti bonum*, that is, 'for everyone who does good.' Erasmus's paraphrase omits any mention of works or actions, although the verse itself reads, 'But glory and honor and peace for every one who does good, the Jew first and also the Greek.'[29] Erasmus also uses 'grace' and 'peace' as interchangeable terms, as he often did after 1532.

Payne points out that Romans 2:10 is one of the seven instances in the *Paraphrases on Romans* where, 'in addition to a somewhat greater emphasis upon the free gift of justification in the 1532 Paraphrase, more prominence is given to faith as the means by which the gift is received.'[30] The slight alterations to the text transform the meaning to some extent and deviate from Erasmus's defence of free will against Luther in the *Hyperaspistes II*. There, Erasmus applied the verse to argue that 'if Paul had meant what Luther interprets him to mean, that the precepts of the Law cannot be kept by anyone and were not given to be kept, he would by no means have said: "Certainly to those who seek glory and honour and immortality with patient persistence in good works, he will give eternal life."' Erasmus continued:

And again: 'But glory and honour and peace to everyone who does good works, first to the Jew and then to the Greek.' That is, he shows that the Law is not useful except to burden the conscience – but useful for whom? For those who do not keep it, even if they seem to be keeping it partly according to the flesh. But who among the ancient exegetes ever proposed the interpretation proposed by Luther? The drift of the context, he says, makes it clear that this is the sense. But in fact I have already shown that the drift is quite otherwise: that is, it charges both the Jews and the gentiles with wickedness and an inclination to sin, and for that reason, when God considered that the Law was not effective in eliminating human wickedness, he removed the burden of the Law and made grace more abundant, proclaiming to everyone salvation by faith in Jesus Christ, whom the Father sent precisely that he might freely forgive the sins of all. But the fact that he here denies that this justice is conferred by the works of the Law does not mean that good works are not required from those who are baptized, but rather it shows that both the gentiles, who were exempt from the Law, and the Jews, who transgressed against it, were to be equally admitted to the grace of baptism, as long as they trust in the promises of the gospel. For the deeds of their former life are not imputed to those who take refuge in the grace of the gospel.[31]

Cochlaeus, in *Adversus cucullatum minotaurum wittenbergensem: de sacramentorum gratia iterum* (1523), likewise used Romans 2:10 to contradict Luther's assertion that works do not contribute to justification:

Ait ergo cap. II: 'Gloria autem et honor et pax omni operanti bonum, Iudaeo primum et Graeco.' Quid putas, Nesene? Est hoc adversus iustitiam operum (ut blaspheme calumniatur vitulus) disputare? Est operibus iustificationem in totum adimere? Nunquid gloria et honor et pax (ut precatur et optat omni operanti bonum Apostolus) est adversus iustitiam operum? Nunquid sine iustificatione? Sed audiamus quomodo statim adhuc//clarius contra vituli blasphemiam subiungat.[32]

The Catholics also cited Romans 2:10 in the *Confutatio* (1530) to the *Confessio Augustana*, in which Cochlaeus also had a hand, as one of the 'Schriftstellern gegen das "sola fide."'[33]

In 1540 Melanchthon offered a response to such assertions in his commentary on Romans 2:6–12: 'It is certain that this is what Paul is driving at in this entire epistle: that men are justified by faith, *gratis*, on account of the son of God, not on account of our worthiness and merits. Although it is certain that is what Paul is driving at, our adversaries twist this statement, "he will reward according to deeds," to conform to their opinions, against the meaning of Paul. They contend that the persons are pronounced just on account of the worthiness of their works. They contend that works are the purchase-price of eternal life.'[34]

Thus, for Catholics and Protestants alike, just as for Erasmus, Romans 2:10 played a role in working out the process of justification according to Paul. Erasmus's paraphrase of Romans 2:10 demonstrates a transition from his clarification of the verse in the *Hyperaspistes II* to that in the later *Paraphrases*, but his interpretation certainly remained within the bounds of Catholic teaching. Without the additions, the paraphrase highlighted the merit of actions and the rewards given to those who have 'lived well' or, as the *Oxford Annotated Bible* translates it, to him who 'does good.'[35] The addition of 'through faith' to the *Paraphrases* emphasizes the role of faith in the efforts to 'live well,' a matter of emphasis surely not unnoticed at the height of the Reformation struggle over the meaning of these terms and these verses in the process of justification.

Romans 3:22

Erasmus and Vulgate: *Iustitia autem Dei per fidem Iesu Christi, in omnes & super omnes qui credunt in eum: non enim est distinctio.*

Erasmus made no changes to Jerome's version of this verse. Nevertheless, in 1532 (change in boldface) he expanded his original interpretation of the verse in the *Paraphrases*. The paraphrase speaks of the way to righteousness and the inability of the law and ceremonies to lead to righteousness:

Righteousness, I say, not of the law but of God, and this not through circumcision or through the ceremonies of the Jews but through faith **and trust** in Jesus Christ, through whom alone true righteousness is conferred, not only upon the Jews, or upon this or that nation, but without distinction upon each and every one who has faith in him.[36]

Through the small addition of 'ac fiduciam,' Erasmus demonstrates what James Tracy has read as a significant development in his theological journey, what amounted to 'a total personal submission to God and not just an intellectual affirmation of the articles of the creed.' The use of *fiducia* indicates a certain abdication of power: 'Hence the fact that Erasmus frequently uses *fiducia* (trust) as a synonym for faith is probably more significant than his use of the phrase *sola fides*.' What Tracy terms a 'fiducial emphasis' in Erasmus's later paraphrases is at work here, as it is in his interpretation of both Romans 1:16–17 and 1 Corinthians 1:21. The later *Paraphrases*, particularly, increasingly identify faith with either 'hope or trust.'[37] Melancthon's 1532 commentary likewise uses the term *fiduciam* to reinforce his understanding of 'faith.' He writes: 'This means, therefore, that "faith" is related to "trust." And this means that justice is delivered not on account of our virtues or newness, not on account of our preceding or subsequent works, but because of Christ through mercy, albeit this mercy is not received without faith or trust.'[38] Melanchthon's 1540 *Commentary on Romans* makes no mention of *fiduciam* and instead focuses on the faith of Christ as '*gratis*'; that is, 'for although new obedience is begun in those who have been justified by faith nevertheless this new obedience, or the Law, is not the reason we receive remission of sins and are accounted righteous or accepted. Truly, these are given *gratis*, on account of Christ.'[39]

In his clarifications of Romans 3:22, as he did for other verses, Erasmus incorporated elements of a nearby annotation into the paraphrase of a different verse. Although there is no annotation to accompany the change in the 1532 paraphrase, since Erasmus did not alter the Vulgate version of Romans 3:22, the annotation to Romans 3:21, for example, demonstrates his increasing preoccupation with the theme of justification and righteousness. In the annotation of Romans 3:21, Erasmus went to great lengths to include a discussion of Augustine's understanding of the significance of the Law. This entire section was added in 1535, after the Romans 3:22 paraphrase was altered in 1532. It is through this annotation that the significance of *iustitia* in Romans 3:22 is emphasized as coming from outside the Law:

[ER] *nunc vero absque lege iustitia dei manifesta est* 'but now apart from the Law the righteousness of God is manifest.'

[VG] *nunc autem sine lege iustitia dei manifestata est* 'now, however, without the Law the righteousness of God has been manifested.'

Augustine points out in his work against Pelagius and Celestius *On the Grace of Christ,* book 1, chapter 8, a way to construe this sentence. It is to be read: *iustitia dei sine lege, nunc manifestata est* [the righteousness of God which is without the Law, now has been manifested]. There would be something in what he says if an article [ἡ 'the'] had been placed before the preposition [χωρίς 'without'], νυνὶ δὲ ἡ χωρὶς νόμου δικαιοσύνη. Since this is not the case, we must understand that the righteousness of God has been made known to all and will be of benefit without the help of the Law. But how you write the phrase makes little difference to the sense. I shall quote Augustine's words: 'How then' he says 'has [the righteousness of God] been manifested *without* the Law, if it has been attested *by* the Law? So here the righteousness which is of God is not 'manifested without the Law' but is the righteousness without the Law.' Thus Augustine. But the difficulty that disturbs Augustine is of no importance. The righteousness of God through faith and grace was manifested in the advent of Christ, but the Law had foretold that this would be.[40]

It is possible that with this addition to his *Annotations on Romans,* Erasmus was placating those who accused him of neglecting Augustine, using Augustine to demonstrate that the 'traditional' interpretation and the one towards which he was moving on the will were not incompatible and/or showing that the text, in the strictest sense, reflects that the righteousness of God 'through faith and grace' is separate from the Law. While his motive for making the change is unclear, this interpretation is an interesting one to focus on as late as 1535. In this elucidation, presented in the annotation of Romans 3:21 and in the paraphrase of Romans 3:22, Erasmus employs the same vocabulary as the *Glossa ordinaria* uses, but in a completely different sense. The *Glossa ordinaria* focuses on the phrase *justitia autem* in Romans 3:22 but asserts the importance of the phrase in its indication of the equity and fairness of God's justice.[41]

Both the Romans 3:22 paraphrase of the 1532 edition and the annotation of Romans 3:21 added in 1535 deviate significantly from Erasmus's treatment of the verse in the *Hyperaspistes II* in 1527. In the latter he responded to Luther's use of Romans 3:21–5 in *De servo arbitrio* in the following way:

> 'Here,' he says, 'Paul speaks in real thunderbolts.' I grant it. But are they 'against free will'? I deny it. Against those who trust in their own powers? I agree. 'The Apostle distinguishes God's justification from that of the Law.' If by 'justification by the Law' Luther means 'pharisaic justification,' I go along with him; but if he means 'justification by the entire Law,' I do not, since the Law also teaches faith and charity, which a person does not achieve merely by his natural powers but with the assistance of grace, which was not lacking ages past to the Jews who lived under the Law.[42]

This use of Romans 3:22 echoes Erasmus's earlier employment of the verse in *Hyperaspistes II*:

> The gospel distinguishes the justice of the Pharisees from that of the gospel, just as the Apostle here distinguishes the justice of mankind from the justice of God: 'Now, however, justice has been revealed without the Law' – but adds 'the justice of God,' and shortly afterwards 'the justice of God, however, through faith in Jesus Christ.' It is incontrovertible that not even the Jews can acquire this justice except by the gift of faith in Christ. That is why Paul says that 'the justice of God is now revealed,' signifying that it had once been with both the gentiles and the Jews but hidden, as it were; now, however, it is poured out more fully and openly upon all the nations of the world.[43]

Both uses of the verse in the *Hyperaspistes II* differ from his assertion in the 1535 annotation that Paul speaks of a righteousness manifest without the Law and that 'the righteousness of God through faith and grace was manifested in the advent of Christ, but the Law had foretold that this would be.'[44]

Romans 12:1

Erasmus: *Obsecro vos fratres per miserationes Dei, ut prae-
beatis corpora vestra, sanctam, Deo placentem, rationalem
cultum vestrum.*[45]

Vulgate: *Obsecro igitur vos fratres per misericordiam Dei, ut exhi-
beatis corpora vestra hostiam viventem, sanctam, Deo placentem,
rationabile obsequium vestrum.*

The annotations on Romans 12:1, numerous and extensive, took
place over a number of years. Almost all of the annotations are
inspired by and dependent on the Greek Fathers, particularly
Chrysostom and Origen, but also Theophylact, although Erasmus
also mentioned Jerome and Thomas.

This entire annotation was added in 1535:

> παραστήσατε τὰ σώματα ὑμῶν [We use the word] *exhibetur*
> when something once promised is in fact made good, or
> something before concealed is produced, as promissory notes
> are 'presented'; frequently in a bad sense, as *exhibere negotium*
> is said of one who causes trouble. [We use] *praebetur* of that
> which is provided for use, as when we 'give' ear to one speak-
> ing, or 'furnish' the expenses for a wedding. Chrysostom and
> Theophylact point out that παραστῆναι is properly used of
> those who furnish war-horses to a general. Thus I have trans-
> lated it *praebere* [to furnish].

> If you reflect that in baptism we have renounced the desires
> of the flesh and dedicated ourselves to Christ, the word *exhi-
> bere* is appropriate, for it admonishes us to make good our
> profession. Or again, if we have in mind that there is an allu-
> sion to the ancient custom of burnt offerings, in which the
> priest placed the victim on the altar while God consumed it
> with fire from heaven, the word 'present' fits well. What has
> once been devoted to God should not be used for any other
> purpose; just as he who has furnished horses for a command-
> er in war has nothing to do with them in the future; he cannot
> recall for his personal use what he has once handed over.

> Chrysostum has also observed that [Paul] did not say ποιήσατε,
> that is, 'make your bodies a sacrifice,' but παραστήσατε, that

is, *tradite* [hand (them) over], so that they no longer belong to you but come under the control of God. And it would be sacrilege to appropriate anew to the service of the devil what you once furnished to your commander, God, for fighting the devil. At the same time we are admonished to take care to treat our bodies in such a way that they are instruments suitable for the divine will and worthy to be presented before his eyes.[46]

The annotation on one aspect of the verse, 'that you furnish your bodies' rather than the Vulgate's 'that you present your bodies,' is relevant to our topic. Here, most important, Erasmus emphasized the power of God and relied on Chrysostom to make his case. Chrysostom had spent a great deal of time discussing this particular verse in his *Homilies*.[47]

In the paraphrase of this verse, Erasmus was also concerned with 'the gift' and its displacement of the 'burden of the Mosaic Law.' While the bulk of the paraphrase remained the same through the seven editions, it was slightly altered in 1532 (changes in boldface):

Therefore, now that by the gift of God you have been brought over from your former superstition to the true religion and are free from the burden of the Mosaic law, I beg and implore you, brethren, through these mercies of God which he has already bestowed on you in many ways and continues now to bestow **(to whose freely given goodness you owe your entire happiness)**, that henceforth you sacrifice victims to him worthy of this profession – not goats or sheep or oxen which are chosen as pure animals and suitable for sacrifices, for this custom belongs to the heathens and Jews. It is enough to have indulged until the present in base sacrifices of such a kind, but in the future God requires from you far different kinds of rites, another kind of worship, other victims, namely, that you offer your own bodies to him.

This should not be done by mutilating your members, but by subduing your evil desires. You should not offer dead beasts but a living, truly pure, and holy sacrifice, pleasing and acceptable to God – a rational sacrifice, in which the mind rather than a brute beast is the victim. As long as the law remained carnal, God allowed the bodies of beasts to be sacrificed to him. But since the law has begun to be spiritual, sacrifices must be made to God with spiritual victims. Sacrifice your disposition to pride rather than a young calf, slay your boiling anger instead of a ram, immolate your lust instead of a goat, sacrifice to God the lascivious and seductive thoughts of your mind instead of pigeons and doves. These are the sacrifices truly worthy of a Christian, these are the victims pleasing to Christ. God is spirit, and he is won over by pure affections. Cut away from your heart superfluous and unbecoming desires instead of cutting away your foreskin from your body. Let the sabbath be for you a mind free from the tumult of disturbing passions. Christ has offered himself for us; it is right that we in turn should sacrifice ourselves for him.[48]

James Tracy notes that in this, as in five other places, Erasmus chose to criticize 'Jewish ceremonies in places where Paul makes no reference to the Law.'[49] Erasmus seems to have adopted Chrysostom's interpretation that Paul is admonishing believers to go a step further and have a worthy conversation, indicating the myriad of ways in which a spiritual sacrifice replaces the sacrifices called for by the Law, including circumcision and animal sacrifice. Perhaps, however, it is most interesting that although Chrysostom's influence on Erasmus's interpretation of the verse is thorough, Erasmus does not follow Chrysostom's homily completely. While Chrysostom asserted, 'Or rather this is not enough but we must have good works also: let the hand do alms, the mouth bless them that cross one, and the hearing find leisure evermore for lections of Scripture,'[50] Erasmus did not mention works at all and instead chose to emphasize that everything human is owed to God's 'freely given goodness.' In a different vein, Erasmus had used the verse in 1527 to support the freedom of the will in the *Hyperaspistes II*: 'After that comes: "I beg you, then, my brothers, to present your bodies, etc." Are these the words of someone who attributes nothing at all to the human will but rather refers everything to sheer necessity?'[51]

Melanchthon very closely followed Erasmus's treatment of Romans 12:1 in the *Paraphrases* (both before and after 1532). In his 1540 *Commentary on Romans*, he, like Erasmus, emphasized the spiritual nature of the sacrifice Paul promotes: 'Sacrifices are either ceremonial or spiritual. In the Old Testament slaughters of cattle and other ceremonies were performed which at that time had a command of God and foreshadowed the benefits of the Gospel. These shadows ceased after the Gospel was revealed. Since the New Testament brings righteousness and life in the hearts, worship and sacrifices should now be true and constant impulses of the heart, a constant glorification of God, as Christ says [Jn 4:24]: "True worshipers will worship God in spirit and in truth," that is, with true and spiritual impulses of the heart.'[52]

Romans 1:16 and 1:17

Erasmus: *Non enim me pudet evangelii. Potentia siquidem est dei in Salutem omni credenti, Iudaeo primum simul & Graeco. Iustita enim Dei in eo revelatur ex fide in fidem: sicut scripturum est; Iustus autem ex fide vivit.*

Vulgate: *Non enim erubesco Euangelium. Virtus enim Dei est in Salutem omni credenti, Iudaeo primum & Graeco. Iustitia enim Dei in eo revelatur ex fide in fidem: sicut scripturum est; Iustus autem ex fide vivit.*

In *De libero arbitrio*, Erasmus first quoted Galatians 2:20 and then paraphrased Romans 1:17: 'Similarly Paul says, "But now it is not I who live; it is Christ who lives in me"; yet also according to Paul, "the just man lives by faith." How can he live and not live? Because he ascribes the fact that he lives to the Spirit of God.'[53] Although Erasmus did not exactly quote his own version, or the Vulgate version for that matter, the meaning is intact. By demonstrating that there are conflicting presentations of the will in Pauline texts, Erasmus hoped to demonstrate that Paul does not altogether exclude free will. Yet in 1527, just three years after the publication of *De libero arbitrio*, Erasmus added an entire annotation in which he defined Romans 1:17 very differently than he had during his exchange with Luther. The annotation demonstrates that Erasmus not only did not stop developing his ideas of faith and the will after *De libero arbitrio*; on the contrary, he spent a great deal of time and energy defining faith and its Pauline uses.

The first portion of the annotation deals with the various uses and meanings of 'faith':

[ER, VG] ex fide in fidem 'from faith unto faith.' The Latin language has no word exactly corresponding to πίστις. In Latin, one who believes the words of another is said to have *confidence* [*fides*] in him; one who makes a solemn promise is said to give a *pledge* [*fides*]; and one who binds himself in obligation to another is said to plight his *faith* [*fides*]. One who performs what he has promised, however, is said to fulfill his *trust* [*fides*]. One who is not believed lacks our *trust* [*fides*] – [we have] no *faith* [*fides*] in the appearances [he puts on]. One who does not adhere to an agreement breaks *faith* [*fides*]; from this one speaks of the *perfidious* [*perfidus*] and *perfidy* [*perfidia*]. A person who causes another not to be believed diminishes the latter's *credibility* [*fides*]. He who does the opposite, inspires *confidence* [*fides*]. We lose *confidence* [*fides*] in one who fails to be responsible for an obligation assumed; we gain *confidence* [*fides*] in one who has carefully done what he could. And we hand over for *security* [*fides*] what we *entrust* [*fidei committimus*] to someone. One who comes into ownership without deception is said to be the *bona fide* purchaser for value; one who does otherwise, [takes possession] in bad *faith* [*fides*] – also *faithful* [*fidelis*] – who runs affairs conscientiously. In Latin, therefore, *fides* belongs sometimes to one who promises, sometimes to one who fulfils a promise, sometimes to one who believes, sometimes to one who is believed; sometimes it is a general term, as when we say 'there is no *faith* [*fides*] left in the world,' meaning that no one fulfils what he promises, and that no one *trusts* [*fidere*] another ... In Latin, the incredulous person is one who *distrusts* [*diffidit*]; for 'credulous' and 'credulity' have a negative connotation, though 'to give credence' [*credere* 'to believe'] is ambiguous. He believes [*credit*] who *relies* [*fidit*], and he entrusts [*credit*] his wife to another who gives her into his charge.

After speaking of faith in terms of reliance and belief, Erasmus turns to another form of faith, one he began to emphasize in his later interpretations of Romans, especially Romans 3:22, 4:21–4, 8:15, and 10:12. He explains the relationship between trust and faith:[54]

Now we speak in a positive way of *trusting* [*fidens*] and of *trust* [*fiducia*], which resides only in the believer [*in credente*]; in a positive way likewise [we use the infinitives] *to entrust* [*confidere*] and *to trust* [*fidere*]; but *self-confident* [*confidens*] and *boldness* [*confidentia*] have a negative connotation. But sacred literature frequently uses these words loosely, for it often uses *fides* [faith] for *fiducia* [trust] in God almost in the sense of hope; sometimes for the belief or conviction by which we assent to the things handed down to us about God – by which even the demons believe. Sometimes the word *faith* [*fides*] embraces all these meanings: that assent to the truth both of the historical record and of the promises, and the *trust* [*fiducia*] that arises from his omnipotent goodness, not without the hope, that is, the expectation, of the promises. So far, indeed, does not speak of the *faith* [*fides*] of human beings.

These first sections of the annotation establish the various meanings and interpretations of the word *fides*. In the last part, Erasmus chose to underscore the fact that in Romans 1:17, faith brings one to trust in the promises of God:

However, one also speaks of the *faith* [*fides*] of God, a faith he manifests in his promises; hence God is said to be *trustworthy* [*fidus*] or *faithful* [*fidelis*], that is, πιστός, because he does not deceive. But a man is said to be *faithful* [*fidelis*] who believes the one who makes a promise. This is not characteristic Latin use, and yet sacred literature frequently speaks in this way. For in Latin a steward is called *faithful* [*fidelis*]; *faithless* [*infidelis*], however, is used in the Scriptures (but not in [secular] Latin) of one who does not believe. The Greek ἄπιστος [unbelieving] or ἀπειθής [not to be persuaded] is better. Sometimes [the Scriptures] speak of the *faith* of God [*fides dei*] by which we *trust* [*fidimus*] in him rather than in man; it is said to be 'of God' not only because it is directed towards him, but also because it is given by him; sometimes [the Scriptures speak of the faith] of both [God and man], as in 'The righteous shall live by *faith* [*fides*] – of God who does not deceive in what he has promised, and also of man who *trusts* [*fidit*] in God.' To both belongs the phrase used here, 'from *faith* [*fides*] to *faith* [*fides*].' For just as God at appointed times began to reveal his nature and to fulfill his promises, so man's knowledge of and *trust* [*fiducia*] in God grew by stages. Few believed the prophets until the Lord displayed before their eyes what they had promised. Again, from what we have seen, and now see, our *faith* [*fides*] is strengthened concerning the things that were predicted about his final coming.[55]

Important for Erasmus is the faith that precedes trust. Trust grows out of knowledge, but faith is a product of belief. Faith, Erasmus emphasized, is not only something to be placed in God, but something one receives from God.

Erasmus added yet another annotation to Romans 1:17 in 1527 (in boldface), which also undermines his interpretation of the verse as presented in *De libero arbitrio*. He located the beginning of true living in faith itself:

> [ER, VG] ἐκ πίστεως; **by faith.** The preposition signifies sources. For life has its beginning in this, that we subordinate our human understanding and trust the divine words. This phrase is directed against the philosophers.[56]

The paraphrase of Romans 1:17 follows the pattern set by the 1527 annotation to the verse. In it, the believer is granted salvation through the gospel (boldface text added in 1532):

> For the majesty of imperial Rome does not deter me from this, nor do I think that I ought to be ashamed of performing my task if I preach the gospel of Christ. For just as to the impious and unbelieving the gospel seems silly and worthless, so to whoever believes it is the power of God capable of conferring salvation on the believer **and truly quieting his conscience**, which neither the traditions of the Jews nor your philosophy nor your wealth is able to do. Although this power is equally effective for all, nevertheless, **as the Lord commanded, it was offered first to the Jews for the sake of honour; soon, through preachers of the gospel, to be spread among the Greeks and all the nations of the world, so that all equally might acknowledge their own unrighteousness and seek the righteousness of God, whether they be Scythians or Britons.** Far, indeed, from salvation is he who neither understands his own sickness nor knows where to seek a remedy for it. (17) For formerly, different people had different views of what righteousness depended upon; but now the righteousness, not of Moses, but of God himself, is disclosed to all through the gospel of Christ. This righteousness does not depend on the superstitious cult of idols or on the legal ceremonies of the Jews. Rather it comes from faith, as long as men acknowledge that God is now offering what

formerly he had promised through the mouth of his own prophets. For instance, Habakkuk prophesied: 'My righteous man shall live by faith.'[57]

Tracy points out that Erasmus adhered in the *Annotations* to an essentially patristic interpretation, even in his lengthy discussion of faith as both belief and trust,[58] and John Payne comments that the annotation reflected a 'balanced interpretation.'[59] Certainly, Erasmus's annotation of the verse is consistent with the interpretation of Chrysostom, who argued: 'This righteousness is not ours but belongs to God, and in saying this Paul hints to us that it is abundantly available and easy to obtain. For we do not get it by toil and labor but by believing.'[60] What is more interesting is the way in which the annotations of the verses reflect Erasmus's preoccupation with the subject in 1527, the year he wrote the *Hyperaspistes II* and a letter to Thomas More about his concern with the subject.[61]

As he clarified the meanings of 'faith' for himself and for his reader, Erasmus demonstrated his concern over the term. Like other reformers and humanists, such as Bullinger in his 1525 Romans commentary, Erasmus selected from different sources based on what made the most sense to him and what most corresponded to the meaning of the text he wanted to convey.[62] However, his treatment of the verse in the *Annotations* and *Paraphrases* is not consistent with his presentation of it in *De libero arbitrio*. In *De servo arbitrio*, Martin Luther also used this verse, albeit very differently from Erasmus. Luther wrote: 'So that this pair of statements by Paul, that "the righteous lives by faith" (Rom. 1:17), and that "whatsoever is not of faith, is sin" (Rom. 14:23), stand confirmed. The latter follows from the former; for if it is only by faith that we are justified, it is evident that they who are without faith are not yet justified.'[63]

Erasmus did not take the interpretation of this verse as a clear statement of *sola fides* in the *Paraphrases* and the *Annotations*, but he did emphasize faith as a form of *fiducia*, just as Melanchthon did to support justification by faith alone in his 1532 commentary on both Romans 1:16 and Romans 1:17. This could be interpreted as a 'halfway' position. In his explication of Romans 1:16, for example, Melanchthon writes: 'Testatur evangelium pertinere ad Iudaeos et gentes. Item testatur salutem offerri non propter opera, sed credentibus. Nam cum dicitur "credenti," fiducia intelligitur

solius misericordiae, non nostrarum virtutm. Sed de hac re infra
prolixius dicendum erit.' Likewise, in his explanation of Romans
1:17, he again emphasizes the importance of 'trust' (*fiducia*) in justification: 'Et haec misericordia non potest accipi nisi fide. Ideo,
inquit, illa iustitia patefit, quae fide accipitur. Nam fides assenti-
tur promissioni Dei et est fiducia promissae misericordiae Dei.'[64]
Insofar as Erasmus mentioned Habakkuk, he followed the *Glossa
ordinaria* on Romans 1:17. In addition, he tracked the *Glossa* closely in seeking different understandings of 'faith,' although the
Glossa does not describe this faith as *fiducia*: '*Ex fide*. Dei promittentis, in fidem hominis qui credit ei ... et spei in fidem rerum et
speciéi. Augustine. Fides est qua creduntur ea quae non videntur
... in fidem rerum qua credita obtinebimus.'[65] Vinzenz Pfnür notes
that contemporary Catholic theologian Johannes Mensing used
the verse to defend free will in the process of salvation, that is,
that 'Gottes Zusage auch mit Bescheid zu vernehmen ist, nämlich,
wenn wir aus ihr nicht herausfallen und uns nicht unwürdig machen. Ich kann in der Schrift keine Zusage finden, die gar ohne
Bescheid unser einem in Sonderheit geschehen wären.'[66]

Romans 2:1–7

Erasmus's interpretation of Romans 2 in *De libero arbitrio* is an
interesting case, because it demonstrates how willing he was to
manipulate verses to support his arguments against the idea of
the enslaved will. The different versions of the scriptures are
aligned here to facilitate comparison. Erasmus's version of the
text with the Vulgate is on the left; on the right is the way Erasmus
rendered the verse for use in *De libero arbitrio* (boldface text indicates differences).

New Testament	De libero arbitrio
Romans 2:2 Erasmus: *Scimus enim quoniam judicium Dei est secundum veritatem in eos qui talia agunt.* Vulgate: *Scimus enim quoniam judicium Dei est secundum veritatem in eos qui talia agunt.*	*Romans 2:2* Et tamen Paulus paulo ante dixerat: 'Scimus enim, quoniam iudicium dei est secundum veritatem in eos, qui talia agunt.'[67]

Romans 2:4
Erasmus: *An **divitias bonitatis illius,** & patientia, & longanimitatis contemnis? **ignorans quod bonitas dei ad poenitentiam te invitat?***

Vulgate: *An diviitas bonitatis ejus, & patientia, & longanimitatis contemnis? ignoras quoniam benignitas, Dei ad poenitentiam te adducit?*

Romans 2:4
Atque in primis occurrit locus in epistola ad Romanos cap. Secundo CW (4): 'An divitias', inquit, 'bonitatis eius et patientiae et longanimitatis contemnis? An ignoras, quod benignitas dei ad paenitentiam te adducit?'

Romans 2:5
Erasmus: *Secundum autem duritiam tuam, & **cor poenitere nescium, colligis tibiipsi** iram in die irae, & **patefiet iustum iudicium** Dei*

Vulgate: *Secundum autem duritiam tuam, & impoenitens cor, thesaurizas tibi iram in die irae, & revelationis iusti iudicii Dei*

Romans 2:5–6
Vide vero, cui malum illorum imputet Paulus: 'Secundum autem duritiem tuam et impaenitens cor thesaurizas tibi iram in die irae et revelationis iusti iudicii dei, qui reddet unicuique secundum opera eius.'

Romans 2:6
Erasmus: *Qui reddet unicuique **iuxta facta sua:***

Vulgate: *Qui reddet unicuique secundum opera ejus:*

Romans 2:7
Erasmus: *Iis quidem, qui **perseverantes** boni operis gloriam, & honorem, & incorruptionem **quaerunt,** vitam aeternam:*

Vulgate: *Iis quidem, qui secundum patientiam boni operis gloriam, & honorem, & incorruptionem quaerentibus vitam aeternam:*

Romans 2:7
Quod si deus sua tantum bona opera, quae per nos operatur, imputaret nobis ad gloriam et honorem et immortalitatem, plausibilis esset benignitas (quamquam et hic admiscet apostolus: 'secundum patientiam boni operis', et rursum: 'quaerentibus vitam aeternam').

When Erasmus used Romans 2:2–7 in *De libero arbitrio* to bolster his arguments on behalf of the freedom of the will, he employed not his own version of the New Testament but rather that of the Vulgate he had rejected and emended beginning with the *Novum*

Instrumentum in 1516. He asked of Romans 2:4, 'How can the accusation of contempt for God's commandment be made if the will is not free? How can God invite us to repent if he is the cause of impenitence?' In reference to Romans 2:2 – 'We know that God's judgment is according to truth against those who do such things' – Erasmus asks how, if 'there is mention of a deed, and a judgment according to truth: where then is absolute necessity, or a completely passive will?' Regarding verses 2:5–7, wherein Paul threatens the wrath of God, Erasmus queries: 'But with what semblance of justice does he visit wrath, indignation, tribulation, and distress on man as an evildoer though man does nothing of his own will, but everything by necessity?'[68]

Erasmus also employed Romans 2:2 in the *Hyperaspistes II*. There, he used Romans 2:2 to poke fun at 'how Luther would have deployed his stock arguments against some of the text he skipped over' in his efforts to promote the servitude of the will. He did so in a long section that pretends to be Luther's defence: 'That one thing is willed by the crucified God, something else by the God who dwells in inaccessible light; that recompense, reward, prize, and similar words do not refer to effort or to the performance of a duty but rather a gratuitous promise of God, so that, when we speak of the merit of the saints, we understand God's promises, by which he consoles those who deserve nothing and do not even want to deserve anything, lest they should grow weary.'[69]

Interestingly, in the paraphrase of Romans 2:7 Erasmus used language similar to that which he had used to mock Luther when he added a phrase stressing the importance of relying on the promises of the gospel (incidentally, one of the uses of the word *fide* he describes in his annotation on Romans 1:16–17) in addition to persevering in pious works:

> Eternal life to those who now **rely on the promises of the gospel and** persevere in pious works. They do not seek the vain and fleeting **advantages of the present life but rather eternal life in heaven. To these he will give eternal glory in place of temporary disgrace, honour in place of contempt, immortality in place of the despised life of the body.**[70]

These verses, changed in 1532 (boldface text), more than any other group of Romans verses addressed by Erasmus in his various theological works, reflect a confused and often uneven theological understanding. In the paraphrase, he added 'rely on the promises of the gospel' to the admonition to persevere in pious works, which in effect negates the previous meaning of the annotation, which had been 'Eternal life to those who now persevere in pious works.'

Erasmus's annotation on the same verse approximates a middle position. While on the one hand he emphasized, 'we are to understand that this outstanding reward is given to those who strive, and that the striving is through good deeds,' on the other hand, towards the end of the same annotation he conceded (and had done so since writing the annotation in 1516) that all of the worries about translating the verse are not particularly important, since 'it makes no difference whether by good works one strives for eternal life, or in glory, honour, and immortality, since God is all these things to us.'[71] Similarly, in the annotation to Romans 2:5, Erasmus changed the verse to read that instead of an 'unrepenting heart,' the human has 'a heart unable to repent' – a subtle shift that indicates the lack of human ability to be truly repentant. At the same time, he had always maintained that humans have 'a heart that no beneficence of God can lead to repentance.' Likewise, in Romans 2:4, he argued that the sinner is invited to repent, rather than led to repent. To invite the sinner leaves more free will to the sinner in his own salvation, but Erasmus nevertheless chose to use the Vulgate translation of 'leads' rather than 'invites' in *De libero arbitrio*, though 'leads' seems to undermine free will more than 'invites,' and though Erasmus had made many annotations to Romans 2:2–7 before *De libero arbitrio* was written.

Other Reformation thinkers also used these verses in defence of their positions on justification. Cochlaeus, for example, employed Romans 2:2 to clarify his argument against Luther's position on works in 'Ein Nötig und Christlich Bedenken auf des Luthers Artickeln' (1538)[72] and in several places in his *Adversus cucullatum minotaurum* (1523) to the same end. In the latter, for example, he used Romans 2:3–6 to ask Luther, 'Ne cum Paulo dicamus ei hodie vel cras: "Existimas autem hoc, o homo" semivitule, "qui iudicas eos, qui talia agunt, et facis ea, quia tu effugies iudicium Dei? An divitas bonitatis eius et patientiae et longanimitatis contemnis?" "Secundum autem duritiam tuam et impoenitens cor thesaurizas tibi iram in die irae et revelationis iusti iudicii Dei, qui reddet unicuique secundum opera eius."' Earlier in the same work, he asks Luther, in reference to Romans 2:6, 'Ubi autem dicit: Reddet Deus unicuique secundum solam fidem eius?'[73] In yet a third place,

Cochlaeus depends on Romans 2:6f to taunt Luther: 'Quid vos ad ista dicits, theologi vitulini? Nonne ex operibus quoque iustifica- tur homo (ut optme et aptissime consentit Iacobo Paulus) et non ex fide tantum, ut mentitur vitulus? Item adhuc manifestius paulo superius contra vos ita dicit idem Apostollus: Deus "reddet uni- cuique secundum opera eius. His quidem, qui secundum patien- tiam boni operis gloriam et honorem et incorruptionem quaerentibus vitam aeternam." Quid obsecro apertius contra vos dici queat, quam hic dicit Paulus?'[74]

Georg Witzel, too, in 1538, referred to Romans 2:7 after accusing Luther's theology of being a wolf masquerading in sheep's cloth- ing. Even so, he used the verse (along with many others) to articu- late a somewhat mediating position: that is, Witzel says, although no one would dispute that Paul challenges the works of the Law in his letters to the Romans and Galatians, belief and faith can and should 'stand with one another' in order to achieve everlasting life.[75] These positions do not necessarily contradict Erasmus's per- spective on the verses in the *Annotations*, his original paraphrase, or his use of the verses in *De libero arbitrio*, although they do not necessarily support his addition to the paraphrase in 1532 (bold- face text).

Romans 3.27–8

Erasmus: *27 Ubi **igitur gloriatio**? Esclusa est. Per quam legem? Factorum? Non: sed per legem fidei. 28 Arbitramur enim **igitur** justificari hominem per fidem sine operibus legis.*

Vulgate: *27 Ubi est ergo gloriatio tua? Esclusa est. Per quam le- gem? Factorum? Non: sed per legem fidei. 28 Arbitramur enim enim justificari hominem per fidem sine operibus legis.*

This verse provides a particularly revealing look into Erasmus's theological development on grace and justification, because it deals directly with faith and works. In *De libero arbitrio*, Erasmus referred to this verse but did not quote it. He claimed that in Pauline usage there are three kinds of Law: nature, works, and faith: 'Unde nasci- tur nobis triplex legis genus: lex naturae, lex operum, lex fidei, ut Paulinis utar verbis.'[76] He went on to describe the relationship be- tween the Law of works and the Law of faith. The Law of works 'increases sin and engenders death, not because it is evil but because it commands things that we cannot achieve without grace.' The Law of faith, on the other hand, requires 'more difficult things than the law of works, and yet, with the addition of abundant grace, it makes things which are intrinsically impossible not merely easy but actually delightful.' Erasmus argued, using this definition of the different kinds of law: 'The Law shows what God wishes. It lays down punishment if you do not obey, and promised reward if you do. For the rest, God leaves the power of choice to their will, which he created free in them and able to turn in either direction.' He then asks why God would have laws and rules 'if we lacked the power of free will,' and continues: 'For although freedom of the will has been wounded by sin, it is not dead.'[77]

In the *Hyperaspistes II*, Erasmus used Romans 3:28 to show that Paul 'distinguishes the justice of the Pharisees from that of the gospel, just as the Apostle here distinguishes the justice of mankind from the justice of God.' He concedes: 'it is incontrovertible that not even the Jews can acquire this justice except by the gift of faith in Christ. That is why Paul says that "the justice of God is not revealed," signifying that it had once been with both the gentiles and the Jews.' Erasmus asserts, however, that Paul emphasizes faith over the Law in this way precisely because of his audience: 'We should also consider against whom Paul is bringing up these points, namely against Jews who were headstrong and took pleasure from the letter of the Law.' As a result, Erasmus argues, Paul 'encourages, he exaggerates, he wounds, he soothes.' He continues:

Thus, when Paul takes aim at the haughty and supercilious Jews, saying that the Law does not confer justice on such persons in the eyes of God, Luther distorts this to mean that the whole Law with all its precepts, even those that command faith, piety, and charity, coupled with exhortations, threats, imprecations, reproaches, flattery, promises, expostulations, which are plentiful everywhere in all of Scripture – accomplishes no more than to make mankind know that it can fulfil nothing that is commanded, even in the presence of grace. I, too, confess that keeping the Law without grace was not enough to gain true justice for the Jews. But it does not follow from this that the Law can do nothing but show that sin is unavoidable. For the reason that the Law reveals sin is so that it may be avoided, and grace is available to anyone who wants to avoid it.[78]

Erasmus explains Paul's emphasis on faith and grace in terms of rhetorical and pastoral flourish: Paul hopes to emphasize to his readers that the way in which the Law had been used by the Jews was not sufficient for pleasing God. Instead, grace was needed in order to find true justice, but this does not negate the role of humans in their own justification.

Erasmus also deployed Romans 3:28 to defend human choices and chastise Luther for oversimplifying Paul's intentions:

> I do not deny that Paul sometimes divides a person into the flesh and the spirit, except that sometimes he adds a third part, the soul, which Luther always refuses to recognize. Certainly here he simply uses 'flesh' to mean 'a human being' 'No flesh will be justified by the words of the Law.' But he adds 'in the sight of God' to distinguish pharisaic justification from that of the gospel. And then, as for the text he quotes from Galatians 3, 'Did you receive the Spirit from the works of the Law or by hearing of the faith' it is clear that the Apostle is speaking of ceremonial works, without which the Galatians received the gift of the Spirit. The same point applies to the texts 'Now justification by God is revealed apart from the Law' and 'We hold that a person is justified by faith apart from the works of the Law.' For Paul does not think that adulterers, murderers, and thieves are justified. But that is what would follow if he thought that justification is bestowed by faith entirely apart from the Law, though, of course, someone who performs of his own accord more than is required by the Law is said to be free from the Law, since by surpassing it voluntarily he is not constrained by it.[79]

These were neither Erasmus's only nor his last interpretations of this verse. His original paraphrase of the verse indicated Paul's insistence on faith, but his 1532 additions to the paraphrase (boldface text) removed any doubt that Erasmus felt that Paul intended the Law of faith to supplant the Law of Moses:

> Tell me, therefore, Jew, where is your boasting? Of course this boasting was taken away from you after the divine will made all the races of the world equal with respect to the gospel. Salvation and righteousness are conferred also on the gentiles. Through what law then? Through that old Mosaic law which

prescribes ceremonies? Not at all, but through a new law which demands nothing except faith **in the Son of God.** For we believe what in fact is the case, that in the future anyone at all will be able to attain righteousness **through faith,** even if he does not observe the prescriptions of the Mosaic law. That law was peculiar to the Jewish nation, but this favour of the grace **of the gospel** proceeds from God himself to all.[80]

The 1532 changes indicate that not just any faith, but faith in the son of God is demanded by the new Law of God. In addition, while Erasmus originally wrote that righteousness could be attained, he reversed that by adding 'through faith' to the sentence. The result is the message that nothing but faith leads to righteousness. Furthermore, Erasmus emphasized that the grace of God is the grace of the gospel.

According to Payne, Erasmus's treatment of Romans 3:27 indicates yet another instance of his choosing to emphasize 'faith as the means or basis of forgiveness or justification.'[81] Tracy has also noticed an increased emphasis on faith in the changes made to this verse in 1532, whereas Erasmus had taken pains in *De libero arbtirio* to maintain 'an eye to "the law of faith" in Romans 3:27 and "the spiritual law" of Romans 7:14.' As Tracy also argues, however, 'identifying the Law with the ceremonial law left room for belief that salvation depended partly on observance of the moral law; ceremonies were works of the flesh, not of the spirit.'[82] The changes Erasmus introduced in 1532 went some distance to reverse this understanding of the relationship between the law and salvation. This verse, in particular, was an important touchstone of the Reformation debate, because Luther's insertion of 'alone' in his translation of the verse sparked controversy about his manipulation of the text, 'lacerating and falsifying' holy scripture.[83] Meanwhile, Melanchthon considered Romans 3:28 one of two texts he used to prove that 'God overlooked our sin and received us into grace.'[84]

This verse also figured prominently in the sights of Catholic polemicists such as Cochlaeus and Witzel. Cochlaeus used Romans 3:28 in his attack on Luther in both 'Ein Nötig und Christlich Bedenken auf des Luthers Artickeln'[85] and in *Adversus cucullatum minotaurum wittenbergensem*, where he employed it to counter Luther's assertion 'Ex operibus legis nemo iustificatur.' Rather, Cochlaeus argued, Romans 3:28 does not state that Christians are justified without works, only without the works of the Law.[86] Witzel, too, employed Romans 3:28 to accuse Luther, this time of misrepresenting 3:38 as testimony to salvation without all works, not just those of the Law.[87]

Romans 8:26

Erasmus: *Consimiliter autem et spiritus auxiliatur infirmitatibus (nostris) siquidem hoc ipsum quid oraturi simus, sicut oportet, nescimus: sed ipse Spiritus intercedit pro nobis gentibus inenarrabilibus.*

Vulgate: *Similiter autem & Spiritus adjuvet infirmitatem nostram: nam quid oremus, sicut oportet, nescimus: sed ipse Spiritus postulat pro nobis gentibus inenarrabilibus.*

In *De libero arbitrio*, Erasmus used Romans 8:26 against the idea that humans are incapable of doing anything on behalf of their own salvation: 'Paul says in Romans, chapter 8[:26], "Likewise the Spirit assists our weakness." "Weak" is never used to describe someone who can do nothing, but rather someone whose strength is not sufficient to complete what he attempts; and someone who does everything by himself is not said to "assist." The whole of Scripture proclaims assistance, aid, succour, help; but how can you be said to "assist" a person unless he is doing something himself? The potter does not "assist" the clay to become a pot, nor does the workman "assist" the axe to make a bench!'[88] He used a strange mixture of his own translation of the verse and of the Vulgate. In the first part of the verse, he uses 'Similiter et spiritus adiuvat,' mixing elements of both translations. The difference is not a great one, and it does not seem that Erasmus would have lost any of the impact of his argument by using his own translation. What is more significant is that he left off the rest of the verse, which he had gone to lengths to annotate from the first appearance of the *Annotations* in the editions published between 1516 and 1527.

In the *Annotations*, Erasmus chose to emphasize, especially in the addition he made in 1519 (boldface text), that humans could not assist themselves even if they wanted to:

τό γὰρ τί προσευξόμεθα. The translator has not expressed the force of the article τό, which refers to the entire phrase immediately following it. Hence I have rendered: 'For indeed we do know this very thing, what we are to pray for as is proper.' **That is, we are so far from being able to help ourselves that we do not even know what kind of help is needed.**[89]

Yet another annotation to this verse demonstrates that the intercession of the Holy Spirit is necessary 'as one in charge of all appeals':

This occurs whenever one **goes to** a person on behalf of another's affairs, as one might approach a prince to commend the cause of a friend. **It must be observed that he has not said simply** ἐντυγχάνει **but** ὑπερεντυγχάνει, **as this preposition [**ὑπέρ **'above'] in Greek usually indicates superiority. For if I am not mistaken, the sense is this: even though one's spirit sometimes seeks things that would be harmful, nevertheless the Holy Spirit breaths upon the souls of some and corrects their misguided demands, as one in charge of all appeals.**[90]

The paraphrase for this verse, particularly the additions made to it in the 1532 edition (boldface text), demonstrate a similar theme:

In the meantime, suffering in the flesh is painful, but perhaps it is useful for us to suffer in this way. Our spirit is sympathetic and fights against the weakness of the body, but the Spirit of God breathes upon us, sustaining our flesh in its weakness and through hope giving us the resolution to bear all things, pointing out clearly what we should desire in our prayers or what we must pray to avoid. Now we ourselves according to human feelings, do not know what we should desire or how to ask for it. Consequently, it is not rare that we pray for pernicious rather than health-giving things. I can testify to this from my own experience. Once when I was bearing an affliction of the body only with great difficulty, I persistently implored divine help, asking three times that Satan, by whom I was then afflicted, might depart from me. My request was denied, **because it was not expedient for me to obtain it.** What I was given brought health, not pleasure. Indeed God does listen to the prayers of those who belong to him if only they pray not according to the desires of the flesh but according to the wish of the Spirit **acting in us in hidden ways**. Even if we ourselves are silent the Spirit solicits God for us, and he does this not in a human way but by indescribable groans. **Sometimes the human spirit prays with great sighs to avert external affliction, or prays for bodily conveniences, thinking that trivial things are of most importance. But that heavenly Spirit which is incorporated into the hearts of the pious demands things which, if they are absent, are to be desired with unspeakable groans; if they are present, they bring true and perfect beatitude.**[91]

All of the changes can be ascribed to influences of those Fathers to whom Erasmus most often looked as he reassessed his original understanding of a verse. The concept of human ignorance, for example, is a theme found in Chrysostom's *Homily on Romans*, and for this verse in particular, Chrysostom argues, 'Since we are ignorant of much that is profitable for us and we ask for things which are not profitable, the gift of prayer used to come into one person in the church.'[92] For Melanchthon's part, his take on the verse in the 1535 *Loci Communes* actually defended the role of the will: 'Sicut inquit Paulus [Rom. 8:26]: Spiritus adiuvat infirmitatem nostram. In hac lucta hortandus est animus, ut omni conatu retineat verbum. Non est dehortandus, ne conetur, sed docendus quod promissio sit universalis, et quod debeat credere. In hoc exemplo videmus coniungi has causas, Verbum, Spiritum sanctum, et voluntatem, non sane otiosam, sed repugnatum infirmitati suae.'[93] In a later version of the *Loci Communes*, Melanchthon clarified this statement, and his clarification echoes Erasmus's addition of 1527 to the annotation to the verse (**'even though one's spirit sometimes seeks things that would be harmful, nevertheless the Holy Spirit breathes upon the souls of some and corrects their misguided demands, as one in charge of all appeals'**)[94]: 'Liberum arbitrium in homine facultatem esse applicandi se ad gratiam, id est, audit promissionem et assentiri conatur et abiicit peccata contra conscientiam.'[95]

Romans 9:16

Erasmus: **Itaque** non volentis est neque currentis, sed miserentis est Dei.

Vulgate: Igitur non volentis, neque curentis, sed miserentis est Dei.

When Erasmus claimed in *De libero arbitrio* that he would 'consider certain scriptural passages that seem to deny free will completely,' he used Romans 9 to show that a God 'who is good as well as just' would not harden a heart merely to demonstrate his own strength:

> The first is in Exodus, chapter 9[:12 and 16], and is discussed by Paul in Romans, chapter 9: 'The Lord hardened Pharaoh's heart, and he did not listen to them.' And later, 'I have raised you up for the very purpose of showing my strength to you, and so that my name shall be declared throughout all the earth.' Paul explains it in this manner, comparing a similar verse in Exodus 33[:19]: 'The Lord said to Moses: 'I will take pity on who[m]ever I pity, and I will show mercy to whoever I will show mercy.' And so it depends not on man's will or exertions, but on God's mercy.'[96]

Thus, Erasmus has admitted that although it appears that this verse seems to put the onus of Pharaoh's behaviour on God, he followed Origen to claim that God 'throws the blame back on to Pharaoh, who as a result of his own evil was made more obstinate by the very events which should have led him to repentance ... so God's lenient toleration of the sinner leads some to repentance and makes others more persistent in their wrongdoing.'[97]

Just a few pages later in *De libero arbitrio*, Erasmus again addressed this verse. To show 'prevenient, cooperating, and persevering grace,' Erasmus argued that 'God in his own hidden wisdom directs men's effort to another end than the one they had intended.' He continued, 'And so, just as evil men's efforts are turned to the advantage of the godly, good men's efforts do not achieve their aims unless aided by God's freely given support.' Erasmus worked very hard to cast this verse as a promotion of free will and the efficacy of works: 'This, of course, is what Paul adds: "And so it depends not on man's will or exertions, but on God's mercy." God's mercy goes before our will, accompanies it in its efforts, and brings about a happy outcome. Yet meanwhile we exercise our will, make progress, reach our goal; but still we attribute what is our own to God, to whom we entirely belong.'[98]

Erasmus used the verse again to discredit any claim that it proves the bondage of the will. As a result, he carefully tried to demonstrate that God's prevenient grace is combined with a believer's active participation. He wanted very much to emphasize the elements of human activity in the process of justification. Likewise, in the *Hyperaspistes II*, Erasmus described Paul's true intention behind Romans 9:15–20 to defend the verses against Luther's assertions that those verses indicate the enslavement of the will.[99]

Erasmus used the Vulgate version of Romans 9:16 in *De libero arbitrio* because he did not alter and annotate that verse until 1527.[100] When he did so, it was to emphasize that this verse reflected not 'Paul's own opinion, but that of an imaginary wicked antagonist who distorts Scripture so as to remove human responsibility.'[101] Further, he argued that 'Chrysostom calls this an *antithesis* [counter-proposition], as if [it were] an objection by an opponent, as is also this: "Therefore he has mercy on whom he will" [9:18]. Where, then, is the response? – "O man, who are you" etc [9:20].'[102] Payne demonstrates that Erasmus also treated this verse as a response to an imaginary opponent in the *Paraphrases* until he radically modified the paraphrase in 1532: 'He changes the *quasi* to *quum* so that it is less clear that he intends these verses to be regarded as the irreverent words of an imaginary opponent of Paul. Even more strikingly, he drops out the words that had affirmed the participation of the human will in the work of salvation.'[103] The paraphrase is as follows (boldface text added in 1532):

> **So then**, it is not by willing or by exertion that salvation is attained, but by the mercy of God, for in vain do we desire, in vain do we strive, unless a willing God draws us to him. Moreover, he draws to himself whomever he chooses, even those who have merited nothing, and rejects those who are guilty of nothing. **However, it does not follow that God is unjust to anyone, but that he is merciful to many.** No one is condemned except by his own guilt. No one is saved except by the kindness of God. Thus, he thinks those worthy whom he wishes, but in such a way that **if you have been drawn to him by his mercy,** you have reason to give thanks; but **if you have been abandoned to your own obduracy,** you have no reason to complain.[104]

The changes to this paraphrase represent a turning point in Erasmus's exegesis. Moving away from the interpretation he had proposed in the *De libero arbitrio* and as late as 1527 in the

Annotations, Erasmus demonstrated that he had reconsidered his earlier qualification of the statement that God attracts and repels others according to his own will.[105]

The verse played an important role in Reformation polemics beyond the debate between Luther and Erasmus. For Johannes Mensing in the early 1530s, for example, the verse did not exclude the role of human action after God's will worked through the Holy Spirit in Christians.[106] For Melanchthon in 1532, the verse represented irrefutable proof that works played no role in salvation: '"Non est volentis neque currentis, sed Dei miserentis." Haec sententia clare testatur eligi homines per misericordiam, non propter dignitatem nostrorum operum.'[107]

Romans 9:21–3

Erasmus and Vulgate	*De libero arbitrio*
Romans 9:21 Erasmus and Vulgate: *An non habet potestatem figulus luti, ex eadem massa facere aliud quidem vas in honorem, aliud vero in contumeliam?*	*Romans 9:21* 'An non habet potestatem figulus luti ex eadem massa facere aliud quidem vas in honorem, aliud vero in contumeliam? Quod si deus volens ostendere iram et notam facere potentiam suam sustinuit in multa patientia vasa irae apta ad interitum, ut ostenderet divitias gloriae suae in vasa misericordiae, quae praeparavit in gloriam' etc.[108]
Romans 9:22 Erasmus: *Quod si Deus volens ostendere iram, & notam facere potentiam suam, **tulit multa animi lenitate**, vasa irae, **apparata in interitum**,*	
Vulgate: *Quod si Deus volens ostendere iram, & notam facere potentiam suam, sustinuit in multa patientia, vasa irae, apta in interitum,*	
Romans 9:23 Erasmus: *Ut ostenderet divitias gloriae suae in vasa misericordiae, quae **praeparaverat** in gloriam.*	
Vulgate: *Ut ostenderet divitias gloriae suae in vasa misericordiae, quae praeparait in gloriam.*	

Although Erasmus had thoroughly annotated and altered Romans 9:21–3 by the time he published *De libero arbitrio,* he chose to go back to the Vulgate's text. He used these verses in *De libero arbitrio* to assert: 'We must submit ourselves to God exactly as the wet clay obeys the potter's hands. And yet this does not do away with free will altogether, nor does it exclude the cooperation of our will with God's will to gain eternal salvation.'[109]

Likewise, in *Hyperaspistes II,* Erasmus called on these verses nine times in his defence of the freedom of the will. In particular, Erasmus used the verses to argue that, though Paul sometimes appears to emphasize the servitude of the will, the overall picture is not, as Luther contends, 'that in the whole epistle Paul is concerned with showing only that mankind does nothing, what he says is manifestly false.' Instead, as Erasmus points out again and again in many different ways, 'God's foreknowledge and will do not always impose necessity on the human will, although in some matters the occurrence imposes a necessity of inevitability, as the scholastics say.'[110]

While Erasmus used this verse to support the idea of cooperative grace in his written polemics with Luther, his comment on the verse was very different in the 1517 paraphrase:

> What clay in the hands of the potter, we all are in the hands of God. So says the Lord himself through the prophet Isaiah. He forms whatever pleases him, making one vessel for a lowly function, another for a noble function. No matter what the reasons for his actions may have been, the potter is answerable to no one, and it is not proper for the clay to demand from him the reason for his decision.

This first portion of the paraphrase reinforces the unknowability of God, a concept Erasmus returned to many times in the *Paraphrases on Romans.* The second part of the paraphrase, introduced in 1532 for the first time, takes on a distinctly different theological tone:

> **The clay in itself is nothing other than clay. If the potter forms an elegant drinking-cup from clay, whatever honour attaches to this belongs to his own artistry. If the potter forms a chamber-pot, no injustice is done to filthy and worthless clay. Therefore if God abandons someone to his sins, thus he was born, there is no injustice. But if he calls**

someone to righteousness, his mercy is a free gift. In the case of the former, God reveals his own righteousness so that he may be feared. To the latter he discloses his own goodness so that he may be loved. It is not part of a man to require a reason from God for his decision – why he calls this one later and that one earlier, why he accepts one who has done nothing to deserve it and abandons a man who has incurred no guilt.

Mercy is here a free gift of God, and, even more interesting, man is either born or not born 'abandoned to his sins.' As Tracy puts it, 'If the notion that God reveals his justice in the reprobate sounds unmistakably Lutheran, it is still Erasmus who holds out the possibility that all men will at some time be called by God.'[111] In this 1532 addition, however, most prominent is the fruitlessness of human works in the process of salvation. In the last section, not altered in 1532, Erasmus returned to the original theme of the paraphrase, the unknowability of God, but with a now typically Erasmian emphasis on the importance of belief and the futility of debate:

A man is far more lowly in comparison with God than is clay in comparison with its human craftsman. If it is monstrous arrogance for the clay to argue with its creator, is it not greater arrogance for a man to dispute about the purposes of God which are so far above us that we are scarcely able to grasp a shadow or a dream of them? Begin to believe and cease to debate, and then you will understand more quickly.[112]

These verses, used carefully by Erasmus in *De libero arbitrio* and the *Hyperaspistes*, had been subject to many alterations and much reconsideration through the various editions of the *Paraphrases* and the *Annotations*. And it was an important verse for the Fathers, to whom he turned so often in his study of scripture. However, although Erasmus frequently called upon Chrysostom to support his own interpretations of verses, particularly after 1532, he could not depend on Chrysostom's understanding of this verse to support his own. Chrysostom argued, 'Why are some people vessels of wrath and others vessels of mercy? It is by their own free choice.'[113] Augustine, whose writings are, like those of Erasmus, full of contradictory interpretations of this verse, finally argued, 'The fact that men become vessels of wrath at birth is due to the penalty they deserve, but that they become vessels of mercy at their second birth is due to an undeserved grace.'[114] Luther, too, called upon Augustine in his *Scholia* (1515/16) to Romans 9:21, and this appears to have had a result similar to Erasmus's 1532 addition to the paraphrase:

> God shows mercy out of His great goodness and hardens with no injustice, so that he who is freed may not boast of his own merits and he who is damned has been overcome by nothing but his own deserts. For grace alone distinguishes the redeemed from the condemned, all having been mingled in one mass of perdition by the common cause of their common origin. Because of such words a man recognizes his own damnation and despairs of saving himself by his own powers, for otherwise he is left cold by the mere thought that he has fallen in Adam, for he hopes that he can raise himself up from that fall by his own free will, indeed he is presumptuous about this. But here he learns that grace has raised him up before every will, including his own.[115]

Romans 11:25–26

Erasmus and Vulgate	De libero arbitrio
Erasmus: *25 Nolo enim vos ignorare fratres mysterium hoc (ut non sitis **apud vosmetipsos elati animo**) quia caecitas ex parte contigit in Israel, donec plenitudo Gentium intraret. 26 Et sic omnis Israel salvus fieret, sicut scriptum est: Veniet ex Sion, qui **liberat et avertet impietates** à Iacob.*	Ac mox: 'Ut non sitis vobismet ipsis sapientes.' Haec nimirum arguunt Paulum hoc illic agere, ut reprimat gentium simul et Iudaeorum arrogantiam.[116]
Vulgate: *25 Nolo enim vos ignorare fratres mysterium hoc. (ut non sitis vobis ipsis sapientes) quia caecitas ex parte contigit in Israel, donec plenitudo Gentium intraret. 26 Et sic omnis Israel salvus fieret, sicut scriptum est: Veniet ex Sion, qui eripiat, & avertat impietatem à Iacob.*	

In *De libero arbitrio*, Erasmus used Romans 11:25 to bolster his claim that Paul 'is concerned to check gentile and Jewish arrogance alike,' but his use of the verse is not very helpful. He insisted that Paul 'inspires those who have been lopped off with the hope of being grafted on again, if they will abandon their unbelief and believe, and instils into those who have been grafted on the fear of being lopped off if they turn away from God's grace.' The passage continued: '"You hold your place by faith," he says, "do not be arrogant, but beware!" and shortly afterwards, "so that you should not congratulate yourselves on your own wisdom."' Erasmus intended that the verse be understood as reinforcing the human role in accepting or turning away from God's grace, an act of the human will.[117]

Erasmus's perspective on the verse changed some time before 1532. Until this point, his paraphrase of Romans 11:25–6 had demonstrated an understanding similar to the one he expressed in *De libero arbitrio*:

> I shall reveal a certain secret to you, my brothers, which would perhaps be better hidden in silence if it were not to your advantage that I speak – to prevent you, that is, from being arrogantly pleased with yourselves because you seem to have been preferred to the Jews. This blindness came upon the Jewish people, but not upon all of them and not forever. A good many of them do acknowledge Christ, and others will persist in their own blindness only until the number of gentiles has been filled for whom the fall of the Jews has now opened an access. But when they see that the whole earth abounds in the profession of the Christian faith, that they await that messiah of theirs in vain, that their city, temple, sacred things, and people have been dispersed and scattered, they will finally begin to regain their vision and to acknowledge their own error, and they will understand that Christ is the true messiah. And thus all of the Israelites will be restored to salvation, although now part of them have fallen away from it.

Again, Erasmus embraced a now familiar theme in his *Annotations* on Romans: the contrast between the Jews and the Christians. The last portion of the paraphrase was altered in 1532 (boldface text), and what had been simply an admonition to believe turned into a critique of works:

For they will truly be worthy of the name of Israelite when they begin to recognize Christ as God and as the Son of God with the eyes of faith, **and when, strong in faith rather than in reliance on works, they have wrung the blessing from the Lord.**[119]

Both Tracy and Payne addressed this verse in their investigation into the changes in Erasmus's paraphrases, and both scholars noted the new emphasis on faith and the futility of works in 1532.[120] Melanchthon's 1532 interpretation of the verse emphasized instead the liberation of the gospel through the remission of sins: 'Addut et vaticinium de conversione Iudaeorum, quod usque ad finem mundi subinde aliqui converti debeant. Et citat [26f.] Esaiam, qui testatur Iudaeos non esse abiectos, sed aliquos esse reliquos, qui consecuturi sint remissionem peccatorum. Est enim hoc dictum propterea maxime observandum, quia clare dicit in novo testamento praedicandam esse remissionem peccatorum.'[121]

ONE ROAD, TWO DESTINATIONS

Erasmus used verses from Paul's Epistle to the Romans in the *De libero arbitrio* and the *Hyperaspistes* very differently than he interpreted them in the later *Annotations* and *Paraphrases*. His desire in his polemics with Luther to emphasize what he believed to be consonant with official Catholic teaching later evolved into a position that sometimes, but not always, reflected Luther's own 'desire to uphold the absolute necessity of God's grace for every human act that has any relevance for salvation (*bonum coram Deo*) and to strike down every doctrine which places the beginning of salvation or the effectiveness of God's grace in the power of fallen man's free will.'[122] While Erasmus's later writings demonstrate that he did not entirely reject, as Luther did, the *fides caritate formata*,[123] that is, the 'faith active in love,'[124] they also demonstrate that by 1527 he had begun to question his own interpretation of the verses in his argument with Luther. Like Melanchthon in the 1530s, Erasmus began to reassess his position on the most important aspects of the reformation debate.[125] This reassessment is evident in the changes he made to Romans, the book of the Bible around which so many of the debates centred for both Catholics and Protestants. Erasmus left a trail of changes in two formats from two stages between 1527 and 1532 to show that he was, indeed, trying very hard to follow in the footsteps of Paul.

Conclusion

The changes in Erasmus's interpretation of Paul, as evidenced in his interpretation of Romans in his published conflict with Luther and in the *Annotations* and *Paraphrases*, indicate that he challenged his own understanding of Pauline teaching in the last years of his life. In 1527, as we have seen, he wrote to his old friend Thomas More of his concerns about his ongoing struggle to understand Paul's presentation of the will in Romans: 'But if we follow Paul and Augustine, very little is to be given to free will. And yet, in the two books he wrote to the old man Valentius, he supports free will ... I admit that grace works in us, but what of merit? Here Augustine gives less to it, there he finds refuge in it.'[1] The letter demonstrates how seriously Erasmus continued to evaluate Augustine's claim that in Paul's theology the power of grace not only overrides any possibility of meritorious action in the economy of salvation but also lacks any room for the human free will to act on behalf of its own salvation. Perhaps more important, this letter shows Erasmus to have been a man of his age, who searched for answers to the questions that preoccupied many thinkers of his day.

Payne wonders if the tone of this 1527 letter mirrors a similar shift on the part of Philip Melanchthon, Luther's friend and collaborator. He asserts that Erasmus's reassessment of Paul's perspective on the will might well have arisen from his 'desire to mediate theological differences between Catholics and Protestants in the early 1530s.' This is possible, but the changes in the *Paraphrases* and *Annotations* on Romans appear too irregularly and inconsistently to give solid support to this assertion. Payne accurately points out that Julius Pflug, the irenic bishop of Naumburg-Zeitz, urged Erasmus and Melanchthon to work towards some sort of theological middle ground. This urging took place in 1531,[2] however, four years after the publication of Erasmus's letter to More, four years after Erasmus began to alter his texts in response to his thoroughgoing reconsideration of Paul's assessment of the will in the *Annotations on Romans*, and one year after the failed negotiations at Augsburg. While the 1532 *Paraphrases on Romans* was indeed the first exegetical text to reflect Erasmus's new interpretation of Paul's concept of the will, additional evidence suggests that he began even earlier to reconsider his position on the will.

Erasmus's struggle to understand Paul did not arise from his encounters with his peers, or from pressure from the Church or the reformers. It is nevertheless helpful to place Erasmus in conversation with Melanchthon and other humanists and polemicists of his age. This will allow us to situate him in his intellectual milieu and its leading theological ideas and opinions. As the previous chapters have shown, Erasmus's changes in his approach to Paul and grace reflected sometimes an affinity for Catholic thinkers (Mensing, Cochlaeus, Witzel) and sometimes – indeed, quite often – to Melanchthon and even Luther. Yet Erasmus's theology always remained distinct from that of these other thinkers. Even while he worked to develop a theology of grace consistent with Paul's epistles, he developed his own Pauline theology in the light of the historical Church community and its grounding in the contributions of the Fathers and tradition. Beyond all influences from his intellectual milieu, Erasmus developed his own theology, and this theology was Pauline, founded on his ideas of grace, free will, and salvation.

A MAN OF HIS AGE

Erasmus won fame primarily as a humanist, and much of his theology sprang from his roots in humanist learning. His theology has often been seen as expressing his 'Christian Humanism,' which Charles Nauert defines as a program 'which conceived humanistic studies as an essential part of religious renewal and concentrated on both pagan and Christian Antiquity as a source of inspiration.'[3] The *Paraphrases* and *Annotations* reflect a theology inspired by and made possible through the application of skills Erasmus achieved in his studies of ancient languages and the classical world. His focus on philology, accuracy, and context; his interest in Greek patristic and manuscript sources; and his dedication to rhetoric and presentation were humanist skills he applied to his theological endeavours. Furthermore, Erasmus moved in a humanist milieu in which, as his letter to More reveals, he sought both refuge and inspiration. While Erasmus also produced other writings on religious subjects, his biblical exegesis and translations are quite distinct from his other ventures, because in them he deployed his humanistic skills to shed light on a deeply personal theological quest to understand Paul's message of salvation.

Among the new breed of humanist reformers who appeared following the onset of Luther's quarrel with Rome was Philip Melanchthon, who had maintained close ties to Erasmus. Melanchthon ranked among Erasmus's most frequent correspondents, and the frequency and intensity of this contact was particularly marked during the years just before Erasmus's death.[4] Melanchthon provides a crucial piece of the picture of Erasmus's later theological work. What helps us to place Erasmus in the Reformation is not necessarily the extent of his agreement or disagreement with Luther, either directly (i.e., through *De libero arbitrio* and the *Hyperaspistes I* and *II*) or indirectly (i.e., through the *Annotations* and *Paraphrases*), but rather the connection between his theology and that of the Reformation legacy. The basis of this placement lies in the striking similarities between Melanchthon's and Erasmus's views on the economy of salvation and the sources of the faith.

E.P. Meijering argues that Melanchthon concurred with Erasmus on several issues. First, the Fathers were to be used as a source of superior erudition and authority in place of the late scholastic doctors.[5] Second, Melanchthon concurred with Erasmus about the significance of Chrysostom's work on grace and faith, though he rated him behind Ambrose and Augustine.[6] Meijering demonstrates Melanchthon's dependence upon Chrysostom, particularly in reference to 'the doctrine of grace and free will,' and 'sees his doctrine of justification confirmed by Chrysostom.' Meijering is nevertheless careful to emphasize that Melanchthon was not 'uncritical of Chrysostomus' doctrine of grace.' He explains: 'The latter's interpretation of Paul's doctrine of justification through faith is given the qualified approval that it is less impure than the one given by Origen, but Melanchthon says that it is also obscure and inconsistent.' Melanchthon criticized homilies in which Chrysostom failed to mention faith as the primary means of receiving forgiveness. Meijering nevertheless believes that Melanchthon may have judged Chrysostom less critically than did Luther, possibly because of Erasmus's influence.[7] In any case, Erasmus was also critical in his employment of Chrysostom, as some of the examples in the preceding chapters demonstrate. After 1527 Erasmus often truncated ideas from Chrysostom to put them in line with his own desire to emphasize faith and grace.

Melanchthon also examined carefully the issue of free will, and, more directly than Erasmus, he addressed the scholastic strains that had influenced the development of thought on the will. His theology, like that of Erasmus, developed and changed over time. While earlier he had been concerned to challenge 'the Scholastic doctrine of free will,' his later theology demonstrates a startling departure from Luther's early insistence on a radical Augustinian denial of the freedom of the will in which 'only God's grace can save.' Here Melanchthon exhibited a new view on the will, in which 'spiritual acts are not *the work of* the Holy Spirit, but they are done *with the help of* the Holy Spirit.' In this view, 'the Holy Spirit, when it is at work in man, needs the Word of God through which it speaks and it needs the consent of human will.' Melanchthon referred to Church Fathers Augustine, Basil, and Chrysostom 'in support of this doctrine.' Meijering argues that it was possibly under the influence of Erasmus that Melanchthon turned to patristic literature and sought a position on grace and the will that would connect him to both scripture and patristic tradition. After all, it is true that 'when the later Melanchthon says that the Fathers taught that man has the ability to turn towards grace he repeats what Erasmus had said before him.'[8]

Interestingly, each theologian seems to have been reaching for the ideas the other had earlier held, which produced an almost perceptible exchange rather than a meeting of ideas. Melanchthon's final position places him 'more in line with mainstream Patristic thought and makes him see light also in some of those Medieval theologians in whom he originally only saw darkness.'[9] Erasmus, meanwhile, reached a position that seems closer to that of the early Melanchthon, which was more in line with Luther's initial insistence on the absolute bondage of the will and the futility of works. This insight suggests that it is distinctly more important to consider Erasmus's selection and interpretation of Biblical verses – as detailed in the foregoing chapters – less as evidence for his belief about the freedom of the will than as evidence for a sense of himself as a guide to others in these matters. How might it have appeared to Erasmus's readers to suddenly see the appearance of the phrase 'by faith' in so many annotations and paraphrases on Romans? How would it have been perceived – given the events of the Reformation between 1527 and 1532 – that Erasmus chose to emphasize *fiducia* much as Melanchthon had done? How would readers have interpreted Erasmus's change from *reputare* to *imputare*, given Luther's insistence on the latter term? How would his contemporaries have reflected on the addition in 1532 of these words: 'the free gift of the truly justifying faith of the gospel'? These questions, I submit, are much more important than opinions as to whether Erasmus came to believe in Luther's theology.

Erasmus's relationship to Luther is, of course, very well documented. Although the two men clashed in their one very public dispute, Erasmus's ongoing struggles with Paul show that he was confronting the same issues and challenges that Luther addressed. Particularly after *De libero arbitrio*, Erasmus's work took on a tone and direction that paralleled rather than mimicked Luther's own journey. Unquestionably, fundamental differences remained between their respective interpretations of Paul, and at moments their theologies seem very far apart. There were also moments, however, when it was (and still is) difficult to tell, as the Prince of Carpi pointed out, which of them authored a particular argument. In the late 1520s and early 1530s both Erasmus and Luther were attempting to tread in Paul's footsteps.

In these years Erasmus's theology gradually assumed specific positions that approximate in content, if not in terminology, Luther's interpretation of the Pauline texts. As the examples in chapters 3, 4, and, 5 demonstrate, this meant a fiducial emphasis, which grew stronger between 1527 and 1535. Take, for example, Romans 1:17: Luther's emphasis on the process of 'God's justification not as active, punitive, and judgmental, but rather better understood as passive and based on man's belief in God'[10] resembles Erasmus's view after 1527, when he added two annotations on the meaning of faith and its role in salvation. Likewise, Luther understood Romans 3:28 as meaning that 'man is justified only through faith (*sola fide*) and not through works of the law.'[11] Erasmus explained the verse in essentially the same way: 'For we believe what in fact is the case, that in the future anyone at all will be able to attain righteousness **through faith**, even if he does not observe the prescriptions of the Mosaic law.' His addition of 'through faith' to this paraphrase in 1532 further demonstrates Erasmus's growing certainty that righteousness was available through faith alone.

In verse after verse, Erasmus reassessed Paul's insistence on the centrality of faith and futility of works in the Epistle to the Romans. More and more he became convinced of an understanding of salvation in terms of *sola fides*. Both he and Luther thus participated in an attempt to give proper emphasis to Paul's insistence on the centrality of grace and belief over works and knowledge. This effort found support within the tradition left by Augustine and his interpreters. Both men turned to the Fathers for corroboration and above all to Augustine and the Augustinian tradition. Erasmus believed that the scholastic tradition had perverted scripture through its endless speculations about God and faith. The patristic tradition, represented by Chrysostom especially but also by Augustine, underpinned Erasmus's theology. Similiarly, Luther's relationship to and use of the Fathers was characterized by a dependence on Augustine, whom he saw as the true luminary.[12]

Although Luther criticized Erasmus for not relying upon, much less understanding, Augustine, we have seen that this critique was misplaced. Particularly after 1527 Erasmus was greatly influenced by a renewed interest in Augustine's interpretation of Paul. While the two men agreed on the importance of Augustine, they differed in their perspectives on him. Erasmus respected Augustine as the backbone of the tradition that he so admired. As Jan den Boeft has pointed out, Erasmus often judged the Fathers on their rhetorical skills, piety, and peacefulness.[13] Luther believed he was fighting the same battle as Augustine – against the Pelagians.[14] While Erasmus greatly admired Chrysostom's contributions and called on him often, Luther was sceptical of Chrysostom's doctrine, partly because of Erasmus's affection for the Greek Father.[15] Erasmus used the Fathers to support his own theology and to connect it to the tradition he respected. Luther, by contrast, employed patristic sources to justify his criticism of the Church and some of its traditions. He used the Fathers to demonstrate that 'the church of his own day differed only terminologically but not in substance from the Pelagians,' to challenge the supremacy of papal power and to deny the Church authority over scriptural interpretation, for 'when the issue is erroneous theological decisions and false directions on the part of the Fathers, Luther does not interpret the authorities but openly attacks them, especially where they are in danger of leading away from Christ.'[16] It may therefore be said that it was not a shared understanding of the Fathers that guided the two men, Erasmus and Luther, to their sometimes similar theological destinations.

Despite the similarities between Luther's mature theology and that of Erasmus and despite their common reliance on the Fathers, they differed in their understanding of the Church. Luther's view of scripture as radically transcendent led him to reject the tradition upon which the existing ecclesiology not only stood but depended. Erasmus, on the other hand, emerged from his tangle with Paul somewhat confused about ecclesiology. Despite the similarity of his interpretation of Romans to Luther's with respect to salvation and the centrality of grace and faith, Erasmus was ultimately unwilling to separate that theology from the sense of the Church to which he remained dedicated, despite his criticisms of it. Instead, Erasmus worked to develop a Pauline theology of grace informed by and shaped by the tradition and historical community that he still believed could serve Christians.

The theological gap between the two men turns out to have been not quite what we might expect, given their respective positions in their polemics on free will. For Erasmus, a concern for the pragmatic implications of the theology most likely inhibited his further embrace of the programmatic inference Luther had already drawn from Pauline theology. Contrary to what has often been said, it was not his concept of *Philosophia Christi* that kept Erasmus from fully articulating a theology of grace without any benefit of human endeavour. Erasmus had already discovered that the Christology associated with the *Philosophia Christi* was fundamentally incompatible with Paul's insistence on faith as the cornerstone of the human relationship to God. Furthermore, while the *Philosophia Christi* may be an accurate label for Erasmus's message in his early works, such as the *Enchiridion*, and in his initial forays into biblical exegesis (the early *Annotations*), the theology he developed in the *Paraphrases*, *Annotations*, *De libero arbitrio*, and the *Hyperaspistes* indicates an increasingly familiar emphasis on grace and justification. James D. Tracy has argued:

> At the deepest level Luther's doctrine of divine grace and human nature involved an unequivocal either/or, as against the both/and implied by the *philosophia Christi*. For Luther, since God was omnipotent and salvation was not an accomplishment of which sinful human beings could boast, it was blasphemy to think that the free gift of irresistible grace could be conditioned by any human act. But in the *philosophia Christi* salvation meant the 'kindling and purifying' of the heart, the imitation of Christ, the 'rebirth' of a nature created

good, in sum the 'transformation' by stages of the life of nature into the life of grace. Thus although Erasmus could for pastoral purposes agree with Luther's understanding of faith as unconditional trust in God, when it came to making dogmatic statements of his own Erasmus parted company with Luther by insisting that 'faith itself is a human work in which free choice has a role.' Further, since as Luther himself maintained 'the faith of the just is joined with fear and trembling,' Erasmus also rejected the reformer's contention that the person of true faith 'must pronounce with certitude that his works are pleasing to God,' on the ground that 'not to do so would be a mark of unbelief.' If Erasmus endorsed Luther's *sola fides*, he did so in a way that Luther himself would find no endorsement at all.[17]

That was the Erasmus of *De libero arbitrio* and the *Hyperaspistes*. The Erasmus of the later *Paraphrases* and *Annotations* appears less concerned to reconcile Pauline justification with the active human life. Perhaps, the *Philosophia Christi* was a younger humanist's sport, not one for someone who had emerged from the battle of a lifetime with Luther the worse for the wear and shaken to the point that he confided to his closest friend that it was time to reassess Paul's message and Augustine's interpretation of it. Erasmus was grasping for truth, and he looked for it in the place he trusted most: scripture.

AND FINALLY, A MAN OF THE CHURCH

Erasmus spent the later years of his life at Freiburg in Breisgau and at Basel. In each city, he sought a tranquility that eluded him. He continued to work on his editions of the *Paraphrases* and the *Annotations* for his publisher, Froben. At the same time, he continued to hope that Christendom would avoid complete fragmentation over doctrine. He believed that he had been misinterpreted by both sides of the debate, and he never truly felt at ease with either side. A man who was considered for elevation to cardinal by one pope had his entire opus placed on the *Index of Forbidden Books* (1555) by another.[18] Nor was he vindicated, twenty-seven years after his death, by the Council of Trent's canon on grace, free will, and salvation.

In response to his own difficulties, Erasmus wondered 'why the writings of the Fathers are accepted by the church given that nearly all of them contain some heterodox statement.' In response to his own question, Erasmus argued that 'error does not make a man into a heretic.'[19] This particular understanding of theology and scripture and its relationship to orthodoxy helps to explain why Erasmus felt comfortable viewing scripture as something that could be interpreted and reshaped, time and again, even by the same theologian. The Church Fathers were truly his fellows, and their methods of interpretation allowed for diversity and sometimes even heterodoxy. Erasmus's orthodoxy, however, can be judged only in the light of a yet to emerge Tridentine ruling on justification and the equally not yet complete evangelical theology. That is to say, when these two standards became set, a generation after Erasmus's death, Erasmus met neither standard. As for the former, the problems of justification by faith and the role of grace and works were not fully solved. Indeed, 'between the idea of belief as assented to or belief as infused,'[20] the Council of Trent left much unsaid, but ultimately its Fathers came to a position that appears closer to the Erasmus of the *De libero arbitrio* than to the Erasmus of the later paraphrases and annotations.[21]

The later Erasmus had travelled a great distance from *De libero arbitrio*. His own mature understanding did not fit exactly with Luther's understanding of faith and the will, but aspects of it reflected a similar theology of grace and justification. Luther's own explanation also was not entirely original. Indeed, as Heiko A. Oberman has written: 'Luther's discovery of the iustitia Dei passiva was not that grace is always prevenient. That would have been nothing new, since after all that was exactly the main theme of the traditional medieval anti-pelagian campaign. With such a discovery Luther would have indeed only attacked the disciples of Occam. Neither was the novelty of his discovery located in the fact that he would have taught that the sinner is justified through sanctifying grace, the gratia gratum faciens, and thus receives into himself the iustitia Christi.' Instead, it was that '*the heart of the Gospel is that the iustitia Christi and the iustitia Dei coincide and are granted simultaneously ...* It is not the task of those who are justified to implement the iusitia Christi by relating themselves in an optimal fashion to the iustitia Dei.' For Luther, Oberman points out, the idea of '"fides Christo formata" replaces the medieval "fides charitate formata"; in other words, "faith living in Christ" has come in the stead of "faith active in love" as it had been formulated and defined in a unanimous medieval tradition and as it can be found with Thomas Aquinas, Duns Scotus, Gabriel Biel, et al., including the Council of Trent.'[22] This position, which took into consideration the relationship between faith and human virtue, reflected the tradition and ecclesiastical structure in which it grew.[23] Erasmus's interpretation of the process of justification after 1527, however, much more than his earlier work, approached a conception of *fides Christo formata*. His Pauline discovery expressed itself in active human transformation, but did not stem primarily from human initiation.

The reformations of sixteenth-century Europe gave voice to a wide range of interpretations of the freedom of the will and the related issues of justification and grace. The positions articulated by Luther (who himself held a variety of positions on these issues in his lifetime) and the Council of Trent were only two in a kaleidoscope of belief and interpretation rooted in the long tradition of European Christian thought. The inherent doctrinal flexibility of the late medieval intellectual habitus made space for a variety of interpretations and thus also for conflicts regarding the issues that affected not only the ideas behind the accepted theologies of the day but also the pastoral lives of many Christians.

Erasmus offered one interpretation, and the fact that it changed during his life does not make him somehow feckless or irresolute regarding theological matters, as has often been said, but rather places him within a long and rich tradition of the searching believer, a traveller in the footsteps of Paul. The relationship between Erasmus and the positions articulated by cardinals Girolamo Seripando (1493–1563) and Gasparo Contarini (1483–542), for example, challenge the assumption that the ideas offered in Erasmus's later works on Romans should be brought into conversation only with Trent's decrees on the freedom of the will, grace, and justification or only with Luther's understanding of the bondage of the will. Contarini wrote in 1541 that Luther's teaching on justification was of particular importance because 'the Christian religion taught that no one can be saved on the basis of works.' Like Erasmus's explanation of the different forms of faith in his annotation to Romans 1:17, Contarini's sought to elucidate the varieties of belief, faith, and trust and to frame salvation in terms of man's relationship to God. He nevertheless held that the process of justification was founded on man's obedience to God, which stems from the will, where it is worked only with the force of God. Contarini's position approximated the Protestant position closely enough, however, that the Council of Trent did not accept it.[24]

Seripando's concept of the will, like Contarini's, demonstrates that, although Erasmus's understanding of the freedom of the will would not be sanctioned by the Council of Trent, it was not far off many of the opinions offered there. Seripando differentiated between justification through faith and justification through love – that is, sanctification. The former deals with sin, for sin can be forgiven only through God and Christ. The latter is active love, which cannot bring forgiveness for sins, as it is built upon the basis of works. His formula, too, was not accepted by the council.[25] The diversity of opinions within Christian tradition also was evident in the debate over justification and the will by the Council of Trent. This situation meant that in the age of Reformation one could frame a Pauline theology similar to Luther's without, in consequence, advocating a break with the Church or even a rejection of Luther's idea of the Church. Erasmus's later Pauline interpretation approximates but does not duplicate those of Seripando and Contarini as well as those of Luther and Melanchthon. Though their dependence on tradition and their commitment to the preservation of the unity of the Church varied, each of these thinkers sought to assess the process of Christian salvation in the light of Paul's writings. Although tracking Erasmus's changes in his theology of the will does not by itself create a new and complete picture of his theology, it does challenge the notion that Erasmus's theology was fundamentally a 'rhetorical theology,' as John O'Malley and Charles Trinkaus assert. A rhetorical theology, the former writes, is one that holds that 'only that theology was genuine which contained and communicated the great truths applicable to practical conduct. Not subtlety of construct but relevant message was important. Besides a content pertinent to life, this message had to be encased in a style that was persuasive. Good theology required a style which would enkindle the affections to love the good and to live it. The very purpose of theology, thus, was to persuade to a "theological life," a more genuinely religious life.'[26] The problem with this assertion is that it depends on an interpretation of Erasmus's theology as a *Philosophia Christi* rather than a Christ-centred theology of grace. Erasmus's later concern for the role of grace in salvation moved him a great distance from his earlier dwelling on a rational and intellectually based theology. He based the *Annotations* less on rhetoric than on textual criticism and philological accuracy. Moreover, Erasmus did not write the *Paraphrases* in order to lend rhetorical flare to the works of

Paul, but rather to present Paul's perspective more clearly and in context. Particularly in his later work, Erasmus's theology was less about 'persuasion' and 'rhetoric' than about doctrine and interpretation.

Finally, it may be helpful to ponder how much Erasmus's fear of poverty and intellectual isolation motivated his very quiet move towards a new Pauline theology. On the one hand, he continued to write against Luther in the *Hyperaspistes I* and *II*; on the other, he was editing and changing his *Annotations* and *Paraphrases* on the New Testament. The battle to do both at the same time must have been exhausting.

In December 1526 Erasmus received a letter from his friend Thomas More. More had heard that Erasmus had been very ill and, indeed, Erasmus may have thought his life was coming to an end. More, like many of his Catholic friends, was concerned that Erasmus was putting off publishing the *Hyperaspistes II*; in fact, that publication was delayed until September of 1527. More encouraged his friend to write again against Luther as soon as possible and argued that Erasmus 'could not produce anything more useful to the world at large.' The letter conveys a tone of great urgency, as More advised Erasmus to take up a discussion of scripture, which he implied Erasmus had not yet done in his debate with Luther. More wrote: 'I am so anxious about the *Hyperaspistes* that I would not want you to concern yourself with anything that might turn your thoughts and interests elsewhere and prevent you from finishing that work as soon as possible.' Erasmus did finish that work. But More's fear that Erasmus would turn his mind, 'a powerful instrument for the defence of truth,'[27] to other matters seems to have been at least partially founded. In 1527 Erasmus's mind began to take him on a journey further in the footsteps of Paul, but never irrevocably away from the Church, as he developed his own theology of grace.

Notes

PREFACE

1 I drew upon the research presented here for two articles: 'Beyond the *Freedom of the Will*: Erasmus' Struggle for Grace,' in *Defining and Redefining Early Modern History: Old Paradigms and New Directions*, ed. Christopher Ocker and Peter Wallace in Studies in Medieval and Reformation Thought (Leiden: Brill, 2007); and 'The Searching Believer: Erasmus in the Footsteps of Paul,' in *Konfessionen und Kulturen*, ed. Kaspar von Greyerz and Thomas Kaufmann (Gütersloher: Schriften des Vereins für Reformationsgeschichte, 2008).

INTRODUCTION

1 Luther's theology also changed and developed over time. For a helpful overview of the evolution of Luther's thought, see, for example, Elert, *Structure of Lutheranism*.
2 Erasmus's connection to Luther's and the other reformers' interest in Paulinism has been referred to as 'Lutheranizing.' The term is not altogether helpful in describing Erasmus's position on grace, justification, and the will, since Erasmus never embraced Luther publicly, never purported to be a Lutheran, and never practised Lutheranism. The problem, however, is that the chronology and circumstances in which Erasmus made changes to his theology of grace meant that his readers, critics, and observers became concerned with the proximity of some of his ideas to those of Luther. Indeed, we know this is the case, since his Catholic critics, in particular, so vociferously decried his theological affinity to Luther's work. Yet we also know that the Lutherans, especially after the publication of *De libero arbitrio*, did not

mistake Erasmus's changes as particularly Lutheran. It is perhaps helpful to distinguish between 'Lutherizing' and 'Lutheranizing' and to assess the accuracy of those terms for describing Erasmus's theology. If 'Lutherizing' indicates that one is following directly and emulating Luther's theology, whereas 'Lutheranizing' encompasses a wide range of theological principles and assertions related to the movement that came to be associated with Luther (i.e., Melanchthonian Lutheranism), then Erasmus's Paulinism can be more closely associated with 'Lutheranizing' elements than with the Council of Trent's definition. Those who perceived this most clearly were Erasmus's Catholic critics. Yet neither term sufficiently articulates Erasmus's place in the Reformation's theological debates. Instead, it is helpful to view Erasmus's changes to his work on Romans as encompassing the development of a reconsideration of a theology of grace and a renewed interest in Paulinism and Pauline theology.

3 The issues Erasmus grappled with in his work on Romans, particularly the issues of grace and free will, had a long history in the medieval and early modern Church. To sketch out that debate for readers, I rely on Karlfried Froehlich, Jill Raitt, Vinzenz Pfnür, Heiko A. Oberman, Harry J. McSorley, Alister E. McGrath, and Eric L. Saak and their understandings of the relationship between Augustinianism, nominalism, the history of justification, and the theology of both the Protestant Reformation generally and the Lutheran trajectory specifically. The debates on the nature of the impact of late medieval Augustinianism on the Reformation continue. The scope of the historical debates has broadened since McSorley and Oberman wrote on the subject, and some have challenged their assertions. McGrath's *Iustitia Dei*, Saak's *High Way to Heaven*, Markus Wriedt's *Gnade und Erwählung*, and the essays in *Via Augustini* (ed. Oberman, James, and Saak), and *Augustine, the Harvest, and Theology (1300–1650)* (ed. Hagen) all present more recent examinations of the place of justification debates in late medieval and Reformation theology. Readers interested in the subject will find a broad range of opinions and histories that address these questions.

4 Gilmore, 'Erasmus and Alberto Pio,' 299–318.

5 Ibid., 303, 304, 304–5.

6 Ibid., 306. Gilmore consulted Folio 29r of *Alberti Pii Carporum comitis illustrissimi ad Erasmi Roterodami expostulationem responsio accurata et pareaenatica, Martini Lutheri et asseclarum eius haeresim vesanam magnis argumentis et iustis rationibus confutans* in the Vatican Library.

7 Ibid., 306–7, 313.

8 See, for example, Olin, *Six Essays on Erasmus*, and Olin, McNally, and Smart, *Luther, Erasmus.*

9 See, for example, Bernhard Lohse's formulation of the Erasmus-Luther debate in *Martin Luther*, especially 62– 9.

10 On the *philosophia Christi*, see Tracy, *Erasmus of the Low Countries*, 45ff. Tracy notes that Erasmus's theology reflected the theme of Christian philosophy, 'his understanding of what he called the *philosophia Christi*, the *doctrina* of the Gospels, which if properly and efficaciously taught could remedy the greed rooted in human hearts and spare the Christian people many wars' (57).

11 See, for example, Heiko Oberman's understanding of Luther's theological breakthrough in *Luther: Man between God and the Devil* , 151–61. Oberman writes: 'At the Last Judgment the righteous God will decide if the faithful have used and truly done justice to Christ's gift. What is completely new about Luther's discovery is that he sees God's righteousness as inseparably united and merged with the righteousness of Christ: already *now* it is received through faith. That is the reason all the faithful will be able to stand the test: That is the long and the short of it: He who believes in the man called Jesus Christ, God's only Son, has eternal life – as He himself says (John 3:16): "For God so loved the world, that he gave his only begotten Son, that whosoever believeth in him should not perish, but have everlasting life"' (152–3).

12 Grane, 'Church Fathers in the First Years of the Reformation,' in *Auctoritas Patrum*, 23. Grane cites Erasmus from the *Ratio verae theolgoiae* (1518) (*Ausgewählte Schriften*, Vol. 3). 'There a golden stream, here almost dry creeks, not even clean, and not in harmony with their sources; there oracles of eternal truth, here petty and insignificant human commentaries, unable to bear a close scrutiny without being dissolved in dreaming phantasies; there a steady course towards the harbor of evangelical truth, here a collusion with human questions, with the papal power, with the rocks of scholastic dogmas, and with human and divine legislations; there the safe foundation of Scripture, here futile human sophistry or adulation; there a splendid garden, here just thorns and thistles' (158–60).

13 Elert, *Structure of Lutheranism*, 83. Elert links this transcendence to Luther's understanding of faith and justification and notes: 'It has already been indicated that for Luther faith is bound to the receiving of forgiveness of sins and that forgiveness of sins is bound to the Person and the work of Christ. Now it is necessary to ask what connection this has with justification and how the statement that all

salvation is bound to Christ can be reconciled with the binding of justification to faith alone. The difficulty consists in this, that the righteousness of faith is centered only in the transcendental subject, and faith itself should in no case be assessed or rewarded as an act defined as having a psychological content.' Later, Elert comments: 'even if we stop for the present at the fact that the believer is 'hostile to sins,' it becomes apparent that the transcendental birth of faith affects man's psyche' (147).

14 Augustijn, 'Hyperaspistes I': 'Une telle pensée est complètement différente de celle de Luther. Ce dernier, lui aussi, est convaincu que l'Écriture a été donnée à l'Église mais en même temps aperçoit un "gegenüber" de l'Écriture et de l'Église. Ainsi l'Écriture peut remplir les fonctions d'un critique dans l'Église de sorte que le seul critère pour pouvoir dire que l'on appartient à l'Église est que l'on écoute l'Écriture' (745).

15 For a Luther scholar's perspective on the conflict, see Lohse, *Martin Luther*, 64–9. Lohse writes: 'Obviously, Erasmus was not, after all, concerned about understanding the Reformation theology at which Luther had arrived from his study of Paul. And his statements in the discourse on the freedom of the will were even inferior to the statements that he customarily made in discussing questions such as the freedom of the will, the hiddenness of God, or the authority of the church' (65).

16 See, for example, Steven Ozment, *A Mighty Fortress: A New History of the German People* (New York: HarperCollins, 2004).

17 Erasmus's contemporaries often confused this matter. See, for example, Rummel, *Erasmus and His Catholic Critics*. Rummel notes that one basis for the criticisms against Erasmus by Catholic theologians was based on 'the question of Erasmus's qualifications.' She explains: 'The traditionalists considered the interpretation of Holy Writ the privilege of professionals' (149). In addition, many Catholic critics considered Erasmus's defence of free will in his exchange with Luther 'purposely feeble' (151). It did not help that Erasmus 'had initially defended Luther and expressed sympathy with his ideas' (151). For Italian responses, see also Gilmore, 'Italian Reactions to Erasmian Humanism,' 61–118. Other scholars have depicted Erasmus as straddling Lutheran and Catholic positions, a stance he bridged with humanistic skills. See Trinkaus, 'Erasmus, Augustine': 'Clearly also, Erasmus was striving for an open, as well as an irenic, Christianity in which all, except the fanatical extremes, could exist together. We know that he lost this struggle, but we should also know that, although always loyal to the Catholic Church, he

represented a position that was both critical and understanding of Catholic orthodoxy, and up to a point, Lutheranism' (31).

18 Tracy, *Erasmus of the Low Countries*, 57.

19 See, for example, Rummel, *Biblical Humanism and Scholasticism*, and Pabel, *Herculean Labours*.

CHAPTER ONE

1 For more on this topic, see Regnerus Richardus Post, *The Modern Devotion: Confrontation with Reformation and Humanism* (Leiden: Brill, 1968).

2 Tracy, *Erasmus of the Low Countries*, 17, 17–18, 22–4, 24. Tracy offers a helpful and succinct description of Erasmus's early life and intellectual development.

3 See Rummel's description in *Erasmus' Annotations*, 6–10.

4 Erasmus, *Paraphrases*, xiii.

5 Gleason, *John Colet*. See chapter 5 for an additional discussion of the humanist milieu Colet and Erasmus shared.

6 Smith, *Erasmus*, 33.

7 Rabil, *Erasmus and the New Testament*, 11.

8 Rummel, *Erasmus' Annotations*, 12, 15, 13–14. Rummel cites Epistle 181, 38–40.

9 Lohse argues: 'Over against Erasmus, Luther emphasized that the Holy Scriptures give clear and unambiguous answers to the basic questions. Since the seal on the grave of Jesus had been broken and the stone rolled away from the entrance of the grave – that is, after the deepest mystery of the incarnation of Christ and the Trinitarian nature of God have been revealed – the Scriptures are never unclear about the central issues: "Take Christ out of the Scriptures , and what will you find left in them?"' (*Martin Luther*, 65).

10 Froehlich, 'Justification Language,' 143.

11 Jedin, *Council of Trent*, 166.

12 Froehlich, 'Justification Language,' 143, 144.

13 Ibid., 144, 147, 147–8. 'Medieval theologians discussed these problems in a new climate of growing confidence in the potential of the human intellect even after the fall, a fervent desire for perfection through ascetic and monastic lifestyles, and sophisticated academic theology' (148).

14 McGrath, *Iustitia Dei*, 94.

15 Froehlich states: 'In this new context, the Augustinian denial of true human merit was retained either by declaring all merit dependent

on God's prior grace or by regarding congruous merit as sufficient for human salvation through God's gracious acceptation. The emphasis on God's 'acceptation' as the proper framework of justification language, and especially of the discussion of merit, was characteristic of most late medieval theologians after Duns Scotus' ('Justification Language,' 150).

16 Ibid., 160, 160–1.

17 Saak, *High Way to Heaven*, 387.

18 Froehlich, 'Justification Language,' 161.

19 Trinkaus, 'Problem of Free Will,' 51, 53.

20 Ibid., 56. Trinkaus asserts that Valla's *Dialogue on Free Will* (1440) took a position 'very close to that of the reformers' (59).

21 Trinkaus, 'Erasmus, Augustine,' 3–4, 6. Trinkaus, however, limits his discussion to the Diatribe and the *Hyperaspistes*.

22 Ibid., 31. While Trinkaus's assessment goes a long way towards establishing the historical roots of Erasmus's position on free will, it does so without acknowledging the change in Erasmus's exegetical work, which in many ways expressed a theology quite distinct from that which he articulated in *De libero arbitrio* and the *Hyperaspistes I* and *II*. See the following chapters for my assessment of the distinction between the theology found in Erasmus's exegetical and polemical works.

23 See also Jedin, *Council of Trent*: 'The doctrine of gratuitous acceptance of the sinner by God, as further developed by the nominalists, ended by undermining the results achieved by the great scholastics. Scotus and his school had, in addition, further elaborated the significance of faith in the process of justification. The Dominican, Robert Holcot, a nominalist, when treating of the doctrine of justification in the article on faith in his commentary on the *Sentences*, did not do so within the framework of sacramental doctrine. The scholastic theology of grace, many-sided as it was, provided a number of openings for a discussion of Luther's theology of justification' (167).

24 McGrath, *Iustitia Dei*, 180.

25 Saak, *High Way to Heaven*, 683ff; see appendix A for a complete historiographical essay on the subject.

26 Ibid., 695.

27 Brecht, *Martin Luther*, 172–5.

28 Tracy, *Erasmus of the Low Countries*, 149–82.

29 McSorley, *Luther: Right or Wrong?* 9.

30 Jedin argues: 'Time was needed before Catholic controversial theology was in a position to bypass particular propositions and catch

words, so as to penetrate to the very core of the Lutheran doctrine of justification, that is, the new conception of the nature of the process of justification ... Following the controversy between Erasmus and Luther on the question of free-will, this article also secured a firm position in Catholic polemics' (*Council of Trent*, 168).

31 Raitt, 'From Augsburg to Trent,' 201.

32 For a detailed discussion of this and later theological dialogues, see Thomas Fuchs, *Konfession und Gespräch: Typologie und Funktion der Reformationszeit* (Cologne: Böhlau, 1995).

33 Ibid., 200–2, 202, 212–13, 213. See also Jedin, *Council of Trent*: 'The Council's aim was to draw a line of demarcation between Catholic dogma and belief and Protestant teaching. This delimitating function of the decree was realized, in the first instance, by means of thirty-three canons which are no mere appendage of the doctrinal chapters' (309).

34 Fuchs, *Konfession und Gespräch*, 214–15, 217. See also Jedin, *Council of Trent*, 168–70.

35 McGrath, *Iustitia Dei*, 198, 202.

36 Ibid., 224.

37 Elert, *Structure of Lutheranism*, 92.

38 For a discussion of Erasmus's intellectual achievements in the period, see Hoffmann, *Rhetoric and Theology*.

39 For more information, see Tracy, *Erasmus of the Low Countries*; Oberman, *Luther*; and Lohse, *Martin Luther*.

40 Luther, *Bondage of the Will*, 42.

41 Anderson, Murphy, and Burgess, *Justification by Faith*, 23–4.

42 For an in depth discussion of Luther's view and its context within both the Catholic tradition and the Protestant Reformation, see Pfnür, *Einig in der Rechtfertigungslehre?* Pfnür notes that by 1516 Luther already had argued that 'the will of man without Grace is not free' (de viribus et volutate hominis sine gratia) (118). Pfnür cites WA, 1: 145–50.

43 Winter, *Discourse on Free Will*, x.

44 Oberman, *Luther*, 218.

45 McGrath, *Iustitia Dei*, 199. McGrath also argues that this conviction was based on 'Luther's inadequate and ill-informed generalizations concerning the theology (especially the *pastoral* theology) of the late medieval Church' (197).

46 For a discussion of the late medieval doctrinal flexibility of the issue, see Froehlich, 'Justification Language,' 143–61. McGrath notes: 'From the analysis of the late medieval schools of thought on justification

presented in the present study, it will be clear that there existed considerable diversity of opinion on the matter during the later medieval
period. This diversity represents a particular instance of the general
pluralism of late medieval religious thought, which usually argued to
originate from the fourteenth century. The Tridentine decree on justification may be regarded as an attempt to define the limits of this pluralism, if not to impose a unity upon it' (*Justitia Dei*, 181–2.

47 Lohse, *Martin Luther*, 41.

48 McGrath explains it thus: 'For Luther, man may thus only progress
in the spiritual life by continually returning to Christ, *semper a novo
incipere*. Thus Luther interprets *semper iustifcandus* as "ever to be justified anew," while Augustine treats it as meaning "ever to be made
more and more righteous"' (*Justitia Dei*, 200). McGrath directs readers to WA, 56: 259.14.

49 Erasmus, *Controversies*, 76: 42. LB, 9: 1228: 'Dispiciamus an & apud
Paulum, strenuum assertorem gratiae, & perpetuum expugnatorem
operum legis, reperire liceat, quod statuat liberum arbitrium.'

50 Ibid. 'Atque in primis occurrit locus in Epistòla ad *Romanos* capite II.
An divitas, inquit, *bonitatis ejus & patientia & longanimitatis contemnis?
An ignoras quod benignitas Dei ad paenitentiam te adducit?* Quomodo
imputatur contemptus praecepti, ubi non est libera voluntas? Aut
quomodo Deus invitat ad poenitentiam, qui auctor est impoeniten-
tiae? Aut quomodo justa est damnatio, ubi judex cogit ad
maleficium?'

51 Ibid., 44. LB, 9: 1229: '*Abiciamus*, inquit *Paulus, opera tenebrarum. Et:
Exspoliantes veterem hominem cum actibus suis.* Quomodo jubemur ab-
jicere & exsuere, si nihil agimus?'

52 Ibid., 60–1. See fn287 for the references to Romans. LB, 9 1236: '*Judaei*
gloriabantur in templo, in praeputio, in victimis: Graeci gloriabantur
in sapientia sua. Verum per Evangelium revelata ira Dei de coelo,
exficcata est omnia illa gloria.'

53 This translation is from Luther, *Bondage of the Will*, 120. The Latin is
from WA, 18: 618, 15–18: 'Et ii qui sapientes voluerunt videri suis
disputationibus eo abierunt, donec obscurato corde stulti fierent,
Roma. 1. Et negarent vel dissimularent ea, quae Poetae et vulgus
atque ipsorummet conscientia pro usitatissimis, certissimis et veris-
simis habent.'

54 Ibid., 212.

55 Ibid., 215–16. The Latin is from WA, 18: 717, 32–9: 'Compescit
itaque imios istis verbis clarissimis offenses, quod nostra necessitate
voluntatem divinam impieri sentiret, ac definitum certo sentirent

sibi nihil libertatis aut liberi arbitrii relictum, sed potentiae et voluntatis divinae, in quam nos nullum ius, ipsa vero in nosh abet plenum
isu faciendi quicquid voluerit. Neque fiery nobis iniuriuam, cum
nihil nobis debeat, nihil a nobis acceperit, nihil promiserit, nisi quantum voluit et placuit.' Luther bases this on Romans 11:35.

56 Galbraith, 'Kant, Luther, and Erasmus,' 70–1.

57 McGrath, *Iustitia Dei*, 203.

58 Erasmus, *Paraphrases*, 16. All Latin paraphrases are from LB, 7. Devi-
ations from that edition are from my collation of Froben manuscripts
of Erasmus's *Paraphrases on Romans* and are noted as individual editions. Romans 1:7: 'Non quam mundus hic vulgato more solet pre-
cari, sed veram novamque gratiam, hoc est, gratuitum donum
Euangelicae fidei vere justificantis, & per hanc penitus abolitis omnibus vitae praeteritae commissis, securae jam conscientiae pacem, sta-
bilemque amicitiam cum Deo: quae duo non praestant vel humanae
sapientiae vires, vel Mosaicae Legis observatio, sed omnibus profi-
ciscuntur à singulari munificentia Dei Patris, & hujus Filii, Domini
nostri Jesu Christi.'

59 Erasmus, *Paraphrases*,16. Romans 1:13. 'Euangelium autem voco,
justificationem per fidem in Jesum Christum Filium Dei, quam Lex
promisit & praefiguaravit.' 60 Ibid., 52. Romans 9:1. 'Ad quem
unitam & Judaei omnes sese convertant, Mose suo relicto, qui nunc
sibi persuadent, satis esse ad consequendam salutem, quod filii sint
Abrahae, quod Legem teneant olim à Deo datam, cum horum nihil
profuturm sit, nisi per fidem se dignos praebeant, qui trahantur ac
diligantur à Deo.'

61 Ibid., 53. Romans 9:5. 'At Christus sic est homo, ut idem & Deus sit,
non hujus aut illius Gentis peculiaris, sed universorum Deus, & idem
cum Patre Deus: qui praesidet omnibus, cujusque inscrutabili consilio
geruntur haec omnia, cui soli ob tam inauditam erga genus humanum
caritatem debetur laus & actio gratiarum in omne aevum, Amen.'

62 Some more recent scholarship focuses on Erasmus's contribution to
the free will debate as shaped primarily by his humanistic interests.
Timothy J. Wengert, writes in his discussion of Melanchthon's role in
the Luther- Erasmus debate on free will: 'Whereas Luther uses high
Latin prose as well as allusion and quotes from Latin literature to
demonstrate his ability to play Erasmus' humanistic game,
Melanchthon criticizes Erasmus' own prose and unethical behavior
on the basis of the Dutch humanist's own game rules. It is almost
as if Melanchthon would shame Erasmus into silence – and silent he
becomes on this subject, admitting to Melanchthon that he will now

stick to his work with texts. Luther elicited from Erasmus "a shape-less mass of commentaries." Melanchthon silenced him' ('Melanch-thon's Contribution to Luther's Debate,'123). Wengert also views Luther and Melanchthon as responding to 'skepticism' (121). For a more traditional view of Erasmus's navigation of the Reformation, see Gilmore, *World of Humanism*. Gilmore writes about Erasmus's Christian humanism: 'Yet it was a Christianity infused also, and perhaps more than Erasmus knew, with the spirit of antique culture. It was a Christianity which recognized the possibility of growth and change in the historic institutions of the church. Erasmus in reality stood for a kind of sixteenth-century modernism. Like the St. Jerome who he so much admired, he was not interested in theology or in metaphysics. He never seems to have felt the acute sense of sin and unworthiness which was characteristic of a Luther or a Savonarola. But in spite of the secularized character of his interpretation of Christianity he did cling to the unity of Christendom as fundamen-tal'(228). For a view of Erasmus's scepticism in the context of humanism and the Reformation, see Rummel, *Confessionalization of Humanism*, 54–61.

63 Erasmus, *Correspondence*, Letter 1804, 13: 17–18. I would like to ex-press special thanks to the editor and the translator of this CWE vol-ume for providing me with a copy of their translation of this letter prior to its publication.

CHAPTER TWO

1 Erasmus, *Paraphrases*, xiii. This may or may not have been the case; see Gleason, *John Colet*. 2 Erasmus, *Paraphrases*, xiii, xiv, xv.

3 Padberg, 'Glaubenstheologie und Glaubensverkündigung,'60. My English translation. 'Sein Reformprogramm findet in den Paraphra-sen zum N.T. eine kerygmatische und pastorale Realisierung.'

4 Ibid., 61.

5 Rummel, *Erasmus' Annotations*, vii.

6 Ibid.

7 Bateman, 'Textual Travail,' 219, 213. Bateman provides convincing evidence that the *Paraphrases* were, indeed, the promised 'commen-tary' from Erasmus: 'Following the noun *Paraphrasis* on the title page there is a new clause, *quae commentarii vice possit esse* ("which could be used in place of a commentary"). This is the first indication in print that the paraphrase is a form of commentary' (219).

8 Ibid., 221, 231, 242.

9 This is contrary to Bateman's contention: 'The difficulties were caused in part by his own inveterate habit of tinkering with texts, in part by the animadversion of both friendly and hostile critics, but mostly by the men employed to put these works into print: editors, correctors, and above all, the compositors' (ibid., 213). The changes introduced in the *Paraphrases on Romans* are more substantial than simple grammatical corrections. Consequently, substantive changes that were introduced in 1532 were not excised in subsequent Froben editions, over which Erasmus would have exerted some editorial control.

10 Erasmus, *Paraphrases*, ix.

11 Bateman contends: 'It would appear, then, that the 1538 folio edition contains corrections or revisions made by Erasmus but also a large number of changes made by someone else. Erasmus presumably left at his death a copy of the 1532 edition into which he had entered the revisions made for the 1534 octavo edition as well as new revisions for a future edition, probably at the same time he was preparing the copy for the 1535 folio edition of the *Paraphrases on the Gospels and Acts*. This copy would have come into the possession of Hieronymous Froben and Nicholaus Episcopius, who were the executors of Erasmus' Last Will and Testament, together with the other materials that were eventually used for the publication of the *Opera Omnia*' ('Textual Travail,' 250). Because it is uncertain what changes, after 1532, were introduced or excised by Erasmus, I have used the 1532 *Paraphrases on Romans* as the last correction of *Paraphrases* over which he exercised complete control.

12 Boisset, 'Le Christianisme Érasme,' 666.

13 Ibid., 660.

14 Charles Trinkaus's introduction to the *Controversies* (Vol. 76) offers a detailed and helpful history of the publication of the three-part debate with Luther and reactions, both Catholic and Protestant, to Erasmus's efforts. See especially lxxix ff. for a discussion of the *Hyperaspistes I* and *II*.

15 Augustijn, 'Hyperaspistes I,' 738.

16 Trinkaus, 'Erasmus, Augustine,' 5–32. See especially 6–11.

17 Erasmus, *Controversies*, 76: lxxxi, fn167.

18 See ibid., lxxx. Trinkaus quotes Erasmus's letter to Thomas More in which Erasmus describes his feeling of helplessness. See Allen, *Opvs Epistolarvm Des*, Letter 1804, 2–13, 49–72.

19 McGrath, *Iustitia Dei*, 71–2.

20 Oakley, *The Western Church*, 135, 134. For a helpful history of the historical contours of the Pelagian controversy and Augustine's role in it, see Bonner, *Augustine and Modern Research*.

21 Bonner, *Augustine and Modern Research*, 18, 40, 48–9.
22 McGrath, *Iustitia Dei*, 25.
23 Oakley, *The Western Church*, 134, 135. Bonner writes: 'On 1 May 418, the day following the promulgation of the imperial rescript, a general council of the African Church assembled at Carthage and there passed the famous series of nine canons against Pelagianism … So was erected by conciliar decree that monument to African doctrine which was destined to remain a permanent force in Latin theology' (*Augustine and Modern Research*, 51).
24 McGrath, *Iustita Dei*: 'Theologians of the medieval period thus did not have access to this definitive statement of an Augustinian doctrine of justification, and appear to have been unaware of its existence. Second, much of Pelagius' work was mistakenly ascribed to Jerome during the medieval period, with the inevitable result that Jerome and Augustine were thought to have radically different theologies of justification' (74).
25 Erasmus, *Paraphrases*, 60, 65–6. See chapter 3 on the content of Erasmus's *Annotations* and *Paraphrases* of Romans and their relationship to his understanding of the will.
26 McSorley, *Luther: Right or Wrong?* 291n63. He notes: 'Feret, "Erasme," in: *Catholicisme*, 4, 373 has called attention to the parallels between the scriptural argument for free will in Origen's *Peri Archon* and in DLA' (ibid.).
27 Rummel, *Erasmus' Annotations*, 59.
28 Erasmus, *Correspondence*, Letter 1579, 11: 119fn4, See also Rummel, *Erasmus' Annotations*, 59.
29 Ibid. Beda also criticized Erasmus for sometimes questioning Augustine or other Fathers. See also Erasmus, *Correspondence*, Letter 1609, 11: 270fn13.
30 Rummel, *Erasmus' Annotations*, 59.
31 For a helpful discussion of Augustine and his work with the Pauline Epistles, see Souter, *Earliest Latin Commentaries*, 143–4.
32 Gorday, *Principles of Patristic Exegesis*, 147.
33 Ibid., 149.
34 See, for example, Erasmus, *Paraphrases*, 11, 22, 29.
35 McGrath, *Iustitia Dei*, 204, 205.
36 Tracy, Review of *Érasme*, 441–4, 442.
37 See, for example, Margolin, 'Le Commentaire d'Érasme au Psaume I,' 71–92; den Boeft, 'Erasmus and the Church Fathers,' 537–72; Chomarat, 'Sur Érasme et Origène,' 89–113.
38 Erasmus, *Correspondence*, Letter 1800, 12: 511.

39 For a discussion of Erasmus's publication of Chrysostom, see Olin, *Six Essays on Erasmus*, 42ff.

40 Erasmus, *Correspondence*, Letter 1736, 12: 285. The editors write, 'Erasmus clearly has in mind not a formal commentary but Chrysostom's thirty-two homilies on Romans' (285fn8).

41 Payne, 'Lutheranizing Changes,' 315.

42 den Boeft, 'Illic aureum quoddam ire flumen,' 172–81, 178; Olin, *Six Essays on Erasmus*, 42.

43 Gorday, *Principles of Patristic Exegesis*, 108 104–5, 105.

44 Ibid., 130, 108–9, 134.

CHAPTER THREE

1 Tracy, 'Luther's Influence.' I would like to thank Professor Tracy for allowing me to read and use this paper. His important findings on Erasmus's evolving understanding of the freedom of the will were fundamental in shaping my own study. Tracy does not see an inconsistency in Erasmus's treatment of the will in *De libero arbitrio* and the subsequent changes in the *Annotations* and the *Paraphrases*. He views Erasmus's perspective as consistent, if increasingly interested in leaving less room for human knowledge and emphasizing the importance of both *fiducia* and *fides*. See below.

2 Others have even suggested that the change in Erasmus's work took place much earlier, between 1522 and 1523, when he began to incorporate 'the theme of justification by faith' into his work. See, for example, Kleinhans, 'Luther and Erasmus,' 469.

3 Wengert, *Human Freedom, Christian Righteousness*, 141, 142.

4 Melanchthon, *Opere quae supersunt omnia*.

5 Dolan, *The Influence of Erasmus*, vi.

6 Henze, *Aus Liebe zur Kirche Reform*, 15, 16–17.

7 Ibid., 18–19. 'Danach erfolgte seiner lutherischen Pfarrei, im Spätsommer 1531, den der erste Brief aus Vacha is vom 7. Oktober 1531 datiert. Witzel nennt als Grund fuer diesen Schritt die Inkongruenz von Leben und Lehre der Lutheraner, Melanchthon hingegen vermutete verletzten Ehrgeiz. Wahrscheinlich kamen mehrere Unstimmigkeiten zusammen. Eventuell aufgrund seiner Studien erschien Witzel recht früh auch die lutherische Kirchenform als nicht ideal' (19).

8 Dolan, *Influence of Erasmus*, vi, 30. This term refers to those theologians on both the Protestant and the Roman Catholic sides of the debate who attempted to discover a theological and pragmatic solution

to the Reformation disputes and salvage the cohesion of the Roman Catholic Church.

9 Henze, *Aus Liebe zur Kirche Reform*, 67–8. Henze offers a comprehensive list of the categories of Witzel's work. Dolan notes: 'The 130 printed works catalogued by Richter embracing almost every facet of the reform considerations of the middle decades of the 16th century are sufficient to warrant the judgment of Frank Falk that it must be undisputedly maintained that George Witzel is one of the most interesting characters of the Reformation. His numerous writings place him as one of the unique personages of the era; no other theologian has approached him in the number of books published. Few reformers of the period exercised such an influence in the various church reforms of the time' (*Influence of Erasmus*, 30).

10 Dolan, *Influence of Erasmus*, v, 31.

11 Ibid., 43, 43–4, 44.

12 Henze, *Aus Liebe zur Kirche Reform*, 110–11. This publishing spurt on justification began in 1532 with *Pro defensione bonorum operum* and continued with an additional ten works ending in 1557 with *Methodus orthodoxae doctrinae de justificatione*.

13 Rummel, *Confessionalization of Humanism*, 139. Rummel agrees with Barbara Henze's assessment that Erasmus and Witzel concurred on 'three points: both men differentiated between immovable divine law and *adiaphora*, which were open to accommodation; both based the doctrinal truth on Scripture and consensus, which favors a historical rather than a systematic approach; and both believed in a spiritual church sustained by and united in love.' Rummel points out, however, that Erasmus 'did not recognize in Witzel a kindred spirit' (140).

14 Vandiver, Keen, and Frazel, *Luther's Lives* 40, 41, 41–2. *Luther's Lives* provides a thorough introduction to Cochlaeus as well as an English translation of his *Commentaria Ioannis Cochaei* [The deeds and writings of Dr Martin Luther from the year of the Lord 1517 to the year 1546 related chronologically to all posterity by Johannes Cochlaeus].

15 Ibid., 43. Keen cites *Commentaria Joannis Cochlaei*.

16 Ibid. Keen cites *Sieben Köpfe Martini Lutheri vom Hochwirdigen Sacrament des Altars* (trans. as *Septiceps Lutherus*) (Leipzig: Valentin Schumann, 1529).

17 Vandiver, Keen, and Frazel, *Luther's Lives*, 256–7.

18 For a helpful summary, see Sanday and Headlam, *International Critical Commentary*. These terms are almost always used in Latin. See also Oberman, *Harvest*, 459–76, for definitions of important nominalist terms.

19 Bateman, 'Textual Travail,' 245.
20 Ibid., 243. Bateman writes: 'Evidently feeling some limitations of
    mortality, Erasmus published in 1529 a list of "criticized passages"
    (*loca notata*) that include selections from the *Paraphrases on the Gospels*
    and from some of the *Paraphrases on the Epistles*' (243).
21 Erasmus, *Paraphrases*.
22 LB, 7.
23 Reeve and Screech, *Erasmus' Annotations*.
24 Schelkle, *Paulus Lehrer der Vaeter*, 21. My English translation of 'ihn
    gegen häretische Deutungen zu sichern.'
25 All English translations are from Erasmus, *Paraphrases*, 16. The Latin
    selections presented in the notes are from LB, 7, unless otherwise
    noted. 'Quotquot igitur estis Romae Deo cari, & à pristinis vitiis ad
    sanctimoniam vitae vocati, gratiam vobis opto pacemque: non quam
    mundus hic vulgato more solet precari, sed veram novamque gra-
    tiam, hoc est, gratuitum donum Euangelicae fidei vere justificantis,
    & per hanc penitus abolitis omnibus vitae praeteritae commissis,
    securae jam conscientiae pacem, stabilemque amicitiam cum Deo:
    quae duo non praestant vel humanae sapientiae vires, vel Mosaicae
    Legis observatio, sed omnibus proficiscuntur à singulari munificen-
    tia Dei Patris, & hujus Filii, Domini nostri Jesu Christi.'
26 Payne, 'Erasmus and Lefèvre d'Étaples,' 81. In this article, Payne
    insists that Erasmus 'sees Paul as repudiating ceremonialism and
    emphasizing a more inward, spiritual – that is, especially ethical –
    Christianity, which is grounded in God's grace and human freedom
    with the emphasis upon the latter,' and also that, 'unlike Erasmus,
    Faber contrasts grace and faith not only with ceremonies but with
    all works of the written or the natural law' (71).
27 Erasmus, *Paraphrases*, 16.
28 Padberg: 'Neben der verdeutlichen Heilswirkung moechte Erasmus
    offensichtlich gerade die Heilswurzel hervorheben: den rechtferti-
    genden evangelischen Glauben. Ebenso deutlich, wie der Geschenk-
    charakter des Glaubens herausgestellt wird, wird das durch ihn
    wurzelhaft mitgetielte Heil auf seine letzte shoepferische und
    personale Ursache zurückgeführt … Jedenfalls erscheint in der
    Paraphrase zum Römerbrief der paulnische Gedanke von der
    Heilsmächtigkeit und Ungeschuldetheit des Glaubens unverkürzt'
    ('Glaubenstheologie und Glaubensverkundigung,' 65).
29 *Biblia latina cum glossa ordinaria*, Romans 1:7. Cited throughout as
    Glossa ordinaria.

30 Erasmus, *Annotations*, 31. See also Reeve and Screech, *Erasmus' Annotations*, 342. All Latin excerpts from the *Annotations* are taken from Reeve and Screech: 'quoniam autem potest aliquis suo merito vocari ac diligi, addit gratiam. Gratia data parit remissionem peccatorum, quam suo more pacem vocat. Peccatum enim inimicitiam ponit inter deum & homines. Ille nos vocauit, non nos illum quaesiuimus: ille nos dilexit prior, quum essemus inimici: ille poenam commeritis impartiit spiritus donum. Per spiritum autem, peccatorum veniam & abundantiam charismatum' (342).

31 Payne, 'Lutheranizing Changes,' 317, 318. Payne also notes:'In addition to a somewhat greater emphasis upon the free gift of justification in the 1532 paraphrase, more prominence is given to faith as the means by which this gift is received. In all there are some nine instances of additions in 1532 which mention faith as the means or basis of forgiveness or justification, seven in the Paraphrase of Romans and two in the Paraphrase of Galatians' (319). It should be noted, however, that Payne finally cannot accept that Erasmus was becoming a Lutheran and that these changing interpretations offer evidence of that move towards a Lutheran, or even Melanchthonian, approach to Paul. Rather, Payne argues, 'one cannot affirm with any confidence that Erasmus has already embarked on a conscious program of ecumenical Pauline interpretation. These modifications may be only little signs of a willingness to move in that direction or may represent in line with the letter to Thomas More of the same year some wavering of interpretation. In any case, in the 1532 paraphrase of Romans and to a considerably lesser extent also in the 1532 paraphrase of Galatians, his changes smack of a much more deliberate program of ecumenical exegesis' (330).

32 Bray, *New Testament*, 13, 14–15. Chrysostom argued: 'Christ told his apostles to make peace their first word when entering into houses. So it is from this that Paul always starts also, for it was no small war which Christ put an end to, but a many-sided and enduring conflict. And it was not because of anything we had done, but by his grace and grace with peace.' The Latin is from Migne, *Patrologiae Cursus Completus*, 60: 399–400: 'Hoc Christus apostolos in domos intrantes primo pronuntiare verbum jubet: ideoque Paulus sic ubique orditur, a gratia nempe et pace. Neque enim Christus modicum perfecit bellum, sed varium, omniodum et diuturnum; ideque non ex laboribus nostris, sed per gratiam suam, gratia pacem dedit.' Gorday notes that Augustine also worked on the connection between grace and peace in his *Inchoata Expositio*, and in this, 'his only sustained treatment of this

introductory section of Romans, Augustine broke off his commentary at 1.7 with a lengthy and rambling discourse on *gratia* and *pax*, relating them to repentance (sec. 9), hardships (sec.10), the trinity (secs 11–12), disciplinary matters and in particular the sin against the Holy Spirit (secs 13ff.). Augustine promised to continue this commentary, but in fact never did' (*Principles of Patristic Exegesis*, 152).

33 Bray, *New Testament*, 15. The Latin is from Migne, *Patrologiae Cursus Completus*, 60: 399: 'Atque ut discas Paulum hoc facientem, non confusionem inducere, nec omnia miscere, sed optimam distinctionem novisse, non simpliciter scripsit, Omnibus qui Romae estis, sed cum distinctione, *Dilectis Dei*. Haec enim optima est distinctio, ostenditque unde sit sanctificatio.'

34 Melanchthon, *Melanchthon's Werke*: '"Gratia" significant favorem Dei relative seu misericordiam. "Pax" significant Hebraico more generaliter felicitatem seu, ut nos dicimus, salute. Complectitur igitur pax pacem conscientiae et reliqua dona, quibus opus est' (30).

35 Luther, *Lectures on Romans*, 5–6, 6n10. (The Latin, from WA, 56, *Schriften*, is found on pp. 6–7.)

36 Erasmus, *Annotations*, 39.

37 Bray, *New Testament*, 26. The Latin is from Migne, *Patrologiae Cursus Completus*, 406: 'Quod si modum ignoras, ne id aegre feras: illud enim maxime ad fidem pertinet, si is, qui economiae modum ignorat, providentiae tame rationem admittat.'

38 Erasmus, *Paraphrases*, 16.

39 Ibid. Latin paraphrase: 'Id quo minus sit factum hactenus, per me quidem haudquaquam stetit. Imo nolim vos llud latere fratres, mihi frequenter in animo fuisse vos invisere, verum ad hunc usque diem non licuit per impedimenta, quae inciderunt: ob hoc autem causae vos tantopere cupiebam invisere, ut inter vos quoque nonnihil fructus reportarem, quemadmodum in caeteris Nationibus antehac feci: neque enim hanc Euangelii praedicandi operam, à Deo mandatam, huic aut illi Genti proprie debeo, sed ut ille Deus est ex aequo omnium, ita Christi Euangelium aeque ad omnes pertinet. Euangelium autem voco, justificationem per fidem in Jesum Christum Filium Dei, quem Lex promisit & praefiguravit.' The Latin addition is 'Euangelium autem voco, justificationem per fidem in Jesum Christum Filium Dei, quem lex promisit & praefiguarvit.'

40 Schelkle: '"Die Gnade Gottes, sagt Paulus, leitet mich"' (*Paulus Lehrer der Vaeter*, 34).

41 Ibid.:'Paulus wollte bei Gott dadurch Frucht seines Dienstes haben, dass er die Roemer zum rechten Glauben fuehrte' (35).

42 LB, 7: 780: 'Euangelium autem voco, justificationem per fidem in
    Jesum Christum Filium Dei, quem lex promisit & praefiguravit.'
    The English version is from Erasmus, *Paraphrases*, 16.

43 Elert explains: 'In this writing [*De libero arbitrio*] Luther also set great
    if not all store by the foundation of faith, namely, by the certainty of
    salvation (604, 33; 605, 6; 646, 2ff.; 656, 9; 783, 24ff.). If the mere
    thought of predestination cannot vouch for this certainty – because,
    to say the least, it does not exclude the possibility of 'despair' (*des-
    peratio*) – the basis of faith has to be something else. And here it is
    nothing else than it is elsewhere in Luther, namely, "the Gospel, by
    which the Spirit and grace are offered for the forgiveness of sins
    through Christ crucified" (*Evangelium, quo offertur spiritus et gratia in
    remissionem peccatorum per Christum crucifixum*) (692, 21)' (*The Struc-
    ture of Lutheranism*, 122). In another change to the *Annotations* and
    Paraphrases, Erasmus chose to emphasize God's power, but in differ-
    ent terms: *Romans 9:5*: Erasmus: *Quorum patres, & ex quibus est Chris-
    tus secundum carnem, qui est **in omnibus** Deus bendictus in Saecula.
    Amen*. Vulgate: *Quorum patres, & ex quibus est Christus secundum car-
    nem, qui est super omnia Deus bendictus in Saecula. Amen*. The annota-
    tion to this verse, one of the longest in the *Annotations* on *Paul's
    Letter to the Romans*, underwent several stages of additions and chan-
    ges. First composed in 1516, it was radically changed in both 1527
    and 1535. The *Paraphrase* of Romans 9:5 covers a broader range of
    ideas, including not only Christ's divinity and birth in the flesh, but
    also the inscrutability of God's will and God's omnipotence. The
    addition (made in 1532; boldface text below) seems unnecessary and
    a bit awkward: 'These trace their ancestry from those famous men
    who were most pleasing to God, the luminaries and founders of our
    nation – Abraham, Isaac, Jacob, and others – and from their stock
    Christ saw fit to be born according to the flesh. In this respect, at
    least, they are, whether they like it or not, already close relatives of
    Christ, who is by far more outstanding than the fathers by whose
    titles they advertise themselves. Indeed, no matter how pious those
    famous men might have been, nevertheless they were nothing more
    than men. But Christ is a man in such a way that at the same time he
    is also God, not the God peculiar to this or that nation, but the God
    of the whole world, **and a God who is one with the Father. He is in
    command of all, and all these things are carried out by his inscrut-
    able wisdom. Because of such an unusual love for the human race,
    praise and thanksgiving are owed to him alone for all eternity.**
    Amen' (Erasmus, *Paraphrases*, 53). Latin: 'Qui genus ducunt ab

inclytis illis, ac Deo gratissimis Gentis nostrae luminibus & auctori-
bus, Abraham, Isaac, Jacob, aliisque , ex quorum stirpe Christus ipse
nasci dignatus est secundum carnem, ut hac certe parte jam illi,
velint, nolint, propinqui cognatique sint Christo, qui longe praestan-
tior est patribus illis, quorum titulis sese venditant. Siquidem illi
quantumvis pii fuerunt, nihil aliud tamen quam homines fuerunt. At
Christus sic est homo, ut idem & Deus sit, non hujus aut illius Gentis
peculiaris, sed universorum Deus, & idem cum Patre Deus: qui praesidet omnibus, cujusque inscrutabili consilio geruntur haec omnia,
cui soli ob tam inauditam erga genus humanum caritatem debetur
laus & actio gratiarum in omne aevum, Amen.'
44 Erasmus, *Annotations*, 103. The latter point is made by the editors of
   CWE.
45 Erasmus, *Paraphrases*, 26. Latin: 'Porro cum unus, idemque sit
   omnium Deus, par est & donum illius omnium esse commune.
   Itaque est alius, qui justificat circumcisum, à fide Legis **servatorem
   promittentis, ad fidem Euangelii** promissum exhibentis **traducens:**
   alius qui justificat incircumcisum, à cultu simulacrorum ad com-
   munem fidem vocans.'
46 Melanchthon, *Commentary on Romans*, 104. This sentence is from the
   section on Romans 3:28–30. The Latin is from Melanchthon, *Philippi
   Melanthonis*: 'Hinc facile intelligi potest, Paulum de tota lege concio-
   nari, non tantum de ceremoniis, sicut etiam infra ostendit eius con-
   firmatio, detrahi iustificationem toti legi' (595).
47 Bentley, *Humanists and Holy Writ*, 124.

CHAPTER FOUR

1 Erasmus, *Paraphrases*, 23. 'Quod ad Euangelii gratiam attinet, nihilo
   potior est Judæorum quam Gentium conditio. Attamen aliquo respectu magni refert omnino Judaicæ gentis esse. Primum enim hoc
   nomine jure illis gloriari licet, quod his proprie commissa sunt verba
   Dei, sive quod his peculiariter Lex & Prophetiae proditae sunt, sive
   quod his solis Deus loqui dignatus est. Primum magnificum est hoc
   honoris habitum fuisse à Deo ei Genti, deinde multo præparatior
   videtur ad fidem Euangelicam, qui Legis promissa tenet: & vero
   propior est, qui veri tenet imaginem. Si quidem Mosi Lex &
   Prophetarum oracula gradus est ad Euangelicam Christi doctrinam.'
2 Payne, 'Lutheranizing Changes,' 319. Payne goes on to say (and thus
   underscores the contrast in the theological interpretation Erasmus
   offered in his polemical and interpretive works): 'While here

Erasmus appears to suggest that the Jews by virtue of the law are
more prepared for the gospel than the heathen, in the *Hyperaspistae II*
he states that the gentiles have the law of nature which for them constitutes just as much a preparation for the Gospel. Erasmus expressly
connects this view with the Occamist doctrine of a *meritum de congruo* prior to the reception of justifying grace, a teaching for which at
an earlier point in the *Hyperaspistae II* he had expressed his approval'
(ibid.).

3 Melanchthon, *Melanchthon's Werke*, 90.

4 Melanchthon, *Commentary on Romans*, 92. The Latin is from CR, 15:
579–80: 'Primum ait Iudaeos praestare Gentibus, et hanc habere
praerogativam, quod habeant promissiones. Praestant igitur non
propter legem, non quod lege mereantur iustificationem, sed quia
habent promissiones.'

5 Erasmus, *Paraphrases*, 25. 'Nec ideo condonat, quod illi meruerint,
sed quod ipse promiserit. Nec ideo passus est hucusque peccantes
homines, quod illorum vitia vel nesciret , vel probaret, sed ut hoc
praefinito tempore palam faceret suam justitiam, ut appareat ipsum
esse natura vereque justium ex sese, & unicum humanae justitiae
auctorem, idque promiscue omnibus quicunque fidem habuerint
Euangelio Jesu Christi. Dic igitur Judaee, ubi gloriatio tua?'

6 Tracy, 'Luther's Influence on Erasmus,' 4.

7 Erasmus, *Paraphrases*, 144. See especially fn15.

8 Chrysostom, *Homilies*, 93–4.

9 Romans 3:27, *New Oxford Annotated Bible*, NRSV.

10 Chrysostom, *Homilies*, 95.

11 Cochlaeus wrote: 'Diesen artikel unterstehet Luther, mit etlichen
sprüchen aus Paul und Esaia zu beweren. Aber es felet ihm weit.
Denn die selbigen sprüche reden von Christo, nicht vom glauben
allein, wie er redet. Wir gestehen, das "Christus und unser sünde
willen gestorben und umb [sic] unser gerechtigkeit willen ausser-
standen ist," das "Christus das lamb Gottes ist, das der welt sünde
tregt," das er uns die sünde vergibt und gerecht macht. Daraus fol-
get aber nicht, das uns der glaube allein gerecht mache, denn der
glaub ist nicht Christus. Glaub und Christus ist nicht ein ding,
sonder der glaub ist ein gab Christi, wie auch die guten werk nicht
von uns selbs herkommen, sonder von Christo, durch welches gen-
ad wir den glauben empfahen und gute werk verbringen' (CC, 18: 8;
see Volz, *Drei Schriften*).

12 Witzel, *Antwort auf Martin Luthers Letzt bekennete Artikel*; 'S. Paulus
disputirt wol wider die werk des gesetzes Mosi zun Roemern und

Galatern, niemand leugnet dis, aber darmit hebt er nicht auff das christlich leben noch gerechte, gute werk, welche der gleubige thut und thun sol, sondern er preiset und foddert solchs von dem, der do selig werden wil' (CC, 18: 67; see ibid.).

13 Romans 3:26, *Glossa ordinaria.*

14 Erasmus, *Paraphrases*, 32. 'Christo igitur non Mosi justitiam & innocentiam nostrum acceptam feramus oportet, qui sponte sese tradidit in mortem, ut gratis per fidem nostra dilueret commissa: atque idem revixit excitatus à mortuis, ut à mortuariis factis abstineremus, neque posthac peccaremus, ea rursus committentes, ob quæ ille mortem oppetisset. Mortuus est, inquam, ut in nobis culpam occideret, & resurrexit à mortuis, ut prius per illum mortui pristinis culpis, mox una cum illo & per illum resuscitati in novam vitam, deinceps justitiæ vivamus, quam illius beneficio accepimus.'

15 Payne, 'Lutheranizing Changes,' 320fn33. Payne lists this verse as one of the seven instances in the *Paraphrases on Romans* that highlights 'faith as the means by which the gift is received' (319).

16 Gorday, *Principles of Patristic Exegesis*, 116.

17 Melanchthon, *Melanchthon's Werke*, 155. This portion of the commentary is for Romans 4:23f.

18 Cochlaeus, in CC, 18: 8; 10, lines 36–41; see Volz, *Drei Schriften.*

19 Erasmus, *Paraphrases*, 52. 'Ad quem utinam & Judaei omnes sese convertant, Mose suo relicto, qui nunc sibi persuadent, satis esse ad consequendam salutem, quod filii sint Abrahae, quod Legem teneant olim à Deo datam, cum horum nihil profuturum sit, nisi per fidem se dignos praebeant, qui trahantur ac diligantur à Deo. Verum ab his pertinaciter rejicitur Christus Lege promissus, quem Gentes recipiunt. Neque vero hoc dixerim odio Gentis meae, licet mihi unique infestae. Quod res est loquar, teste Christo omnium conscio, neque quicquam mentiar, teste mihi mea conscientia, cujus auctor & inspector est Spiritus Sanctus.' *Romans 9:1.* Erasmus *Veritatem dico in Christo, non mentior,* **attestante mihi simul conscientia mea** in *Spiritu Sancto*: Vulgate: *Veritatem dico in Christo, non mentior, testimonium mihi perhibente conscientia mea in Spiritu Sancto.*

20 Ibid., 49. 'Nec hîc ulla fidei fuerit laus aut spei, si jam exstarent omnia, quae Christus nobis promisit: verum ita demum fide commendamur Deo, si ea, quae corporeis oculis cerni non possunt, oculis fidei cernimus, & interim perseverantes in doloribus, spe pertinaci expectamus quod promissum est.'

21 Althaus, *Theology of Martin Luther*, 235.

22 Erasmus, *Paraphrases*, 49.

23 Melanchthon, *Melanchthon on Christian Doctrine*, 168–9.
24 Gorday, *Principles of Patristic Exegesis*, 166. Gorday sees this in
    Augustine's *De gratia et libero arbitrio*, 18, 39.
25 Romans 8:24, *Glossa ordinaria*.
26 Erasmus, *Paraphrases*, 58. 'Propterea quod quemadmodum idem dix-
    it Esaias: Sermonem in compendium contractum faciet Dominus
    super terram. Fuci nonnihil habere videntur umbrae, ac multiloqua
    Lex est, promittens, adumbrans, praecipiens, minitans, consolans. At
    Christus missus semel exhibuit quicquid erat promissum, expressit
    quicquid erat adumbratum, ac praescriptionum multiloquium re-
    degit ad unicum praeceptum caritatis Euangelicae. Sparsit coelestis
    doctrinae semen, quod licet infrugiferum sit in multis meae Gentis,
    non desunt tamen in quibus fructum attulerit.'
27 Bray, *New Testament*, 267. The Latin is from Migne, *Patrologiae Cursus
    Completus*, 562: 'Id est: Non circuitione opus est et labore, et afflic-
    tione illa legalium operum, sed magna cum brevitate erit salus. Talis
    quippe est fides, in paucis verbis habet salutem.'
28 Gorday, *Principles of Patristic Exegesis*, 170.
29 Luther, *Lectures on Romans*, 396. The Latin is from WA, 56: 406, *Ro-
    emervorlesung 1515/16*: 'Nam antequam hoc verbum fidei, verbum
    spiritus, reuelaretur, Erant omnia in figura et vmbra propter
    Iudaeorum tarditatem, Erat verbum inconsummatum et imperfec-
    tum ac ideo omnibus facile intelligibile, Quia de sensibilibus loque-
    batur in figuris. At vbi exclusis sensibilibus et figuris cepit Deus
    loqui verbum spiritus et absconditum, quod est verbum fidei, Et sic
    Consummatum ac perfectum verbum proferre, tunc simul necess-
    ario est etiam abbreuiatum ab omnibus significatis, sensibilibus ac
    figuralibus.'
30 Erasmus, *Paraphrases*, 61. 'Qui praedicabunt autem Apostoli, nisi missi
    sint ab eo, cujus est Euangelium? De quibus idem meminit Esaias
    Cap. XXV. Cum inquit: Quam decori pedes Euangelizantium pacem,
    Euangelizantium bona? Auditis quid jubeantur praedicare Christi
    praecones, non circumcisionem & sabbatismos, sed pacem, quae per
    fidem abolitis peccatis nos mutua caritate in Christo conglutinet, & ea
    bona quae semper bona sint, quia suapte natura bona sunt.'
31 Ibid., 16. See the paraphrase for Romans 1.7. This is another instance
    where Erasmus sets up grace and peace as flowing from justifying
    faith. See pp. 49–50, above, for a discussion of the uses of grace and
    peace in Erasmus's paraphrases and annotations of Romans.
32 Melanchthon, *Commentary on Romans*, 203. The Latin is from CR, 15:
    992: 'Citat autem Paulus dulcissimum dictum Esaiae ex cap. 52.:

Quam speciosi pedes Evangelizantium pacem. Loquitur et dictum de voce sonante in ministerio, et docet sic colligi Ecclesiam, scilicet voce Evangelii. Metaphora pedum significat cursorem seu nuncium, et hos ait formosos et amabiles esse, quia adferunt laetissimam promissionem gratiae et vitae aeternae.'

33 Erasmus, *Paraphrases*, 61. 'Qui praedicabunt autem Apostoli, nisi missi sint ab eo, cujus est Euangelium? De quibus idem meminit Esaias Cap. XXV. Cum inquit: Quam decori pedes Euangelizantium pacem, Euangelizantium bona? Auditis quid jubeantur praedicare Christi praecones, non circumcisionem & sabbatismos, sed pacem, quae per fidem abolitis peccatis nos mutua caritate in Christo conglutinet, & ea bona quae semper bona sint, quia suapte natura bona sunt.'

34 Romans 10:15, *Glossa ordinaria*.

35 Erasmus, *Annotations*, 6. In 1527 Erasmus added the following: 'Haec vox peculiaris est Paulo, cui studium est omnibus adimere fiduciam operum humanorum, totamque gloriam transferre ad vocantem deum, cuit vocanti qui auscultat suus est. Ita Paulus è caelo vocatus mox obedit.' This addition can be found in Reeve and Screech, *Erasmus' Annotations*, 335.

36 See Paula Fredriksen Landes, *Augustine on Romans: Propositions from the Epistle to the Romans, Unfinished Commentary on the Epistle to the Romans* (Chico, Calif.: Scholars Press, 1982), 53; see also 52–3, 60–1.

37 Chrysostom, *Homilies*, 4. The Latin is from Migne, *Patrologiae Cursus Completus*, 395: 'Ubique se vocatum appellat, gratum animum exhibens, indicansque se non quaerentem invenisse, sed vocatum obedivisse.'

38 Erasmus, *Annotations*, 7–8.

39 Melanchthon, *Commentary on Romans*, 61. The Latin is from CR, 15: 549: 'Ideo autem Paulus initio statim proposuit definitionem, ut sciremus quid professus sit, et diligenter discerneremus legem ab Evangelio, quasi dicat, Paulus divinitus vocatus ad docendum Evanglium de Christo, non ad docendum legem aut philosophiam.'

40 Erasmus, *Annotations*, 27.

41 Romans 1:5, *New Oxford Annotated Bible*, NRSV.

42 Erasmus, *Annotations*, 19.

43 Schäfer, 'Melanchthon's Interpretation of Romans 5.15,' 83.

44 Romans 1:5, *Glossa ordinaria*.

45 Erasmus, *Annotations*, 196–7. I will provide here the Latin for only the last part of the annotation, the portion added in 1535: 'Certe hoc agit Augustinus aduersus duas epistolas Pelagianorum libro primo, capite octauo, & aliquot sequentibus: ut totus hic locus competat

Paulo, uel puero, uel sub lege peccati, uel sub gratia sentienti motus affectuum, licet non assentienti: sed adeo dure multa torquens, ut magis conueniat Paulum humani generis personam in se recipere, in qua est ethnicus ex lex, Iudaeus carnalis sub lege, spiritualis per gratiam liberatus' (Reeve and Screech, *Erasmus' Annotations*, 381).

46 Pelikan, *Reformation of Church and Dogma*, 135. Pelikan quotes Luther from *Against Latomus* (WA, 8: 119): 'Unus est homo Paulus, qui utrunque de se confitetur, alio et alio respectu, sub gratia est spiritualis, sed sub lege carnalis, idem idem Paulus utrobique.'

47 Melanchthon, *Commentary on Romans*, 161–2. The Latin is from CR, 15: 653–4: 'Rursus etiam hic monendus est lector de discrimine interioris et exterioris hominis, de mente et de carne. Interior homo significat hominem, quatenus renovatus est Spiritu sancto, hoc est, quatenus habet verum timorem et veram fiduciam. Ita et mens non signifcat hic tantum partem cognoscentem, sed utramque partem, cognoscentem et appetentem, quatenus renovata est Spiritu sancto, sicut inquit: Ego autem mente servio legi Dei. Econtra exterior homo, seu Caro, significant totum hominem, quatenus non est renovatus Spiritu sancto: et significant non tantum appetitiones sensuum aut externa membra, sed etiam potentias superiores, rationem et voluntatem, quatenus non sunt renovati: sicut infra rursus dicendum est.'

48 See my discussion of this letter, above, pp. 26–7.

49 Erasmus, *Annotations*, 224. I provide the Latin for only the last paragraph: 'Neque uero apud Graecos adiungitur Sancti, tantum est Vocati. Atque ita legisse Origenem ex ipsius liuet interpretatione, quum ait, Videndum est ne forte ex hoc quod dicit, iis qui secundum propositum vocati sunt & quos praesciuit & quos praede stinauit, & caetera. Neque secus legit Ambrosius, sic enim edisserit, Hi autem secundum propositum uocantur, quos credentes praesciuit deus futuros sibi idoneos, ut antequam crederent, scirentur. Legit idem Augustinus libro de correptione & gratia. Sequitur hanc tum lectionem tum sententiam Chrysostomus & Theophylactus, quanquam refragatur Thormas & uetusti Latinorum codices plerique. Apparet autem Sancti, additum ex aliis locis, in quibus hae duae uoces, Vocati sancti, saepenumero copulantur' (Reeve and Screech, *Erasmus' Annotations*, 387).

50 Cochlaeus, *Ein Nötig und Christlich Bedenken*, 8, 8–9; see Volz, *Drei Schriften*. Cochlaeus refutes the Schmalcaldic assertion, 'Das allein der glaube an Christum uns gerecht mache.'

51 Luther, *Lectures on Romans*, 371. The Latin is from WA, 56: 381: 'immo incipit ab hinc de materia predestinationis et electionis disserere, quę non tam est profunda, vt putatur, Sed potius

dulcissima electis et iis, qui spiritum habent, amara vero et dura pru-
dentię carnis super omnia; ibid., 372. The Latin is from ibid., 382:
'Sane nostri theologi, velut acutuli nescio quid magnum sibi effecisse
Videntur, quando suum contingens adduxerint, dicentes Electos sa-
luari necessario, Necessitate scil. consequentię, Sed non consequen-
tis. Hęc tantum vacua verba sunt.'

52 This translation is from Lohse, *Martin Luther*, 68. See WA, 18: 786.

53 Erasmus, *Annotations*, 225–26.

54 I am grateful to Professor Christopher Ocker for his insights into this
verse, especially his suggestion to look to Melanchthon for similarities of interpretation.

55 Meijering, *Melanchthon and Patristic Thought*, 5. For references see
5nn7–8. For Melanchthon's thoughts on this subject, see his *Melanchthon on Christian Doctrine*. For Melanchthon on justification and faith
in 1521, see Melanchthon, *St.A*, Vol. 2, pt 1, 'Loci Communes,' ed.
Hans Engelland (Gütersloh: C. Bertelsmann Verlag, 1951), 86–125.
For his later views on the subject, see the 1535 version of the *Loci
Communes Theologici*, CR, 21.

56 Meijering, *Melanchthon and Patristic Thought*, 114, 134. Meijering directs readers to *St.A.*, Vol. 2, 236–43, where Melanchthon wrote in
1559: 'Sed cum mens audiens ac se sustentans non repugnat, non
indulget diffidentiae, sed adiuvante etiam Spiritu sancto conatur
assentiri, in hoc certamine voluntas non est otiosa' (243).

57 Elert, *Structure of Lutheranism*, 25.

58 Erasmus, *Annotations*, 226, 225.

59 Ibid., 294–5. I provide a portion of the Latin here, from Reeve and
Screech, *Erasmus' Annotations*, 403: 'subest tacita exceptio, ut & alias
hac voce usus est Paulus. Ita sensus erat: Si gratia, non igitur ex
operibus: quod ni esset, gratia non esset gratia: hoc est, falso dicer-
etur gratia. Atque ut Latinae lectioni magis faueam, facit quod Paulus non hic agit, an opus sit opus, sed gratiam astruit, quam Iudaei
conabantur expellere.'

60 Chrysostom, *Homilies*, 330–7.

61 Melanchthon, *Commentary on Romans*, 204. The Latin is from CC, 15:
697: 'Et addit doctrinam, quod Ecclesia non sit electa propter legem,
propter politiam, sed populum Dei esse electos, qui Evangelium fide
apprehendunt. Ideo addit misericordium esse causam electionis, non
legem, non politiam, sicut supra de discrimine duorum populorum
dictum est.'

62 Luther, *Lectures on Romans*, 96. The Latin is from WA, 56: 107 (Romans 2:6) '**Si autem gratia** i. e. ex gratia Vel per gratiam **iam non ex**

operibus: i.e. Iustitia propria Et hic infert ex necessario Impossibile **Alioquin** | nisi stet illud; stat autem, ergo istud non stat | **gratia** Si meritis Iustitię et operibus data est **iam non est gratia.'**

63 Pfnür, *Einig in der Rechtfertigungslehre?* 276.

64 Erasmus, *Annotations*, 107.

65 Romans 4:3, *New Oxford Annotated Bible*, NRSV.

66 Elert, *Structure of Lutheranism*, 109 (Elert quotes from Luther [WA, 2: 490, 26]); 86–7. Elert notes the importance of imputed righteousness to the very essence of the Reformation: 'But if imputed righteousness is actually an "alien righteousness" (*justitia aliena*) – only when it is this, can it be imputed or, in some other way, be declared, granted, promised, imparted; and without this there would have been no Reformation – the "right" (*jus*) inherent in the new righteousness would have to belong to a transsubjective reality. And this is not something new that would be added to the doctrine of justification or would even destroy it; it belongs to its absolutely necessary presuppositions' (110).

67 *St.A*, Vol. 2, pt 1, 89.

68 Melanchthon, *Melanchthon's Werke*, 126. See the editor's footnote 6 for a discussion of Melanchthon's reliance on Erasmus's 1516 NT and annotation.

69 Melanchthon, *Philippi Melanthonis*, 595.

70 Hausammann, *Römerbriefauslegung zwischen Humanismus und Reformation*. The Engish is my translation of 'die Gerechtigkeit beruht allein auf der Guete des anrechnenden Gottes "ohne alles hinzuthun der werchen"' (112–13). Heiko A. Oberman sees the use of *imputare* as critical to understanding Luther's theology: 'The central concept "extra nos" does not stand on the side of an imputatio-justification over against a unio-justification. It does not prove that we are justified "outside ourselves" before the chair of God the judge (*in foro Dei*), in such a way that grace would not be imparted but "only" imputed. The intention of the "extra nos" is to show that justification is not based on a claim of man, on a debitum iustitiae. The righteousness granted is not one's property but one's possession. It is not *proprietas* but rather *possessio* … We point here so emphatically to the difference between proprietas and possessio because we believe that an understanding of the meaning of both implies a terminological advance after centuries of debate in this history of Luther interpretation between those who have argued in favor of a justification by imputation against those who claimed that impartation was definitely the best one-word summary' (*Dawn of the Reformation*, 121–2).

71 Contarini, *De iustificatione*, CC, 7: 29. For a discussion of the importance of pre-Tridentine formulations of 'double justification,' see
McGrath, *Iustitia Dei*, 246–9.

72 Jedin, *Council of Trent*, 2: 243f. See also McGrath: 'Those in Rome
who read the letter were sceptical about its catholicity' (*Iustitia Dei*,
314fn25)

73 Romans 4:3, *Glossa ordinaria*.

74 McGrath, *Iustitia Dei*, 315–16.

75 Erasmus, *Annotations*, 128fn2.

76 Ibid., 127–8.

77 Melanchthon, *Melanchthon on Christian Doctrine*, 157.

78 Melanchthon, *Commentary on Romans*, 122. The Latin is from CC, 15:
611: 'Secundo, usurpandum est hoc dictum, ut erudiat et consoletur
pios agnoscentes suam infirmitatem, ut videlicet revocentur ad
mediatorem Christum, et discant se iustos reputari propter Christum
fide, non propter propriam dignitatem. Itaque infirmitas, quae adhuc in ipsis haeret, condonatur eis, nec sunt iusti propter illam in-
coatam et imperfectam obdedientiam, sed fide propter Christum.'

79 Pfnür, *Einig in der Rechtfertigungslehre?* 176. He cites *Apologia Confes-
sionis Augustanae*, 4: S305.

80 Ibid., 371.

81 All of these verses are discussed earlier in this chapter.

82 Tracy, 'Luther's Influence,' 4.

83 Ibid., 8–9.

84 Raitt, 'From Augsburg to Trent,' 213.

85 Ibid., 217. See also Cameron, *The European Reformation*, 344–9 for a
discussion of the breakdown in efforts to prevent a permanent split
of Christendom.

CHAPTER FIVE

1 For a discussion of Erasmus's religious program, see Hoffmann,
'Faith and Piety,': 'Thus Erasmus can stress the Protestant principle
of *sola Scriptura*, according to which salvation is revealed by Scripture alone. But a true understanding of Scripture hinges, as we have
seen, on the allegorical interpretation, otherwise the word would
yield at most a broader tropological sense like the *bonae littera*, or
nothing at all. And to expound the word allegorically, one needs the
eye of faith. For Scripture has been generated by Christ's spirit. Consequently, no one can grasp its essential truth except those who by
evangelical faith partake in his spirit' (249).

2 Erasmus, *Controversies*, 76: xii

3 McSorley, *Luther: Right or Wrong*, 277. McSorley asserts that Luther's response was a masterpiece and a fundamental articulation of his theological program, while Erasmus's attack was the work of a theological dilletante.

4 Ibid., 188, 284, 273, 279.

5 Bainton, *Erasmus of Christendom*, 187. Manfred Hoffmann's study of the role of rhetoric in Erasmus's theology may provide a helpful explanation of why so many theologians and scholars have viewed Erasmus's polemic against Luther as particularly unclear. Hoffman notes that Erasmus rejected an overly aggressive style and embraced allegory in theology. This may, indeed, explain the way in which Erasmus wrote against Luther as well as the accusation that he was unclear and inadequate in his efforts. See Hoffmann, *Rhetoric and Theology*, especially 213. See also Hoffmann, 'Erasmus on Free Will: An Issue Revisited,' *Erasmus of Rotterdam Society Yearbook*, 10 (1990): 101–21.

6 Rummel, *Erasmus and His Catholic Critics*, 151.

7 Tracy, 'Two Erasmuses, Two Luthers,' *Archiv für Reformationsgeschichte* 78 (1987): 37.

8 Oberman, *Luther*, 152.

9 Oberman, *Dawn of the Reformation*, 120.

10 Pelikan, *Reformation of Church and Dogma*, 138ff, 139, 140.

11 As C. Augustijn has noted in 'Le dialogue Érasme-Luther dans l'Hyperaspistes II,' in *Actes du Colloque International Erasme Tours, 1986* (Geneva: Droz, 1990): '*L'Hyperaspistes*, la résponse d'Érasme au *De servo arbitrio* de Luther, a toujours en une mauvaise presse: "simplement ennuyeux," dit André Meyer, "rien qu'un épilogue," déclare Johan Huizinga' (171).

12 The Peasants War and the theologies of Zwingli, Carlstadt, and the Anabaptists, for example, evidence such 'misunderstandings' or alleged misunderstandings. See, for example, Blickle, *Revolution of 1525*.

13 See the Introduction.

14 Luther, *Bondage of the Will*, 63. The Latin is from WA, 18: 601: 'Cui tuus libellus comparatus, ita mihi sorduit ac viluit, ut tibi vehementer compaterer, qui pulcherrimam tuam et ingeniosam dictionem in istis sordibus pollueres, ac materiae indignissimae indignarer, quae tam praeciosis eloquentiae ornamentis veheretur, tanquam si quisquiliae vel stercora aureis argenteisque vasis portarentur. Id quod tu ipse quoque persensisse videris, qui tam difficilis fuisti ad hoc scriptionis munus obeundum, nempe quod conscientia tua te

monuit, forte, ut quantislibet eloquentiae viribus rem tentares, non posse tamen mihi fucum fieri, quin feces ipsas, semotis verborum lenociniis perspicerem.'

15 Hoffmann, 'Faith and Piety,' 249.

16 Tracy, *Erasmus of the Low Countries*, 150.

17 Bainton, *Erasmus of Christendom*, 178. Bainton quotes Erasmus's *Sponge to Wipe Away the Aspersions of Hutten* (LB, 10, 1672 C-D) and indicates the myriad of issues Erasmus saw as central to Luther's conflict with Rome: 'It is not a question of the articles of faith but as to whether the Roman primacy was instituted by Christ, whether the order of the cardinals is a necessary member of the Church, whether confession was instituted by Christ, whether bishops by their constitutions can obligate any one to commit a mortal sin, whether free will contributes to salvation, whether any work of man can be called good, whether the Mass can be called a sacrifice, whether faith alone confers salvation.'

18 Tracy, *Erasmus of the Low Countries*, 155.

19 Tracy, 'Luther's Influence,' 9.

20 Erasmus, *Annotations*, 113–14.

21 Erasmus, *Controversies*, 77: 360. Erasmus refers to Romans 4:9–12.

22 Cochlaeus, *Adversus cucullatum minotaurum wittenbergensem*, 39.

23 Erasmus, *Paraphrases*, 53: 'Quo magis exsecranda est quorundam Judaeorum impietas, qui dum maledici sunt in Filium, Patrem, qui per Filium voluit illustrari, contumelia afficiunt. Neque tamen tantum valet istorum impietas, ut ideo non praestet Deus, quod Prophetarum oraculis se praestaturum promisit. Populo Israelitico, ac posteris Abrahae promissa fuit ista felicitas, verum non quibuslibet, sed iis modo, qui vere essent horum posteri. Neque enim omnes, qui genus ducunt ab Israele, veri sunt Israelitae, sed qui fidei robore fortes sunt & invicti adversus hujus Mundi incommoda, quibus Deus explorat animi nostri pietatem, in hos vere competit cognomen Israelitae, hoc est, potentis Deo.' The CWE editors note (referring to 63fn5): 'The 1517 edition reads: "only those who see with the eye of faith truly fit the name of Israel." In 1521 the passage was changed to read as it is translated in our text, except that the final words, "that is, of one powerful with God," were added in 1523' (153). My collation indicated that they were added in 1532.

24 Chrysostom, *Homilies*, 285.

25 Gorday, *Principles of Patristic Exegesis*, 168.

26 Erasmus, *Controversies*, 77: 526–7. Erasmus also used the verse later in the text to defend free will against Luther; see 555.

27 Jedin, *Council of Trent*, 2: 186. Jedin says the argument 'runs thus: "In
the act of justification God prevents man with his grace, enlightens,
or moves his intelligence not only inwardly but from outside as well,
through the preaching of the word of God (Rom. x, 14ff). If this call
is heeded, God brings home to man his unbelief, ungodliness and
unrighteousness and offers him justification and remission of his
sins through Christ. Where this preventing grace is accepted, there
follows faith in the divine promise concerning Christ and in the im-
parting of Christ's merits by God's mercy to man, a sinner." If to
these statements of the *Summarium* of the second half of the debate
we add the one sentence that "the good works done in God's grace
do not only preserve and increase justice, but likewise merit eternal
life," we are in possession of the Council's answer, as yet incomplete
it is true, to the seven questions which we set down at the beginning
for the purpose of orientation' (186–7).

28 Erasmus, *Paraphrases*, 20. 'E diverso gloria, honor, & pax, ex aequo
rependetur omnibus, quicunque per fidem bene vixerint, sed in
primis Judaeo, mox Graeco, dein Barbaris omnibus.'

29 Romans 2:10, *New Oxford Annotated Bible*, NRSV.

30 Payne, 'Lutheranizing Changes,' 319; see especially 320fn33.

31 Erasmus, *Controversies*, 77: 361–2.

32 Cochlaeus, *Adversus cullatum minotaurum wittenbergensem*, 36–7.

33 Pfnür, *Einig in der Rechtfertigungslehre?* 238; for a thorough discussion
of the content of the *Confutatio Pontifica*, see 222–50.

34 Melanchthon, *Commentary on Romans*, 87. The Latin is from the *Comentarii in Epistola Pauli ad Romanos* in CR, 15: 576: 'Constat hoc
agere Paulum in hac tota Epistola, Fide gratis propter filium Dei
iustificari homines, non propter dignitatem nostra aut merita. Hoc
verge agi a Paulo cum constet, tamen adversarii hoc dictum, reddet
iuxta facta, detorquent ad suas opiniones, contra Pauli sententiam.
Contendunt homines pronunciari iustos propter dignitatem operum,
contendunt opera esse pretium vitae aeternae'

35 Romans 2:10, *New Oxford Annotated Bible*, NRSV.

36 Erasmus, *Paraphrases*, 25fn124. 'Justitia, inquam, non legalis, sed Dei,
idque non per circumcisionem aut Judaicas ceremonias, sed per fidem **ac fiduciam** erga Jesum Christum, per quem unum vera justitia
confertur, non Juadeis modo, aut his aut illis Nationibus, sed citra
delectum omnibus & singulis, quicunque illi fidem habuerint.'

37 Tracy, 'Luther's Influence,' 4, 4–5.

38 Melanchthon, *Melanchthons Werke*, 107. My English translation.
'Quod addit, 'per fidem Iesu Christi', saepe iam dixi non pronuntiari

homines iustos propter fidem, quia fides sit quedam novitas ac
dignitas in nobis, sed quia aliter apprehendi misericordia non potest.
Significat igitur 'fides' correlative fiduciam misericordiae. Estque
sententia, quod iusti pronuntiemur non propter nostras virtutes aut
novitatem, non propter opera praecedentia aut sequentia, sed propter Christum per misericordiam, etsi haec misericordia non potest
accipi nisi per fidem seu fiduciam.'

39 Melanchthon, *Comentarii in Epistola Pauli ad Romanos*, CR, 15: 587.
The English is from *Commentary on Romans*, 99. Latin: 'Etsi enim in
his, qui fide iustificati sunt, incoatur nova obedientia, tamen illa
nova obedientia seu lex, non est causa propter quam consequimur
remissionem peccatorum, et reputamur iusti seu accepti, verum haec
gratis donantur propter Christum.'

40 Erasmus, *Annotations*, 100–1.

41 Romans 3:21–2, *Glossa ordinaria*: 'Justitia dei. Non qua ipse justus est
essentialiter, sed qua induit impium: quando misericorditer de in-
fideli facit fidélem. *Justitia autem, etc.* Justitia dixit. Non misericordia
utcunque quod promisserat deus in lege et prophetis sed adventum
christi reddidit.'

42 Erasmus, *Controversies*, 77: 669–70; see also 669n1433.

43 Ibid., 360.

44 Erasmus, *Annotations*, 100–1.

45 See ibid., 320–3. See also Reeve and Screech, *Erasmus' Annotations*,
409–10. The CWE editor does not note that the Vulgate was, indeed,
different and therefore altered by Erasmus. See his annotations in
Reeve and Screech, *Erasmus' Annotations*, 409.

46 Erasmus, *Annotations*, 320. Reeve and Screech, *Erasmus' Annotations*,
409: 'Exhibetur quod ante promissum re praestatur, aut quod prius
occultum profertur, velut exhibentur syngraphae: frequenter in
malam partmen, ut dicitur exhibere negocium, qui facesit negocium:
praebetur, quod ad usum subministratur: ita praebemus aureies di-
centi, praebemus sumptum ad nuptias. Chrysostomus & Theophylactus indicant eos proprie παραστηναι, qui imperatori praebant
equos bellicos. Unde nos vertimus, praebere. Si respicias quod in
baptismo abiurauimus desideria carnis nosque Christo dedicavimus,
quadrat exhil bendi verbum, quo monemur hoc praestare, quod
sumus professi. Rursum si consideremus allusum esse ad veterem
morem holocautomatum, quo sacerdos hostiam imponebat altari,
deus autem igni coelitus demisso eam absumebat, non male congruit
exhibendi verbum. Quod enim semel deo dicatum est, non oportet
in alios usus accommodare: quemadmodum qui praebuit equos

imperatori ad bellum, postea nihil habet cum illis commercii: nec ad priuatos usus revocat, quos semel tradidit. Annotauit & illud Chrysostomus, quo non dixit, ποιήσατε id est, facite corpora vestra hostiam: sed παραστήσατε, hoc est, tradite, ut iam disinant esse uestri iuris, sed incipiant esse diuini, nefasque sit quae semel praebuistis imperatori deo ad bellandum aduersus diabolum, ea denuo diaboli obsequiis accomodare: simulque monemur, ut curemus sic tractare corpora nostra, ut idonea sint instrumenta diuinae voluntati, dignaque quae illius oculis exhibeantur.'

47 See Migne, *Patrologiae Cursus Completus*, 595–8.

48 Erasmus, *Paraphrases*, 69. 'Ergo posteaquam vobis Dei munere contigit, ut à pristina superstitione sitis ad veram translati Religionem, ut ab onere Mosaicae Legis sitis liberi, obsecro & obtestor vos fratres per **eas misericordias** Dei, **quas multifariam erga vos praestitit praestatque, cujus gratuitae bonitati** summam vestrae felicitatis debetis, ut posthac immoletis illis victimas ista professione dignas, non hircos, aut oves, bovesve, quae ut pura deliguntur animalia, & rebus divinis apta, quemadmodum mos est Ethnicis ac Judaeis. Hactenus indulsisse sat est crassis istiusmodi sacrificiis, posthac longe alios ritus, alium cultum, alias victimas Deus à vobis requirit, nimirum ut offeratis illi vestra ipsorum corpora: non mutilandis membris, sed subigendis malis affectibus: hoc est, non mortuas pecudes, sed viventem hostiam, vere puram ac sanctam, Deo gratam & acceptam, sacrificium rationale, **victimam animi**, non brutae pecudis. Dum lex durabat carnalis, patiebatur Deus sibi corporeas immolari pecudes: posteaquam Lex coepit esse spiritualis, spiritualibus illi victimis litandum est. Pro vitulo immola superbiae affectum, pro ariete iram effervescentem jugula, pro hirco exure libidinem, pro columbis & turturibus lascivas ac lubricas animi cogitationes Deo sacrifica. Haec demum sunt Christianis digna sacra, hae Christo gratae victimae. Deus est animus, & animi donariis conciliatur: nec ceremoniis, sed affectibus puris coli postulat. Pro praeputio, ab animo supervacaneos & indecoros affectus reseca. Sabbatismus tibi sit, mens à tumultu perturbationum vacans. Christus semetipsum obtulit pro nobis, par est ut ipsi nosmet illi vicissim immolemus.'

49 Tracy, 'Luther's Influence,' 3.

50 Chrysostom, *Homilies*, 360.

51 Erasmus, *Controversies*, 77: 424.

52 Melanchthon, *Commentary on Romans*, 211.

53 Erasmus, *Ausgewählte Schriften*, 4: 146–7; *Controversies*, 76: 69. Romans 1:17 is used in Erasmus's argument: 'Ita Paulus: "Vivo autem

iam non ego, vivit vero in me Christus," et tamen iustus apud eundem ex fide vivit. Quomodo igitur vivens non vivit? Quia spiritui
dei fert acceptum quod vivit.'

54 Both Padberg and Tracy note this phenomenon. See Tracy, 'Luther's
Influence,' 4; Padberg, 'Glaubenstheologie und Glaubensverkündigung,'68.

55 This annotation and others added to the same verse demonstrate
Erasmus's preoccupation with 'faith' in the 1527 *Annotations*, 42–5.
I offer a portion of the Latin here, from Reeve and Screech,
Erasmus'Annotations, 345: '(Ex fide in fidem.) … Latinis enim, habere
fidem alicui dicitur, qui credit dictis illius: & dare fidem dicitur, qui
sancte promittit: & astringit fidem suam, qui se obligat alicui. Liberat
autem fidem suam, qui praestat quod promisit. Fide caret, cui non
creditur, Fronti nulla fides. Fidem violat, qui non praestat conuenta:
unde & perfidus dicitur & perfidia. Fidem derogat alicui, qui facit ne
illi credatur.'

56 Erasmus, *Annotations* , 46.

57 Erasmus, *Paraphrases*, 42: 17, paraphrase of Romans 1:16–17: '16 Non
enim erubesco Euangelium. Virtus enim Dei est in Salutem omni credenti, Iudaeo primum & Graeco. Nec enim hinc me deterret Imperii
Romani majestas, neque pudendam mihi duco functionem, si prae-
dicem Euangelium Christi. Nam ut impiis & incredulis res ridicula
frivolaque videtur hoc Euangelium, ita quisquis crediderit, huic virtus est Dei efficax ad conferendam salutem, vereque tranquillandam
conscientiam, quod nec Judaedorum traditiones, nec vestra Philosophia, opesve conferre queant. Ea vis cum aeque valeat omnibus, ta
men ita ut jussit Dominus honoris causa primum Judaeis oblata est,
mox in Graecos & omnes orbis nationes propaganda per Euangelii
praecones, ut omnes pariter & suam agnoscerent injustitiam, & Dei
quaererent justitiam, sive Scythae sint, sive Britanni. Procul autem
abest à salute, qui aut morbum suum non intelligit, aut unde peten-
dum sit remedium, ignorat. 17 Iustitia enim Dei in eo revelatur ex
fide in fidem: sicut scriptum est: Iustus autem ex fide vivit. Cum
enim antehac aliis in rebus alii sitam esse justitiam existimarent,
nunc Euangelio Christi palam sit omnibus justitia, non Mosi, sed
ipsius Dei, quae non sita sit in superstitioso cultu simulacrorum, aut
legalibus Judaeorum ceremoniis, sed ex fide contingat , dum
agnoscunt homines, id nunc praestare Deum, quod olim ore
Prophetarum suorum promiserat. Quemadmodum & Abacuc prae-
dixit: Justus, inquiens, meus ex fide victurus est.'

58 Tracy, 'Luther's Influence,' 4–5.

59 Payne, 'Lutheranizing Changes,' 318.
60 Bray, *Romans*, 32. The Latin is from Migne, *Patrologiae Cursus Completus*, 409: 'et justitiam non tuam, sed Dei; ejus largitatem et facilitatem subindicans. Neque enim ex sudore et labore illam perficis, sed ex superno dono accipis, hoc unum ex teipso afferens, quod credas.'
61 Erasmus, *Correspondence*, Letter 1804, 13: 17–18. See my discussion of this letter in chapter 1, pp. 26–7.
62 See Hausammann, *Römerbriefauslegung zwischen Humanismus und Reformation*, 64, for Bullinger's dependence on Origen and his use of this verse.
63 The English used here is found in Luther, *Bondage of the Will*, 300–1. See also WA, 18: 774–5.
64 Melanchthon, *Melanchthon's Werke*, 64, 65.
65 Romans 1:16–17, *Glossa ordinaria*.
66 Pfnür, *Einig in der Rechtfertigungslehre?* 353. Pfnür quotes from Mensing's *Antapologie*.
67 Erasmus, *Ausgewählte Schriften*, 4: 80. The English translation is from *Controversies*, 76: 42. All extracts from *De libero arbitrio* in the right-hand panel are from the same source.
68 Erasmus, *Controversies*, 76: 42.
69 Ibid., 77: 443fn449, 443, 444.
70 Erasmus, *Paraphrases*, 20. 'Nempe his, qui nunc freti promissis Euangelicis preseverant in piis operibus, ambiuntque non caduca, vanaque vitae praesentis commoda, sed vitam in coelis aeternam, pro temporaria ignominia dabit sempiternam gloriam, pro contemtu honorem, pro neglecta corporis vita immortalitatem.'
71 Erasmus, *Annotations*, 77.
72 This, in a section on Indulgences. See Cochlaeus, *Nötig und Christlich Bedenken*, 26; see Volz, *Drei Schriften*.
73 Cochlaeus, *Adversus cucullatum minotaurum wittenbergensem*, 52, 41.
74 Ibid., 37. See also Pfnür, *Einig in der Rechtfertigungslehre?* 298–9 for more on Cochlaeus's use of Romans 2:6. Pfnür notes that Johannes Dietenberger used Romans 2:6 to argue: '"Es machen also die guten Werke ihre Täter selig, d.h. sie bewegen hin zur Seligkeit und führen verdienstlich zu ihr hin"' (279).
75 Witzel, *Antwort auf Martin Luthers Artikel*, 67; see Volz, *Drei Schriften*.
76 Erasmus, *Ausgewählte Schriften*, 4: 42; *Controversies*, 76: 24.
77 Erasmus, *Controversies*, 76: 25, 26.
78 Ibid., 360, 360–1.
79 Ibid., 667–8.

80 Erasmus, *Paraphrases*, 25. Latin: '27 Ubi est ergo gloriatio tua? Esclusa est. Per quam legem? Factorum? Non: sed per legem fidei. Nimirum ademta est tibi, posteaquam divina voluntas omnes orbis
nationes aequat in negotio Euangelii, Defertur & Gentibus salus ac
justitia. At per quam tandem legem? Num veterem illam Mosaicam,
quae ceremonias praescribit? Nequaquam, imo per novam legem,
quae nihil exigit nisi fidem erga Filium Dei. 28 Arbitramur enim
enim justificari hominem per fidem sine operibus legis. Existimamus
enim, id quod res est, posthac quemvis hominem per fidem justitiam
consequi posse, etiamsi Mosaicae Legis praescripta non servet. Lex
illa peculiaris erat Genti Judaicae, verum, hoc beneficium Euangelicae gratiae ab ipso Deo proficiscitur in universos.'
81 Payne, 'Lutheranizing Changes,' 319.
82 Tracy, 'Luther's Influence,' 4, 8.
83 Pelikan, *Reformation of Church and Dogma*, 252; for additional information, see 266. Pfnür also notes that this verse served as an important foundation for the *Confessio Augustana* in establishing
justification 'through faith, not earned on the basis of the works of
the law' (Durch den Glauben = nicht durch Verdienste auf Grund
von Gestzswerken) (*Einig in der Rechtfertigungslehre?*150).
84 Wengert, *Human Freedom, Christian Righteousness*, 84. Wengert points
to Melanchthon's use of the verse in the *Dissertatio* on Col. 2:8.
85 Cochlaeus, *Nötig und Christlich Bedenken*, 8; see Volz, *Drei Schriften*.
86 Cochlaeus, *Adversus cucullatum minotaurum wittenbergensem*, 38:
'Caeterum adversus iustitiam operum legis evangelicae nusquam
disputat aut loquitur, sed bonis operibus attribuit gloriam,
honorem, pacem, mercedem, denique a Deo vitam aeternam. Iam
vides, opinor, quam facile repelantur hac una solutione omnes
impotentis vituli huius contra bona opera insultus, crepitus et
mugitus. Nam quod secundo loco ait: "Arbitramur hominem iustificari ex fide sine operibus legis," in eandem sententiam, quam dix-
imus, dictum esse accipio. Non enim simpliciter dicit: sine operibus
(ut contendit vitulus), sed ait: "sine operibus legis." Nec dicit: ex sola
fide, ut falsarius ait vitulus, sed simpliciter et sine adddito dicit: "ex
fide," quae scilicet charitate et bonis operibus est adornata et in-
structa, fides enim sola sine operibus "mortua est in semetipsa,"
teste Iacobo.'
87 Witzel, *Antwort auf Martin Luthers Artikel*, 67; see Volz, *Drei Schriften*.
Witzel also uses Romans 2:7 in the same section. See the discussion
above.

88 Erasmus, *Ausgewählte Schriften*, 4: 156; *Controversies*, 76: 73. Romans
8:26: 'Quod architectus est discipluo, hoc gratia est voluntati nostrae.
Ita Paulus ad Romanos cap. 8 (26): "Similiter et spiritus adiuvat infirmitatem nostram." Nemo vocat infirmum, qui nihil potest, sed cui
vires non sufficiunt peragendo, quod conatur, nec adiutor dicitur,
qui totum solus facit. Tota scriptura clamat adiutorium, opem, auxilium, subsidium. Quis autem adiuvare dicitur, nisi aliquid agen-
tem? Neque enim figulus adiuvat lutum, ut fiat vas, nec faber
securim, ut fiat scamnum.'

89 Erasmus, *Annotations*, 222.

90 Ibid. Boldface additions were made in 1527. Underlined text shows
change from 'addresses' to 'goes to' in 1519.

91 Erasmus, *Paraphrases*, 49–50. Latin: 'Molesta est interim afflictio juxta
carnem, verum fortasse sic expedit nobis affligi. Spiritus tamen boni
consulit, & cum corporis infirmitate pugnat, sed adspirat Dei Spiritus
adjuvans imbecillitatem carnis nostrae, & spe erigens ad omnia toler-
anda, commonstrans quid votis optandum sit, aut quid deprecandum.
Nam ipsi juxta humanum affectum nescimus quid sit optandum,
neque quomodo sit optandum. Unde non raro sit, ut pro salubribus
oremus pestifera. Quod mihi ipsi usu venit, cum aegre ferens corporis
afflictionem, improbus implorabam opem divinam, ter rogans, ut re-
linqueret me Satanas, à quo tum affligebar, & ob id negatum est, quod
postulabam, quia non expediebat impetrare. Pro jucundis data sunt
salubria. Audit quidem Deus vota suorum, si modo non precentur
juxta carnis affectum, sed juxta vocem Spiritus arcanis rationibus
agentis in nobis. Is, etiamsi ipsi sileamus, tamen pro nobis interpellat
Deum, idque non humano more, sed gemitibus inenarrabilibus.
Spiritus hominis interdum magnis suspiriis deprecatur externam af-
flicitonem, aut precatur corporalia commoda, existimans esse maxima
quae levia sunt: sed coelestis ille Spiritus insitus piorum cordibus ea
postulat, quae si absint, non referendis gemitibus sint desideranda; si
adsint, veram & absolutam adferunt beatitudinem.'

92 Bray, *Romans*, 230. The Latin is from Migne, *Patrologiae Cursus Completus*, 533: 'Quia enim multa corum, quae nobis utilia sunt, ignor-
antes, inutilia postulamus, donum orationis ad quempiam corum,
qui tun erant, veniebat, et quod toti Ecclesiae conducebat, id ille
stans postulabat, aliosque docebat.'

93 Melanchthon, *Opera quae supersunt omnia*, 21: 376. See also Pfnür,
Einig in der Rechtfertigungslehre? 130–1, for a discussion of this point.
Pfnür notes that in the 1559 edition of *Loci Communes* Melanchthon
clarified the point.

94 Erasmus, *Annotations*, 222.

95 Malanchthon, *Opera quae supersunt omnia*, 21: 659.

96 Erasmus, *Controversies*, 76: 46; *Ausgewählte Schriften*, 4: 90: 'Nunc tempus est, ut ex adverso recenseamus aliquot scripturarum testimonia, quae videntur prorsus tollere liberum arbitrium. Ea sane nonnulla sunt obvia nobis in sacris voluminibus, sed in his duo praecipua sunt ac ceteris evidentiora, quorum utrumque sic tractat Paulus apostolus, ut prima specie nihil omnino tribuere videatur vel operibus nostris vel liberi arbitrii viribus. Alter locus est Exodi cap. 9 (12,16) et tractatur a Paulo epistolae ad Romans cap. non (14sq): "Induravitque dominus cor Pharonis et non audivit eos." Et rursus: "Idcirco autem posui te, ut ostendam in te fortitudinem meam et narretur nomen meum in omni terra." Paulus sic explicat adducens similem locum, qui est Exodi trigesimosecundo: "Mosi enim dixit: Miserebor, cuicumque misereor, et commiserabor, quemcumque commiseror. Igitur non volentis neque currentis, sen miserentis est dei."'

97 Erasmus, *Controversies*, 76: 46.

98 Ibid., 48, 46. See especially fn216. The editors of CWE, Vol. 76, add in footnote 16: 'Erasmus refers to prevenient, cooperating, and persevering grace.' The Latin is from *Ausgewählte Schriften*, 4: 96: 'Quemadmodum igitur malorum conatus vertit in bonum piorum, ita bonorum conatus non assequuntur, quod expentunt, nisi adiuti gratuito dei favore. Nimirum hoc est, quod subicit Paulus: "Igitur non volentis neque currentis, sed miserentis est dei." Praevenit dei misericordia voluntatem nostram, comitatur eandem in conando, dat felicem eventum. Et tamen interim volumus, currimus, assequimur, sic tamen, ut hoc ipsum, quod nostrum est, ascribamus deo, cuius sumus toti.'

99 Erasmus, *Controversies* 77: 500, 502, 532.

100 Erasmus, *Annotations*, 261fnn1, 2.

101 Payne, 'Lutheranizing Changes,' 323.

102 Erasmus, *Annotations*, 261.

103 Payne, 'Lutheranizing Changes,' 324.

104 Erasmus, *Paraphrases*, 55. Latin: 'Quum non sit volentis aut currentis assequi salutem, sed miserentis Dei, quandoquidem frustra cupimus, frustra adnitimur, nisi Deus volens nos attraxerit: attrahit autem, quos illis visum est, etiam nihil promeritos, & rejicit nihil commeritos. Nec tamen hinc consequitur, Deum in quenquam esse injurium, sed in multos misericordem. Nemo damnatur, nisi sua culpa: nemo servatur, nisi Dei beneficio: eo dignatur quos vult, sed ita, ut sit de quo gratias agas, misericorditer attractus, non sit quod quereris tuae malitiae derelictus.'

105 Tracy, 'Luther's Influence,' 7. Tracy says that the change in the paraphrase took place 'between 1521 and 1523,' but I find the first evidence of this change in the 1532 Froben edition.
106 See Pfnür, *Einig in der Rechtfertigungslehre?* 361–2.
107 Melanchthon, *Melanchthon's Werke*, 261.
108 Erasmus, *Ausgewählte Schriften*, 4: 110; *Controversies*, 76: 54–6. 'For Paul recounts them as follows: "Does the potter not have power to make the same lump of clay into one vessel for honourable use, and another for menial use? What if God, wishing to show his anger and make known his power, has very patiently tolerated vessels of anger due for destruction, so as to manifest the riches of his glory for the vessels of mercy which he has prepared for glory? Etc."'
109 Erasmus, *Controversies*, 76: 55.
110 Ibid., 77: 482, 501, 503, 506, 510, 548, 551, 553–7, 565, 510, 503.
111 Tracy, 'Luther's Influence,' 8.
112 Erasmus, *Paraphrases*, 56. Latin: 'Quod lutum est in manu figuli, hoc omnes sumus in manu Dei: quemadmodum per Esaiam Prophetam loguitur ipse Dominus. Ille fingit quodcunque animo suo collibuit, aliud vas in sordidos usus, aliud in honestos producens. Quocunque judicio id facit, suo jure facit figulus, nec convenit lutum consilii rationem ab illo exigere. Lutum ex sese nihil aliud est quam lutum. Ex eo si figulus fingit poculum elegans, quicquid hoc est honoris debet suo artifici: sin matulam, nulla sordido vilique luto fit injuria. Ita si Deus deserit hominem in peccatis, sic natus est, nulla est injuria: sin vocat ad justitiam, gratuita est misercordia. In illis Deus declarat suam justitiam, ut timeatur: in his patefacit suam bonitatem, ut ametur. Nec est hominis à Deo consilii rationem exigere, cur hunc vocet serius, illum maturius, hunc attrahat immeritum, illum deserat nihil promeritum. Longe vilior est homo collatus cum Deo, quam argilla collata cum homine figulo. Si prodigiosae sit arrogantiae, lutum argutari cum figulo: quanto majoris arrogantiae est, hominem de consiliis Dei disceptare? Quae tanto supra nos sunt, ut vix umbram aut somnium possimus assequi? Incipe credere, & desine disceptare, atque ita citius intelliges. Et figulus errare potest, Deus non potest. Illud tibi satis est credere, Deum, cum sit omnipotens, posse quicquid vult: sed eundem cum sit optimus, non velle nisi quod optimum est. Neque culpari debet, si nostris malis bene utitur. Immo hoc ipsum summae bonitatis est argumentum, quod aliena mala vertat in bonum. Deus non finxit te vas immundum. Tu teipsum conspurcasti, & inhonestis usibus addixisti. Post haec, si ille pro sua sapientia, tuo malo abutitur ad

salutem piorum, suique nominis gloriam, nihil est hinc tibi quod
queraris. Tu tuae malitiae justas poenas luis, pii tuo exemplo cau-
tiores redduntur, & alacrius agunt gratias, dum ex tua caecitate,
tuoque exitio magis agnoscunt, quantum debeant divinae benefi-
centiae. Non habebat Pharao quod incusaret Deum, suapte malitia
subversus est, & tamen hujus malitia gloriam Dei illustravit apud
Hebraeos. Quid vero sit quod incusent, si nunc item Deus ut olim
distulit exitium Pharaonis, diu multaque lenitate sustinet ac tolerat
incredulos ac pertinaces Judaeos, ceu vasa merita, quae mox con-
fringantur, quo magis evidens fiat omnibus, illos esse exitio dignos,
qui tot modis provocati, corrigi non queant: simulque ut illorum
supplicio caeteri metuant Deum omnipotentem, quem non oportet
sine fine peccando ad certam iram provocare:Utque copiosius os-
tendat gloriae suae magnitudinem erga pios, quos prius vasa im-
munda purgavit, & honestis usibus consecravit, non ex
circumcisionis aut Legis, sed ex fidei merito, cujus unius commen-
datione adsciti sunt ad hoc honoris.'

113 Bray, *Romans*, 264. The Latin is from Migne, *Patrologiae Cursus Completus*, 561: 'Unde igitur hi vasa irae, illi misericordiae? Ex proprio
voluntatis proposito Deus autem valde bonus cum sit, in ambobus
eamdem ostendit benignitatem.'

114 Ibid., 262.

115 Luther, *Lectures on Romans*, 395. WA, 56: 405: 'Sola enim gratia dis-
cernit redemptos a perditis, Quos in vnam perditionis massam con-
creuerat ab origine ducta causa communis.' Istis itaque verbis
efficitur, vt homo agnoscat suam damnationem et desperet suis
viribus saluus fieri, Quod alias frigide cogitat, si tantummodo in
Adam se cecidisse intelligit. vnde se per liberum arbitrium surrec-
turum sperat, immo presumit. Hic autem discit, quod gratia ipsum
suscitat ante omne arbitrium et supra arbitrium suum.'

116 Erasmus, *Ausgewählte Schriften*, 4: 108–9; *Controversies*, 76: 54. Note
that the portion of this excerpt reproduced here shows only the
quotation of Romans 11:25, not Romans 11:20.

117 Erasmus, *Controversies*, 76: 54.

118 Erasmus also refers to the verse in the *Hyperaspistes II*; see *Controversies*, 77: 545fn835.

119 Erasmus, *Paraphrases*, 67. Latin: '25 Aperiam vobis fratres arcanum
quiddam, quod fortasse silentio tegendum erat, nisi vestra referret
me loqui, videlicet ne vobis arroganter placeatis, quod Judaeis
praelati videamini. Incidit haec caecitas in gentem Judaicam, sed
nec in universam, nec in perpetuum. Complures & hinc agnoscunt

Christum, & caeteri tantisper in sua caecitate persistent, donec
Gentium numerus fuerit expletus, quibus nunc Judaeorum lapsus
aditum aperuit. 26 Verum ubi viderint universum orbem florere
professione fidei Christianae, suum illum Messiam frustra ex-
spectari, urbem, templum, sacra, gentem dissipatam ac sparsam,
incipient receptis oculis tandem errorem suum agnoscere, & intel-
ligent Christum verum esse Messiam. Atque ita totus Israeliticus
populus ad salutem restituetur, quamvis nunc ex parte degenerarit.
Tum enim vere dignus erit hoc cognomine, cum Chistum Deum ac
Dei Filium oculis fidei cernere coeperit, ac fide robustus, magis
quam operum fiducia, à Domino extorserit benedicitonem. Quod
quo magis credatis, praedictum est hoc quoque ab Esaia Propheta.
Utrunque praedictum est, fore ut deciderent, fore ut resipiscant:
alterum videmus evenisse, atque ipsa res fidem arrogat vaticinio:
alterum exspectamus simili fide eventurum. Sic autem habet vaticinium Cap. V. Veniet ex Sion, qui eripiet & avertet impietatem ab
Jacob, & hoc illis à me testamentum, cum abstulero peccata eorum.'

120 Payne, 'Lutheranizing Changes,' 320fn33. Tracy, 'Luther's Influence,'
     8fn49.
121 Melanchthon, *Melanchthon's Werke*, 279.
122 McSorley, *Luther: Right or Wrong*, 304. Paul Althaus explains it this
     way: 'For the believer it is a great comfort to know that God himself
     works faith in him. This takes salvation out of his own hand, so that
     his weakness and tendency to fall into Satan's traps need not destroy
     the unshakeable basis of his faith. The fact that God works all things
     in my heart, that is, that my will is bound, makes me certain of salva-
     tion. For the godless, however, God's almighty working in the heart
     is a terrible reality. God works even in Satan and in the godless. They
     too – just as they are – are moved, driven, and pulled along by the
     energy of God's working in all' (*Theology of Martin Luther*, 113).
123 For a complete explanation of Luther's rejection, see Petri, *Glaube
     und Gotteserkenntnis*, 13. For Melanchthon's relationship to the doc-
     trine, see the same volume, 19.
124 Heiko Oberman writes: 'The "fides Christo formata" replaces the
     medieval "fides charitate formata"; in other words, "faith living in
     Christ" has come in the stead of "faith active in love" as it had been
     formulated and defined in a unanimous medieval tradition and as
     it can be found with Thomas Aquinas, Duns Scotus, Gabriel Biel, et
     al., including the Council of Trent' (*Dawn of the Reformation*, 120).
125 See Meijering, *Human Freedom, Christian Righteousness*, 156ff.
     Meijering notes: 'Melanchthon, evangelical theologian and

humanist, was no Erasmian and that especially in the late 1520s he staked out positions in biblical interpretation and theology that expressly contradicted Erasmus' own,' 156. He also notes a 'shift in Melanchthon's theological position and its expression in the 1530s. He did develop what has been termed a hermeneutics of moderation in the years after the 1530 diet of Augsburg in order to avoid speculation and to comfort the weak. However, the identification of these shifts with Erasmus misses the mark' (157).

CONCLUSION

1 Note that John Payne also discusses the importance of this letter; see 'Lutheranizing Changes,' 325. Allen, *Opvs Epistolarvm Des*, 7: 8, lines 75–95. My English translation. 'Iam mihi finge nec ocium deesse nec vires. Si tractauero materiam ex animo monachorum ac theologorum, qui nimium tribuunt hominum meritis ob questum hinc redeuntem, profecto loquar aduersus conscientiam meam, et sciens obscurabo gloriam Christi. Sin temperauero stilum ut aliquid tribuam libero arbitrio, gratiae plurimum, offendam vtranque partmem: quod mihi venit vsu in Diatriba. Quod si sequar Paulum et Augustinum, perpusillum est quod relinquitur libero arbitrio: Hic enim duobus libris quods scripsit ad Valentinum iam senex, asseuerat quidem liberum arbitrium. Sed gratiam sic probat vt ego non perspiciam quid reliquum faciat libero arbitrio. Fatetur opera ante gratiam facta esse mortua, tribuit gratiae quod resipisciumus, quod voumus benefacetere, quod bene facimus, quod perseueramus. Fatetur hec omnia gratiam in nobis operari. Vbi igitur merita? Hic constrictus Augustinus huc confugit, vt dictat Deum sua bona opera nobis imputare pro meritis et sua dona coronare in nobis. Nonne belle que putat nos ex meris nature viribus absque peculiari gratia posse de congruo, vt illi loquuntur, gratiam instituere, nisi refragaretur Paulus: quanquam ne scholastici quidem hanc recipiunt sententiam.'
2 Payne, 'Lutheranizing Changes,' 326.
3 Nauert, *Humanism*, 144.
4 See Tracy, 'Erasmus among the Postmodernists,' 14.
5 Meijering, *Melanchthon and Patristic Thought* , 45.
6 Ibid., fn129: '*Postilla Melanchthonia (CR 25), p. 320:* ... errata non pauca sunt in Ambrosio et Augustino, multo plura in Chrysostomo.'
7 Ibid., 46, 48, 49, 84.
8 Ibid., 133, 134, 138, 134–5 (fnn130, 131), 136.

9 Ibid., 137.

10 This is my translation of Petri, *Glaube und Gotteserkenntnis*, 11.

11 Ibid.

12 Schulze, 'Martin Luther,' 573–626.

13 den Boeft, 'Erasmus and the Church Fathers,' 557–60.

14 Schulze, 'Martin Luther,' 579.

15 Meijering, *Melanchthon and Patristic Thought*, 49.

16 Schulze, 'Martin Luther,' 583, 597–8, 601–3.

17 Tracy, *Erasmus of the Low Countries*, 152–3.

18 Ibid., 179–82, 185.

19 Backus, 'Erasmus and Spirituality,' 112.

20 Petri, *Glaube und Gotteserkenntnis*, 44.

21 Ibid., 35. 'Das Konzil tat sich mit dieser Materie so schwer, weil es in der Lehre über die Rechtfertigung einen entscheidenden Differenzpunkt zur Reformation gesehen hat und weil es in dieser Frage auch unter katholischen Theologen beträchtliche Meinungsverschiedenheiten gab … Schliesslich betont das Konzil, dass keineswegs mit jeder schwere Sünde auch der Glaube selber verloren geht (Kap. 15).'

22 Oberman, *Dawn of the Reformation*, 119, 120.

23 Petri, *Glaube und Gotteserkenntnis*: 'Schliesslich waren eine Reihe von Konsequenzen, die sich aus dem Sola- fide-Prinzip der Reformation ergeben konnten oder auch tatsächlich gezogen worden waren, zurückzuwiesen und positive das Verhaeltnis des Glaubens zu den anderen Tugenden (wie Hoffnung und Liebe) aber auch zu den Sakramenten und den guten Werken aufzuzeigen' (36).

24 Ibid.: 'Der Geist bewirkt die Rechtfertigung dadurch, dass er den Willen und den Verstand des Menschen zur Umkehr zu Gott bewegt. Die Bewegung der menschlichen Seele beginnt im Willen, der nun im Gehorsam gegenüber Gott dem Vertsand befiehlt, der Offenbarung Gottes zuzustimmen und seinen Verheissungen zu vertauen. Als Inhalt der Verheissungen nennt Contarini die Vergebung der Sünden und die Rechtfertigung des Sünders um Christi Willen. Damit stellt auch er den Glauben zunächst in den Kontext der Vorbereitung und der Disposition auf die eigentliche Rechtfertigung' (33).

25 Ibid.: 'Diese in der Auseinanderesetzung mit der protestantischen Theologie entwickelte Lehre fand nicht die Bestätigung des Konzils, wozu nach Jedin u. a. wohl auch beigetragen hat, dass die diesbezügliche, den Theologen vorgelegte Frage nicht ganz der Auffassung Seripandos entsprach. Vor allem hätte die positive Beantwortung des zweiten Teils der Frage zur Folge gehabt, dass man eine weitere Applikation oder Imputation der Gerechtikeit Christi bei Endgericht

hätte annehmen müssen. Die Lehre von der doppelten Gerechtigkeit konnte sicher als ein gewisses Entgegenkommen gegenüber der reformatorischen Auffassung verstanden werden, zumal sie ja auch in der Auseinandersetzung mit den Protestanten entwicket worden war und in reformatischen Äusserungen einige Anhaltspunkte besass. Bei Seripando zum mindesten ist aber auch auf ein spirituelles Anliegen hinzuweisen. Danach steht es dem Menschen nicht an, auf die eigene, durch gute Werke zu erringende Gerechtigkeit zu vertrauen, selbst wenn diese Werke nur im Gnadenstand und mt Hilfe der Gnade getan werden koennen. Wenn das Konzil diese Auffassung nicht billigte, ist sie doch nicht formell verurteilt worden. Das Berechtigte an dieser Lehre hat das Konzil wohl in dem Abschnitt ueber die Heilsgewissheit zur Geltung kommen lassen' (39–40).

26 O'Malley, 'Erasmus and Luther,' 50.
27 Erasmus, *Correspondence*, Letter 1770, 12: 415, 417, 419.

Bibliography

꽃

Allen, P.S., H.M. Allen, and H.W. Garrod ed. *Opvs Epistolarvm Des. Erasmi Roterodami* [1527–8]. Vol. 7. 11 vols. Oxford: Oxford University Press, 1928.

Althaus, Paul. *The Theology of Martin Luther*. Trans. *Robert C. Schultz*. Philadelphia: Fortress Press, 1966.

Anderson, H.G., T. Austin Murphy, and Joseph A. Burgess, eds. *Justification by Faith: Lutherans and Catholics in Dialogue VII*. Minneapolis: Augsburg, 1985.

Augustijn, C. 'Hyperaspistes I et 'Claritas Scripturae.' In *Le Christianisme D'Érasme: Sources, Modalités, Controverses, Influences*. Vol. 5. Limoges, France: Imprimerie A. Bontemps, 1972.

Backus, Irena. 'Erasmus and the Spirituality of the Early Church.' In *Erasmus' Vision of the Church*, ed. Hilmer Pabel. Kirksville, Mo.: Sixteenth Century Journal, 1995.

Bainton, R.H. *Erasmus of Christendom*. New York: Scribner, 1969.

Bateman, John J. 'The Textual Travail of the *Tomus Secundus* of the *Paraphrases*.' In *Holy Scripture Speaks: The Production and Reception of Erasmus' 'Paraphrases on the New Testament,'* ed. Hilmar M. Pabel and Mark Vessey. Toronto: University of Toronto Press, 2002.

Bentley, Jerry H. *Humanists and Holy Writ: New Testament Scholarship in the Renaissance*. Princeton, N.J.: Princeton University Press, 1983.

Biblia latina cum glossa ordinaria. Facsimile reprint of the Edition of Princeps Adolph Rusch of Strassburg, 1480/81. Vol. 4. Ed. Karlfried Froehlich and Margaret T. Gibson. Brepols: Turnhout, 1992.

Blickle, Peter. *The Revolution of 1525: The German Peasants' War from a New Perspective*. Baltimore: Johns Hopkins University Press, 1981.

Bonner, Gerald. *Augustine and Modern Research on Pelagianism*. Wetteren, Belgium: Villanova University Press, 1972.

Boisset, J. 'Le Christianisme Érasme dans la *Diatribe sur le Libre Arbitre.'*
    In *Le Christianisme D'Érasme: Sources, Modalités, Controverses,*
    Influences. Vol. 5. Limoges, France: Imprimerie A. Bontemps, 1972.
Bray, Gerald, ed. *Romans.* Vol. 6 of Ancient Christian Commentary on
    Scripture. Downers Grove, Ill.: Intervarsity Press, 1998.
Brecht, Martin. *Martin Luther: Shaping and Defining the Reformation,*
    1521–1532. Vol. 2. Trans. James L. Schaaf. Minneapolis: Fortress Press,
    1990.
Cameron, Euan. *The European Reformation.* Oxford: Oxford University
    Press, 1991.
Chomarat, J. 'Sur Érasme et Origène.' In *Colloque Érasmien de Liège,*
    ed. J.-P. Massaut. Paris: Les Belles Lettres, 1987.
Chrysostom, John. *The Homilies of S. John Chrysostom, Archbishop of*
    Constantinople, on the Epistle of St. Paul the Apostle to the Romans. Trans.
    Members of the English Church. Vol. 7 of A Library of Fathers of the
    Holy Catholic Church, Anterior to the Division of the East and West.
    Oxford: John Henry Parker, 1841.
Cochlaeus, J. *Adversus cucullatum minotaurum wittenbergensem: de*
    sacramentorum gratia iterum 1523. Vol. 3 of CC. 1920.
– *Commentaria Ioannis Cochlaei, de actis et scriptis Martini Lutheri Saxonis.*
    Mainz: Franz Behem, 1549. Reprint Farnborough, U.K.: Gregg Press,
    1968.
– *Ein Nötig und Christlich Bedenken auf des Luthers Artikeln.* In CC,
    Vol. 18. See Volz, *Drei Schriften.*
– *Philippicae I–VII.* Vols 1 and 2. Ed. Ralph Keen. Nieuwkoop: De Graaf,
    1995.
Contarini, Gasparo. *De justificatione* In *Gasparo Contarini: Gegenreforma-*
    torische Schriften (1530–c.1542). Ed. Dr Friedrich Hunermann. Vol. 7 of
    CC. 1923.
Corpus Catholicorum (CC). Werke katholischer Schriftsteller im Zeitalter
    der Glaubensspaltung. Collected writings of leading sixteeth-century
    defenders of the Roman Catholic Church in the time of the
    Reformation. 48 vols. Reprint Münster in Westfalen: Aschendorff, 1919–
Corpus Reformatorum (CR). Collected works of Reformation writings
    by John Calvin, Philip Melanchthon, and Huldrych Zwingli. 101 vols.
    Halle, 1834–. Reprint New York: Johnson Reprint Corp., 1963.
den Boeft, Jan. 'Erasmus and the Church Fathers.' In *The Reception of the*
    Church Fathers in the West: From the Carolingians to the Maurists. 2 vols.
    Ed. I. Backus. Leiden: Brill, 1997.
– 'Illic aureum quoddam ire flumen.' In Weiland and Frijhoff, *Erasmus*
    of Rotterdam.

Dolan, John Patrick, C.S.C. *The Influence of Erasmus, Witzel and Cassander in the Church Ordinances and Reform Proposals of the United Duchees of Cleve during the Middle Decades of the 16th Century*. Münster in Westfalen: Aschendorffsche, 1957.
– 'Liturgical Reform among the Irenicists.' *Sixteenth Century Essays and Studies* 2 (January 1971): 72–94.
Elert, Werner. *The Structure of Lutheranism*. Vol. 1. Trans. Walter A. Hansen. St. Louis, Mo.: Concordia, 1962.
Erasmus, Desiderius. *Ausgewählte Schriften*. Vol. 3. Ed. and trans. Gerhard B. Winkler. Darmstadt: Wissenschaftliche Buchgesellschaft, 1967. Vol. 4. Ed. and trans. Winfried Lesowsky. Darmstadt: Wissenschaftliche Buchgesellschaft, 1969.
– *Controversies: De libero arbitrio / Hyperaspistes I*. Ed. Charles Trinkaus. Vol. 76 of Collected Works of Erasmus. Toronto: University of Toronto Press, 1999.
– *Controversies: Hyperaspistes II*. Ed. Charles Trinkaus. Trans. Clarence H. Miller. Vol. 77 of Collected Works of Erasmus. Toronto: University of Toronto Press, 2000.
– *The Correspondence of Erasmus: Letters 1535–1657 (1525)*. Trans. Alexander Dalzell. Ann. Charles G. Nauert. Vol. 11 of Collected Works of Erasmus. Toronto: University of Toronto Press, 1994.
– *The Correspondence of Erasmus: Letters 1658–1801 (1526–27)*. Trans. Alexander Dalzell. Ann. Charles G. Nauert. Vol. 12 of Collected Works of Erasmus. Toronto: University of Toronto Press, 2003.
– *The Correspondence of Erasmus*. Ed. James Farge. Trans. Charles Fantazzi. Vol. 13 of Collected Works of Erasmus. Toronto: University of Toronto Press, forthcoming.
– *New Testament Scholarship: Annotations on Romans*. Ed. Robert D. Sider. Vol. 56 of Collected Works of Erasmus. Toronto: University of Toronto Press, 1994.
– *New Testament Scholarship: Paraphrases on Romans and Galatians*. Ed. Robert D. Sider. Trans. John B. Payne, Albert Rabil Jr, and Warren S. Smith Jr. Vol. 42 of Collected Works of Erasmus. Toronto: University of Toronto Press, 1984.
– *Opera omnia* (LB) [1703–6]. Ed. Jean Leclerc. 10 vols. Hildesheim: G. Holms, 1961–2.
Fredriksen Landes, Paula. *Augustine on Romans: Propositions from the Epistle to the Romans Unfinished Commentary on the Epistle to the Romans*. Chico, Calif.: Scholars Press, 1982.
Froehlich, Karlfried. 'Justification Language in the Middle Ages.' In Anderson, Murphy, and Burgess, *Justification by Faith*.

Galbraith, Elizabeth. 'Kant, Luther, and Erasmus on the Freedom of the Will.' In *Human and Divine Agency: Anglican, Catholic, and Lutheran Perspectives*. Ed. F. Michael McLain and W. Mark Richardson. New York: University Press of America, 1999.

Gilmore, Myron P. 'Erasmus and Alberto Pio, Prince of Carpi.' In *Action and Conviction in Early Modern Europe: Essays in Memory of E.H. Harbison*. Ed. Theodore K. Rabb and Jerrold E. Seigel. Princeton: Princeton University Press, 1969.

– 'Italian Reactions to Erasmian Humanism.' In *Itinerarium Italicum: The Profile of the Italian Renaissance in the Mirror of its European Transformations*. Leiden: Brill, 1975.

– *The World of Humanism, 1453–1517*. New York: Harper and Row, 1952.

Gleason, John B. *John Colet*. Berkeley: University of California Press, 1989.

Gorday, Peter. *Principles of Patristic Exegesis: Romans 9–11 in Origen, John Chrysostom, and Augustine*. Vol. 4 of Studies in the Bible and Early Christianity. New York: Edwin Mellen Press, 1983.

Grane, Leif, et al. *Auctoritas Patrum*. Mainz: Verlag Philipp von Zabern, 1993.

Hagen, Kenneth, ed. *Augustine, the Harvest, and Theology (1300–1650): Essays Dedicated to Heiko Augustinus Oberman in Honor of His Sixtieth Birthday*. Leiden: Brill, 1990.

Hausammann, Susi. *Römerbriefauslegung zwischen Humanismus und Reformation: Eine Studie zu Heinrich Bullingers Römerbriefvorlesung von 1525*. Zurich: Zwingli Verlag, 1970.

Henze, Barbara. *Aus Liebe zur Kirche Reform: Die Bemühungen Georg Witzels (1501–1573) um die Kircheneinheit*. Münster in Westfalen: Aschendorff, 1995.

Hoffmann, Manfred. 'Faith and Piety in Erasmus's Thought.' *Sixteenth Century Journal* 20, 2 (1989): 241–58.

– *Rhetoric and Theology: The Hermeneutic of Erasmus*. Toronto: University of Toronto Press, 1994.

Jedin, Hubert. *A History of the Council of Trent*. 2 vols. Trans. Ernest Graf. Edinburgh: Thomas Nelson, 1961.

Junghans, Helmar. *Junge Luther und die Humanisten*. Tübingen: Buchhandlung Gastl, 1985.

Kleinhans, Robert G. 'Luther and Erasmus: Another Perspective.' *Church History* 39 (1970): 469.

Lohse, Bernhard. *Martin Luther: An Introduction to His Life and Work*. Ed. Robert C. Schultz. Philadelphia: Fortress Press, 1986.

Luther, Martin. *The Bondage of the Will*. Trans. J.R. Packer and O.R. Johnston. Grand Rapids, Mich.: Revell, 1998.

– *D. Martin Luthers Werke, Kritische Gesamtausgabe* (WA). 65 vols. Weimar: Hermann Böhlaus, 1883–.
– *Lectures on Romans. Glosses and Scholia.* Ed. Hilton C. Oswald. Vol. 25 of *Luther's Works*. Philadelphia: Westminster, 1961.
Margolin, Jean-Claude. 'Le Commentaire d'Érasme au Psaume I.' In *Les Paraphrases Bibliques aux XVIᵉ et XVIIᵉ Siècles: Actes du Colloque de Bordeaux des 22, 23, et 24 Septembre 2004*, ed. Véronique Ferrer and Anne Mantero. Geneva: Librairie Droz, 2006.
McGrath, Alister E. *Iustitia Dei: A History of the Christian Doctrine of Justification.* 1986. 2nd ed. Cambridge: Cambridge University Press, 1998.
– *Reformation Thought: An Introduction.* 3rd ed. Oxford: Blackwell, 1999.
McSorley, Harry J., C.S.P. *Luther: Right or Wrong? An Ecumenical-Theological Study of Luther's Major Work,* The Bondage of the Will. New York: Newman Press, 1969.
Meijering, E. P. *Melanchthon and Patristic Thought: The Doctrines of Christ and Grace, the Trinity and the Creation.* Leiden: Brill, 1983.
Melanchthon, Philip. *Commentary on Romans* (1540). Trans. Fred Kramer. St. Louis, Mo.: Concordia, 1992.
– *Melanchthon on Christian Doctrine: Loci Communes, 1555.* Ed. and trans. Clyde L. Manschreck. New York: Oxford University Press, 1965.
– *Melanchthon's Werke.* Ed. Rolf Schäfer. Vol. 5 of Römerbrief-Kommentar 1532. Gütersloh: Verlagshaus Gerd Mohn, 1983.
– *Philipp Melanchthon: Werke in Auswahl.* [Studienausgabe]. (St.A). 9 vols. Ed. Robert Stupperich. Gütersloh: Gerd Mohn, 1951–75.
– *Opera quae supersunt omnia.* Vol. 15. Ed. Carolus Gottlieb Bretschneider. Halle: C.A. Schwetschke, 1848. Vol. 21. Ed. Henricus Ernestus Bindseil. Brunswick: C.A. Schwetschke, 1854. CR
Migne, J.-P. *Patrologiae Cursus Completus.* Brepols: Turnholt, 1978.
Nauert, Charles. *Humanism and the Culture of Renaissance Europe.* Cambridge: Cambridge University Press, 1995.
New Oxford Annotated Bible, The. New Revised Standard Version (NRSV). Ed. Michael D. Coogan et al. 3rd ed. Oxford: Oxford University Press, 2001.
Oakley, Francis. *The Western Church in the Later Middle Ages.* Ithaca, N.Y.: Cornell University Press, 1979.
Oberman, Heiko A. *The Dawn of the Reformation: Essays in Late Medieval and Early Reformation Thought.* Edinburgh: T. and T. Clark, 1986.
– *The Harvest of Medieval Theology.* Grand Rapids, Mich.: Baker Academic, 1983.
– *Luther: Man between God and the Devil.* Trans. Eileen Walliser-Schwarzbart. New York: Image, 1992.

Oberman, Heiko A., and Frank A. James III, with Eric Leland Saak, eds. *Via Augustini: Augustine in the later Middle Ages, Renaissance, and Reformation. Essays in Honor of Damasus Trapp.* Leiden: Brill, 1991.

Olin, John C. *Six Essays on Erasmus and a Translation of Erasmus' Letter to Carondelet, 1523.* New York: Fordham University Press, 1979.

Olin, John C., Robert E. McNally, and James D. Smart, eds. *Luther, Erasmus and the Reformation: A Catholic Reappraisal.* New York: Fordham University Press, 1969.

O'Malley, John W. 'Erasmus and Luther: Continuity and Discontinuity as Key to their Conflict.' *Sixteenth Century Journal* 5 (October 1974): 47–65.

Pabel, Hilmar. *Herculean Labours: Erasmus and the Editing of St. Jerome's Letters in the Renaissance.* Leiden: Brill, 2008.

Padberg, Rudolf. 'Glaubenstheologie und Glaubensverkundigung bei Erasmus: Dargestellt auf der Grundlage der Paraphrase zum Römerbrief.' In *Verkundigung und Glaube: Festgabe für Franz X. Arnold,* ed. Theodor Filthaut and Josepf Andreas Jungmann. Freiburg: Verlag Herder, 1958.

Payne, John B. 'Erasmus and Lefèvre d'Étaples as Interpreters of Paul.' *Archiv für Reformationsgeschichte* 65 (1974): 54–9.

– 'The Significance of Lutheranizing Changes in Erasmus' Interpretation of Paul's Letters to the Romans and Galatians in His *Annotations* (1527) and *Paraphrases* (1532).' In *Histoire de l'exégèse au XVIe siècle: Textes du colloque international tenu à Genève en 1976,* ed. Olivier Fatio and Pierre Fraenkel. Geneva: Droz, 1978.

Pelikan, Jaroslav. *The Growth of Medieval Theology (600–1300).* Vol. 3 of Pelikan, *The Christian Tradition: A History of the Development of Doctrine.* Chicago: University of Chicago Press, 1978.

– *The Reformation of Church and Dogma (1300–1700).* Vol. 4 of *The Christian Tradition,* 1983.

Petri, Heinrich. *Glaube und Gotteserkenntnis: Von der Reformation bis zur Gegenwart.* Vol. 1 in Handbuch der Dogmengeschichte. Freiburg: Herder, 1985.

Pfnür, Vinzenz. *Einig in der Rechtfertigungslehre? Die Rechtfertigungslehre der Confessio Augustana (1530) und die Stellungnahme der katholischen Kontroverstheologie zwischen 1530 und 1535.* Wiesbaden: Steiner, 1970.

Rabil, Albert. *Erasmus and the New Testament: The Mind of a Christian Humanist.* San Antonio, Tex.: Trinity University Press, 1971.

Raitt, Jill. 'From Augsburg to Trent.' In *Justification by Faith: Lutherans and Catholics in Dialogue VII,* ed. H. George Anderson, T. Austin Murphy, and Joseph A. Burgess. Minneapolis: Augsburg, 1985.

Reeve, Anne, with M.A. Screech, eds. *Erasmus' Annotations on the New Testament: Acts, Romans, I and II Corinthians; Facsimile of the Final Latin Text with All Earlier Variants.* Leiden: Brill, 1990.

Rummel, Erika, ed. *Biblical Humanism and Scholasticism in the Age of Erasmus.* Leiden: Brill, 2008.

– *The Confessionalization of Humanism in Reformation Germany.* Oxford: Oxford University Press, 2000.

– *Erasmus' Annotations on the New Testament: From Philologist to Theologian.* Toronto: University of Toronto Press, 1986.

– *Erasmus and His Catholic Critics.* Nieuwkoop: De Graaf, 1989.

Saak, Eric L. *High Way to Heaven: The Augustinian Platform between Reform and Reformation, 1292–1524.* Leiden: Brill, 2002.

Sanday, W., and B.D. Headlam. *The International Critical Commentary: Romans.* Edinburgh: T. and T. Clark, 1869.

Schäfer, Rolf. 'Melanchthon's Interpretation of Romans 5.15: His Departure from the Augustinian Concept of Grace Compared to Luther's.' In *Philip Melanchthon (1497–1560) and the Commentary,* ed. Timothy J. Wengert and M. Patrick Graham. Sheffield, U.K.: Sheffield Academic Press, 1997.

Schelkle, Karl Hermann. *Paulus Lehrer der Väter: Die altkirchliche Auslegung von Römer 1–11.* Dusseldorf: Patmos-Verlag, 1956.

Schulze, Manfred. 'Martin Luther and the Church Fathers.' In *The Reception of the Church Fathers in the West: From the Carolingians to the Maurists.* Vol. 2. Ed. Irena Backus. Leiden: Brill, 1997.

Smith, Preserved. *Erasmus: A Study of His Life, Ideals and Place in History.* New York: Frederick Ungar, 1962.

Souter, Alexander. *The Earliest Latin Commentaries on the Epistles of St. Paul: A Study.* Oxford: Clarendon Press, 1927.

Tracy, James D. Review of *Érasme: Lecteur d'Origène* by André Godin. *Renaissance Quarterly* 37 (1984): 441–4.

– 'Erasmus among the Postmodernists.' In *Erasmus' Vision of the Church,* ed. Hilmar M. Pabel. Kirksville, Mo.: Sixteenth Century Journal, 1995.

– *Erasmus of the Low Countries.* Berkeley: University of California Press, 1996.

– 'Luther's Influence on Erasmus' Concept of Faith.' Paper presented at the Central Renaissance Conference, Denton, Tex., 1968.

– 'Two Erasmuses, Two Luthers: Erasmus's Strategy in Defense of *De Libero Arbitrio.*' *Archiv für Reformationsgeschichte* 78 (1987): 37–60.

Trinkaus, Charles. 'Erasmus, Augustine, and the Nominalists.' In *Archiv für Reformationsgeschichte* 67 (1976): 5–32.

– 'The Problem of Free Will in the Renaissance and the Reformation.'
  Journal of the History of Ideas 10, 1 (1949): 51–62.
Vandiver, Elizabeth, Ralph Keen, and Thomas D. Frazel, trans. and ann.
  Luther's Lives: Two Contemporary Accounts of Martin Luther.
  Manchester: Manchester University Press, 2002.
Volz, Hans., ed. *Drei Schriften gegen Luthers Schmalkaldische Artikel von
  Cochläus, Witzel und Hoffmeister (1538 und 1539).* Vol. 18 in CC, 1932.
Weiland, Jan Sperna, and Willem Frijhoff, eds. *Erasmus of Rotterdam: The
  Man and the Scholar.* Proceedings of the symposium held at the
  Erasmus University Rotterdam, 9–11 November 1986. Leiden: Brill,
  1988.
Wengert, Timothy. *Human Freedom, Christian Righteousness: Philip
  Melanchthon's Exegetical Dispute with Erasmus of Rotterdam.* Oxford:
  Oxford University Press, 1998.
– 'Melanchthon's Contribution to Luther's Debate with Erasmus.' In *By
  Faith Alone: Essays on Justification in Honor of Gerhard O. Forde,* ed.
  Joseph A. Burgess and Marc Kolden. Grand Rapids, Mich.: Eerdmans,
  2004.
White, Graham. *Luther as Nominalist: A Study of the Logical Methods Used
  in Martin Luther's Disputations in the Light of Their Medieval Background.*
  Helsinki: Luther-Agricola-Society, 1994.
Winter, Ernest F., ed. and trans. *Discourse on Free Will.* New York:
  Continuum, 1999.
Witzel, *Antwort auf Martin Luthers Letzt bekennete Artikel.* In CC, Vol. 18.
  See Volz, *Drei Schriften.*
Wriedt, Markus. *Gnade und Erwählung: Eine Untersuchung zu Johann von
  Staupitz und Martin Luther.* Mainz: von Zabern, 1991.

Index